W9-DFN-546

# HMCS HAIDA
## BATTLE ENSIGN FLYING

**BARRY M. GOUGH**

**Vanwell Publishing Limited**
St. Catharines, Ontario

Vanwell Publishing acknowledges the financial support of the Government of Canada through the Book Publishing Industry Development Program for our publishing activities.

Design: Linda Moroz-Irvine
Cover painting by Bo Hermanson

Vanwell Publishing Limited
1 Northrup Crescent
P.O. Box 2131
St. Catharines, Ontario  L2R 7S2

Printed in Canada

Canadian Cataloguing in Publication Data

Gough, Barry M. 1938-.
    HMCS Haida : battle ensign flying

Includes bibliographical references and index.
ISBN 1-55125-058-6

1. Haida (Ship) – History.  2. World War, 1939-1945 – Naval operations, Canadian.
3. Korean War, 1950-1953 – Naval Operations, Canadian.  I. Title.

VA400.5.H35G68 2000        359.3'254'0971        C00-9302057-1

Dedicated to the officers and men of HMCS *Haida*
and to all who keep alive the memory of
her noble calling

*If we mean either to maintain the honour and reputation of our country, or to defend ourselves against the enemy ... or to prosecute injuries done unto us, or to aid our friends that crave our help, we must have diligent regard to our seafaring men, and shipping, that both may be maintained and kept in order ...*

*The use of the Navy is great in peace, greater in wars. Thereby traffic and intercourse betwixt friends is maintained, victuals that go to the enemy are stopped, our wants of victuals, arms, munitions, and other necessaries are supplied; the enemy's coast is spoiled, our own defended, the coast towns of the enemy's country that live upon the sea are brought to great extremities, our own maintained ... [without it] the trade of merchandise cannot be maintained ... [nor] the sea towns of the enemy be besieged, nor can we understand the enemy's proceedings, nor help or well defend our friends or ourselves ...*

*Let the practice of war in maritime causes be diligently followed.*

Matthew Sutcliffe
*The Practice, Proceedings and Lawes of Arms*
(London, 1593)

---

*It is not sufficient to say that successful trade defence is a consequence of gaining command of the sea for this begs the questions of what is meant by command of the sea and how that command is gained.*

*What Matthew Sutcliffe called "the use of the Navy," of what, today, we call the object of maritime forces, is this:*

> *To enable us to use ships where and when we want to and to prevent the enemy from using ships where and when he wants to.*

*The extent to which we are able to achieve this object of using and of denying to the enemy the use of ships is the measure of the extent to which we may be said to command the sea. This extent can be expressed quantitatively in terms of shipping movements and cargoes; in terms of merchant ships sailed, and lost; of mercantile cargoes carried, and lost; and of military transports sailed, and lost; of military troops and stores carried, and lost; and of the various movements of these ships across the seas. In the face of enemy opposition these ships can sail successfully to their various destinations only by virtue of the concurrent movements of our maritime forces made in their defence and in offence against the enemy. In fact command of the sea is achieved by effecting local and temporary superiority of maritime force at places and at times where and when we wish to move ships, either for the purpose of carrying trade, or for the purpose of carrying troops and munitions to fight the enemy on land, or to prevent the enemy from carrying trade, or troops and munitions to fight us on land. The core of maritime warfare is thus ships and the movements of ships; it is emphatically not a question of 'controlling sea areas,' or 'sea-routes,' it is a question of ships – merchant ships, transports and warships – and their use at sea.*

Lieutenant-Commander D.W. Waters
*A Study of the Philosophy and Conduct of Maritime War, 1815-1945*
(Admiralty Historical Section, 1957)

# HONOURS, AWARDS AND DECORATIONS HMCS HAIDA

## BATTLE HONOURS HMCS HAIDA

| | |
|---|---|
| ARCTIC | 1943-1945 |
| ENGLISH CHANNEL | 1944 |
| NORMANDY | 1944 |
| BISCAY | 1944 |
| KOREA | 1952-1953 |

## AWARDS AND DECORATIONS

### HMCS Haida 1944

**Distinguished Service Order**

Commander H.G. DeWolf

**Distinguished Service Cross**

Commander H.G. DeWolf
Commander H.G. DeWolf
Captain H.G. DeWolf
Lieutenant R.M. Hesslam, RCNVR
Lieutenant C. Mawer, RCNVR

**Conspicuous Gallantry Medal**

Able Seaman M. Kerwin, RCNVR

**Distinguished Service Medal**

Chief Petty Officer G/M D. Abbott (2)
Chief Petty Officer D. Moon
Chief Ordinance Artificer M. Pederson
Stoker Petty Officer H.D. Richards
Leading Seaman M. White
Able Seaman P.P. Wispinski

**Mention in Despatches**

Commander H.G. DeWolf (2)
Lieutenant J.C.L. Annesley
Lieutenant (E) H.B. Bolus
A/Lieutenant J. Coates
Lieutenant P. Frewer, RCNVR
Lieutenant R.M. Heslam, RCNVR

Lieutenant D. Jeffreys, RCNVR

Lieutenant C. Mawer, RCNVR

Lieutenant R. Phillips

Gunner T.L.T. Jones

Yeoman of Signals A.J. Andrews

Petty Officer R.E. Armstrong

Chief Petty Officer C. Aveling

Chief Petty Officer R.A. Barker

Engine Room Artificer C. Boutilier

Leading Seaman J.L. Brechan

Stoker First Class W.A. Cummings

Able Seaman T.F. Cuthbert, RCNVR

Able Seaman J.W. Dance

Leading Seaman J.R. Finch

Able Seaman J. Hannam

Chief Petty Officer R.C. Hockley

Able Seaman R.H. MacLeod

Able Seaman K.G. MacWhirter

Able Seaman J. Manning

Signalman G.H. Mannix

Leading Radar Mechanic J.L. Taylor, RNVR

Able Seaman M. Williams, RCNVR

Petty Officer Telegraphist W.J.H. Wilson

Acting Petty Officer A.J. Worall

**Korea 1952**

**Distinguished Service Cross**     Commander D. Lantier

**Mention in Desptaches**     Petty Officer R. Smith

# CONTENTS

# ABBREVIATIONS

| | |
|---|---|
| Asdic | Allied Submarine Detection Investigation Committee (see SONAR) |
| AA | Anti-aircraft |
| A/C | Action Information Centre, or Plot |
| A/S | Anti-submarine |
| ASW | Anti-submarine warfare |
| ATW | Ahead-throwing weapon |
| CANCOMDESFE | Canadian Commander of Destroyers Far East |
| CAT | Canadian Anti-Torpedo |
| C-in-C | Commander-in-Chief |
| CNAV | Canadian Navy auxiliary vessel |
| CO | Commanding Officer |
| DF | Destroyer Flotilla |
| D/F | Direction Finding |
| DSC | Distinguished Service Cross |
| DSO | Distinguished Service Order |
| E-boat | German motor torpedo boat |
| FFI | *Forces Françaises de l'Intérieur* (French Forces of the Interior) |
| GNAT | German Navy Acoustic Torpedo |
| HEDA | High Explosive Direct Action |
| HF/DF | High Frequency Direction Finding |
| HMAS | His/Her Majesty's Australian Ship |
| HMCS | His/Her Majesty's Canadian Ship |
| HMS | His/Her Majesty's Ship |
| HNorMS | His Norwegian Majesty's Ship |
| IFF | Identification Friend or Foe |
| LCT | Landing Craft Tank |
| LST | Landing Ship Tank |
| MGB | Motor Gunboat |
| Mk | Mark |
| ML | Motor Launch |
| MTB | Motor Torpedo Boat |
| MV | Merchant Vessel |
| NATO | North Atlantic Treaty Organization |
| ORP | *Okret Rzeczypospolitej Polskiej* (Ship of the Polish Republic) |
| PCO | Principal Control Officer |
| Radar | Radio Detection and Ranging |
| RAF | Royal Air Force |
| RAN | Royal Australian Navy |
| RATOG | Rocket Assist Take-off Gear |
| R-boat | German Motor Minesweeper |
| RCAF | Royal Canadian Air Force |
| RCN | Royal Canadian Navy |
| RCNVR | Royal Canadian Naval Volunteer Reserve |
| RCNR | Royal Canadian Naval Reserve |
| RDF | Radio Direction Finding |
| RN | Royal Navy |
| ROK | Republic of Korea |
| R/T | Radio Telephone |
| SNO | Senior Naval Officer |
| SBNO | Senior Base Naval Officer |
| SIGINT | Signals Intelligence |
| SO | Senior Officer |
| S/M | Submarine (British) |
| SONAR | Sound Navigation and Ranging |
| TAS | Torpedo Anti-Submarine |
| TBC | Train Buster's Club |
| TBF | Torpedo Boat Flotilla |
| TF | Task Force |
| U-boat | *Unterseeboot* (German submarine) |
| Ultra | Deciphered information from *Enigma*, German secret naval code |
| UN | United Nations |
| USAF | United States Air Force |
| USS | United States Ship |
| V/S | Visual Signalling |

THIS IS THE STORY OF A GREAT WARSHIP. Her tale is Canada's best kept secret. Her Majesty's Canadian Ship *Haida*, bearing number DDE 215 at the time of her decommissioning on 11 October 1963, ranks as one of the finest warships of historical record. *Haida*'s service was as worldwide as it was various.

Her class, or design, derived from the era between the First and Second World Wars. This class of fleet destroyers resembled pocket cruisers, for they boasted a powerful armament to match their remarkable engines and hull design. As such, they heralded an age of sea warfare in which inshore and channel operations, as well as offshore cruising and patrol duties, called for a special type of destroyer. That class bore the name "Tribal."

They were a breed of their own: fast, heavily-gunned, and capable of working independently, in groups, or in conjunction with larger units, including battleships, cruisers and aircraft carriers. Their duties extended beyond fleet protection and distant surveillance. Their tasks included blockade and convoy work, support for amphibious operations, and providing aid to partisans ashore. Their obligations involved shore bombardment, "train busting," patrol work, and surveillance. Their work also ranged to hunting and killing submarines. Not least, their duties encompassed search and rescue, humanitarian relief, ceremonial functions, and "showing the flag," that indispensable duty of naval services everywhere.

In all of these actions *Haida* proved the versatility of the class. Now lying dockside at Ontario Place, Toronto, she is the only surviving Tribal of twenty-seven built. She is of telling importance to naval history generally and to these kinds of activities in particular.

This is proudly a Canadian story. It speaks to the past and the present. It speaks to tradition and to memory. As biographer of this ship, I recall a grand day in April 1997, when I was aboard the most recent innovation of the Canadian Navy, the state-of-the-art patrol frigate HMCS *Ville de Québec*, when salutes were exchanged in Toronto Harbour with the aging and venerable *Haida*. It may have been a day to relive old memories for some, but to me it seemed as if the past was melding beautifully with the present, thereby promising good omens for the future. *Haida*'s guns were exchanging salute with the newest breed of Canadian warship, and the legacy seemed assured. The traditions of the Canadian naval service were surely alive on that glorious day on Lake Ontario. How long will the memory of the Canadian naval experience of the Second World War, the Korean War, and the Cold War endure? We await the answers.

The number of warships still surviving that were involved in D-Day and the invasion of Normandy (6 June 1944) can be counted on the fingers of one hand. *Haida* is the only Canadian warship, of that famous day in the liberation of France from Nazi tyranny, to survive. The others are the cruiser HMS *Belfast*, London; the battleship USS *Texas*, Houston; the Polish destroyer *Blyskawica*, Gdansk; and one Liberty Ship, *Jeremiah O'Brien*, San Francisco. Apart from the celebrated corvette HMCS *Sackville* (in Halifax), *Haida* is the last surviving RCN warship of the Second World War. Canada's largest historical artifact, her importance grows with time. Her significance is emerging from the mists of the past.

At one time a junior partner, if not a child of the Royal Navy, the Canadian Navy came to occupy a powerful and respected position in the North Atlantic Treaty Organization (NATO). Its special duties included but were not restricted to surveillance, ocean patrol, anti-submarine operations, minesweeping, and convoy work. *Haida* and her sister Tribals of the Canadian Navy stood the long Cold War watch. One by one, they were dropped from service and were designated for sale or scrap.

Until 1963, when her engines gave out and her hull groaned under the extended obligations of twenty years of steaming and sea-keeping, *Haida* answered every call. She steamed 688,534.25 nautical miles in those two decades, a colossal twenty-seven times around the world. She did every duty known to fleet destroyers. With her companion Canadian vessels of the Second World War, which numbered 324 by official account, *Haida* served in many seas. And with her companion Canadian vessels of the Cold War, she waged a different sort of conflict, this time in Asian waters. It is one of the remarkable ironies of history that she never sailed the waters of British Columbia or visited Canada's Pacific Coast naval base at Esquimalt, Vancouver Island. This is strange, given her name.

*Haida* means "the people," spelled *hidu* according to recent orthography. The ship's name recognizes what anthropologist John Swanton said about the native habitat of the Haida, the Queen Charlotte Islands, also known nowadays as Haida Gwai: "More than any other land on the northwest coast the Queen Charlotte Islands are homes for seamen." The Haida, known to some outside observers as "Vikings of the North Pacific," ranged the coast at ease in their majestic cedar canoes. They defied the rough, open passage across Hecate Strait and Queen Charlotte Sound; and their chiefs and warriors, male and female, risked death at Tsimshian, Kwakiutl and Salish hands to visit distant Victoria or the adjacent Alaskan shore. The Haida knew intimately the seas, hidden haunts, inlets and terrain of their own islands. These consummate sea rovers were a distinct, homogeneous people. They took their lineage through their mother's side, and they were either Ravens or Eagles. Their fabulous exploits gave them a deserved reputation, one made more fascinating, even elusive, by their splendid isolation from their native rivals and trading partners on the mainland of North America.

Violence constituted a way of life to the Haida. Killing, beheading and enslaving remained a traditional way of Haida warfare until the introduction of the government's pacification policies. The reputation of the Haida was legendary, and even today their position in the aboriginal history of the world is assured, inviting respect and wonder. It is appropriate that a great Canadian Tribal destroyer bore the name of this mighty nation. And this, like many another Canadian story, has a United States connection, for the Haida are a cross-border people. Nowadays, kin of the Haida Gwai, the Kaigani Haida, live on the Alaskan islands of Dall, Long, and Prince of Wales.

Lieutenant-Commander William Sclater, RCN, inspired by *Haida*'s history, composed an award-winning portrait entitled *HAIDA*, published in 1946 which, without mentioning a single officer or member of the crew, sought to describe the ship's first tour of duty during the Second World War. He excluded *Haida*'s return to Murmansk, the liberation of Norway and the rest of the story. In the end, Sclater's was less than half of *Haida*'s story. My late friend E.C. Russell, Naval Historian, Directorate of History, Ottawa, recognized the value of the full story and wrote a brief account in 1959, a work still in print. He crafted numerous other histories of ships of the Canadian Navy. The third history of the ship was written by Alan D. Butcher, *I Remember Haida*, published in Hantsport, Nova Scotia, in 1985. Drawing together crew accounts and reminiscences, this book deals extensively with activities in Korean waters. In my own account I have attempted to provide a ship's history of a functioning unit of officers and men.

What I have sought to accomplish above all is to show how *Haida* operated singly or, more often than not, with other vessels of war to the credit of the naval service and to the Allied nations. It will fall to others to write the gallant, glorious and at times tragic history of other HMC ships. In one way or another, they all share in the triumphs and tragedies that were *Haida*'s.

This book is a narrative, a ship's tale. To be sure, in several chapters I provide an analysis of the events as they unfold. On occasion I give a situational report of the circumstances in which *Haida* found herself. In the main, the ship's progress through time and space is the featured subject. The ship's history is worked out against a mighty panorama of competing forces and of struggles not always brought to a logical conclusion. Throughout, my obligation has been to tell the tale. I have let facts speak for themselves, everywhere avoiding moral tendencies, "might have beens," or counterfactual postulations for the benefit of telling a straightforward account characterized by simplicity and clarity.

As will be revealed, this is primarily a story of night fighting at sea. Radar had stripped away darkness, and permitted enormous improvement in gun ranging and fire control. *Haida* won most of her battles at night. She was a technically superior, state-of-the-art ship, and her officers and crew were proficient in the operation of wireless, asdic or sonar, radar and gunlaying. They brought the daily work of the fleet destroyer to a high level of efficiency and effectiveness. With good fortune matched in equal proportion with battle readiness, they carried the war to the enemy with resolve and courage.

How does this book fit into the larger history? The Canadian Navy has had many historians, official and otherwise. Strange to say, few ships of that service have been the subject of detailed historical investigation. An exception to this is Marc Milner's *HMCS* Sackville*, 1941- 1985* (St. Catharines, 1998). Captain Stephen W. Roskill's *HMS* Warspite*: The Story of a Famous Battleship* (London, 1957) provided the inspiration for this book, and I am convinced that *Haida*'s tale is as profoundly significant for Canada's past as *Warspite* was for Britain, or the USS *Constitution* was for the United States. All too often naval history in Canada is recounted as bureaucratic struggle, interservice rivalry, or political intrigue. This book takes Canadian naval history—a special and neglected slice of it, so to speak—to the places of naval influence; at sea, especially in

time of war. This book aims to be "sharp end" history. In doing so it follows recent trends instituted by Roger Sarty, *Canada and the Battle of the Atlantic* (Montreal, 1998) and David J. Bercuson and Holger H. Herwig, *Deadly Seas: the Duel between the* St. Croix *and* U305 *in the Battle of the Atlantic* (Toronto, 1997).

I have benefited more from the work of my associates in Canadian, British, American, German and Norwegian naval history than my bibliography and reference notes can attest. Owing to space restrictions I am unable to make adequate reference to the work of my many colleagues which has revolutionized our understanding of these matters. For this I ask their professional indulgence. To Marc Milner, Roger Sarty, Michael Hadley, David Zimmerman and the late James Lamb I owe deep gratitude. I am especially grateful to Michael Whitby, whose research into the history of the Canadian Tribals and naval operations in the English Channel and Norway revealed an appreciation of naval warfare previously untold.

I am aware that this history of the *Haida* is not a sailor's history nor is it a history of the lower deck of the Royal Canadian Navy—the latter is still the great and yet-to-be-revealed account of the Second World War. I have chosen to tell the story of the proceedings and operations of *Haida*, to put in place an accurate and authentic record of the ship's activities. I hope that others will follow and take up the task of interviewing those who remain to tell the stories (and the secrets) of the great Tribal's wars at sea. It is my hope that this tribute to the ship's past may lead others to recount experiences or write the history of a disappearing historical source.

The sources on which this history is based are many and various. These are listed chiefly in the bibliography. Wherever possible I have based my narrative on reports of actions and of proceedings. Source references are given by chapter, including the specific report of proceedings, logbook or other source from which details, or quotations, are derived.

Speeds are indicated in knots. All distances are in nautical miles (one nautical mile equals one sixtieth of a degree of latitude, and a nautical mile for speed trials is 1.151 statute miles).

This history could not have been written without the support of The Friends of HMCS *Haida*, who assisted with certain costs. Many officers and men of the ship have provided information or given advice, and in this regard I am particularly grateful to the late Vice-Admiral H.G. DeWolf, Rear-Admiral Robert Welland, and Surgeon-Commander David Ernst, all of whom provided perspectives on *Haida*'s years 1943, 1944 and 1945. The staff and volunteers of the ship have shown every kindness, and in particular I thank Lieutenant (N) Peter Dixon, Carla Morse, Edward J. Anderson and Jerry Proc. Captain William H. Wilson and, above all, Commander Robert Willson have been immensely encouraging. Advice on Norway's Liberation, 1945 was provided by Captain Erik Guldhav, Royal Norwegian Embassy, and Nils Naastad, Airforce Academy, Trondheim. For information on Royal Navy sources I thank Captain Christopher Page, Lieutenant-Commander W.J.R. Gardner, and Kate Tildesley. For data from German sources I thank Kapitänleutnant Steffen, Militärgeschichtliches Forschungsamt, Potsdam. Various persons too numerous to mention have answered my plea for documents, photographs and reminiscences. In particular I thank Jan Drent, J. Earl Insley, Jim Lister, Joseph H. Peters, Jerry Proc, Ed Stewart, Mike Bechtold, John D. Harbron, Dave McGrath and Bob Garant. Research advice was given by Lieutenant-Commander Kenneth Hansen, William Schliehauf, Wesley Ferris, Mike Bechtold, Rob Davison, Norman Socha and David Ernst. I am most grateful to them. This book could not have been completed without the research and writing skills of three leading hands, James Wood, Peter Dixon and Rob Bromley, who in several ways helped draft materials that became the final text under my hand. Roger Sarty, Michael Whitby and Richard Gimblett read the manuscript and offered advice. None of them is responsible for any errors of omission or commission, as the responsibility rests completely with me as author. For the use of illustrations I thank The Canadian War Museum, Frank Stockwell, Edward Stewart, William Wilson, Peter Dixon, Ken Macpherson and Douglas B. Munro. I thank Simon Taylor and Royal Canadian Legion Branch 110, Trenton, for materials on the history of the Tribals. Thanks are due to the Marine Museum of the Great Lakes at Kingston for permission to reproduce items from the Grant Macdonald Collection, to Leslie K. Redman of the Canadian War Museum for arrangements for the publication of certain items in their images collection, and to Janice Mullin of the Imperial War Museum in London for arrangements to publish certain photographs from their holdings. Not least, I thank Angela Dobler for fine editorial work that brought this book to fruition.

I close these thanks with this reminder: that *Haida* is Canada's equivalent to Britain's HMS *Warspite* or the United States's USS *Constitution*. Her history and her preservation are of the highest importance to the remembrance of Canada's national achievements at sea, in peace and in war. This ship and her crew stood the long watch for all those who passed on the seas on their lawful occasions, during three wars: the Second World War, the Korean War and the Cold War. Hers is a story well worth the telling, and I am honoured to have been tasked with this weighty and immense obligation.

All proceeds from the sale of this book will go to the Friends of HMCS *Haida* for the maintenance of the ship as a Canadian naval museum. For further information on HMCS *Haida*, visit the website: www3.sympatico.ca/hrc/haida. Also visit the Canadian Tribal Association web page: http://webhome.idirect.com/~jproc/cta.

Barry M. Gough
Professor of History
Wilfrid Laurier University
Waterloo, Ontario

# HMCS HAIDA
## Tribal Class Destroyer

Comissioned: 30 August 1943
Displacement: 3000 tons
Length: 377 feet
Width: 37½ feet
Crew: 18 Officers, 230 Crew

HMCS HAIDA served two very successful years in WWII followed by two tours of duty in the Pacific during the Korean War. Her peacetime activities proved equally exciting as she was involved in a rescue operation off Bermuda in 1949 and took part in many training cruises including NATO exercises in European and North American waters as well as a cruise of the Great Lakes. Since 1965, she has been in Toronto operating as a naval museum.

Top: HMCS *Haida, Action at Dawn* by C.G. Evers

Bottom: *Haida*'s crest displays a two-headed Thunderbird. Legend states that lightning flashed from its eyes and thunder occurs whten it flaps its wings. Its two heads indicate a constant lookout and its wings are unfolded to signify the loud thunder of *Haida*'s guns.

*Vanity - The Hard Way.* Ldg. Sick Berth Attendant H.G. Elliott finds shaving in a rough sea a hazardous process unmitigated by the jeers of his bearded mess-mates, Leading Seaman H.F. Howes, Able Seaman L.W. Blackwell, and Coder T.W. Veysey. (Drawings by Grant Macdonald, courtesy Marine Museum of the Great Lakes [MMGL])

# CHAPTER 1

## THE TRIBALS AND THE WAR AT SEA

●

HER KEEL WAS LAID ON 30 AUGUST 1941, and on 25 August 1942 *Haida* slid down the ways of Vickers-Armstrong Limited, Newcastle, and met the waters of the North Sea. Her launch was sponsored by the Lord Mayoress of London, the Canadian-born Lady Laurie. After *Haida* had slipped into the stream tradesmen continued their tasks. In due course, all systems had been readied and tested. Two days before her commissioning an all-out test had been undertaken. "She did everything asked of her from high speed to slow and full astern," wrote a reporter, who added, "they passed her A1 and, when Haida stopped momentarily to allow the shipyard and Admiralty officials to go ashore, everyone felt well satisfied that this heavily gunned warship will give a good account of herself in any action." Her acceptance trial was completed and passed. Thus, on 30 August 1943,

twelve months after her launching, HMCS *Haida* was first commissioned, under the White Ensign.

*Haida* continued to be fitted with mechanisms to make her fit for war at sea. On 17 September the High Commissioner to the United Kingdom for Canada, Vincent Massey, paid a visit to the ship, had a tour and chatted with men at their work. The next day, with final requirements completed, *Haida* disembarked her trials party and shaped a course north to Scapa Flow in the Orkney Islands, operations base of the Royal Navy's Home Fleet.

*Haida*, the fourth British-built Tribal class fleet destroyer ordered by Canada, joined her sister ships *Athabaskan*, *Iroquois* and *Huron*. *Haida* was designated G63 by the Admiralty, and she carried this, her pennant number, prominently on port and starboard sides until she was redesignated DD215 by the Government of Canada in 1949.

In the late 1930s the Royal Canadian Navy, as the naval service was then called, decided to order new ships to replace the older destroyers previously transferred from the RN. Senior officers in the RCN stuck by their guns that what Canada's navy needed was a heavily gunned vessel in a strong platform with good speed and range, a warship that could stand in the front rank with the fleet destroyers of the RN. These vessels would be of such fine quality that the government could never scrap them after the war. The Government of Canada would have preferred the Tribals to have been built in Canada but this was impossible in the first instance and, accordingly, four Tribals were ordered to be built in English yards. *Athabaskan* was the first of these, *Iroquois* the second and *Huron* the third. *Haida* was the fourth and last of the Canadian Tribals built in England. Canada built four Tribals in Halifax: *Micmac, Cayuga, Nootka* and the last, *Athabaskan II,* named for *Athabaskan* which had been lost on 29 April 1944. Sixteen Tribals were built for the Royal Navy and three for the Royal Australian Navy. The Australian ships were built in Australian yards. All of the Tribals, except HMAS *Bataan* (ex-*Kurnai*), carried tribal designations, as various as *Zulu, Cossack, Bedouin, Matabele.* Each of these vessels has a tale to tell, and their stories are told in Appendix 5. The RCN never had cause to doubt the wisdom of the decision made in 1939 to order and build Tribals. In the end, the Tribals not only had long lives, and the canny Canadians got their money's worth, but these ships were a first-class investment in top quality equipment. The RCN learned an important fact with its Tribals: quality is expensive but has accrued dividends. At one time, it may be mentioned, Winston Churchill, then at the Admiralty, advised the Canadians to buy American destroyers. For various reasons, all of them good ones (including getting necessary equipment stores and

replacements), the Canadians stuck to their decision to adopt a British design and to acquire British-built ships in the first instance.

**Armament**

Tribals were fast and heavily-gunned. They were to be a powerful platform in a naval war for which the British and the Canadian governments were preparing in the late 1930s. Regarded as the most famous of all British destroyers, the Tribals had a long lineage. They emerged from the design modifications of earlier destroyer classes dating from 1892. Tribals were planned to match the most powerful Fubuki class of Japanese destroyers, launched 1928 to 1932. Tribals were also meant to be at least equal in design characteristics to those being built with calculated haste by the Germans, commencing in 1933. The intention of all these design improvements was to allow the gun to replace the torpedo as the primary weapon. Tribals were the first, as well as the last, British destroyers capable of firing an eight gun broadside.

British naval concepts of destroyer operations emphasized the likelihood of a surface fleet action, and for this reason the Tribals carried a main armament intended to take out enemy destroyers. Thus, destroyer guns emphasized weight of shell and muzzle velocity so as to give a flat trajectory with a high probability of hitting rapidly-maneuvering surface ships. The British looked for a high rate of fire, and a well-trained and efficient gun crew in *Haida* could fire twelve rounds a minute from each 4.7-inch gun.

Good ahead fire was required, and originally the designers had considered five pairs of guns. But when ultimate speed and top-weight were taken into consideration the architects called for four twin mountings of 4.7-inch guns—that is, eight guns in all—and these would be A, B, X and Y mounts, with A located on the forecastle, B ranged above it, X positioned on a raised gun deck aft, and Y mount on the main deck aft. These were called twin 4.7-inch Mk XIXs on a CP [central pivot] mount, a pair of quick firing guns in a common cast steel cradle. Each mounting weighed 25.5 tons, had a maximum elevation of 40 degrees and a maximum depression of 10 degrees. It had a maximum training arc of 320 degrees and could shift position, laterally and vertically as required, at 10 degrees a second. The after guns had a training arc of 180 degrees. The 4.7-inch gun had a maximum effective surface range of 16,900 yards. The shell weighed 50 pounds and the cartridge 35, and a power-ramming system allowed the round and its charge to be placed in the breech by a manually operated loading tray. Designers knew that Tribals were likely to engage targets difficult to select, and that concentration of fire would be required. Accordingly, a Director was needed so as to enable the guns to be trained by calculation and mechanisms.

It was further intended that Tribals would have AA armament mainly for the defence of the fleet, convoys and harbours and not just for self-defence. In other words, long-range AA fire was an urgent requirement. Because German military aircraft played havoc with British destroyers in Norway, at Dunkirk, in the Mediterranean and elsewhere early in the war, and the main armament proved useless for high elevation work, the 4.7-inch twin mount at X position was scrapped in favour of a twin 4-inch anti-aircraft mount. The maximum elevation of the new gun allowed the target to be engaged to the bomb release point.

A quad pom-pom, a quick-firing cluster of four guns firing high explosive 2-pdr shells, was located immediately abaft the funnel, between the mainmast and X mount. Designers would have preferred the more powerful "Chicago Piano," but top weight considerations ruled that out, and the famous quad pom-pom, a cut-down version of the larger 8-barrelled one installed on capital ships, provided a powerful AA armament at close range, up to 5000 yards horizontally and 10,000 feet vertically. Each gun theoretically fired at 115 rounds per minute, and they were triggered to operate in pairs. They had a powered drive and automatic loading. As with the 4.7s they were not automatic weapons, requiring six men to serve them. The Layer and Trainer worked the mounting as required at the direction of the Captain of the mounting. There were fourteen rounds to a disintegrating link belt, which were clipped to existing rounds in the ammunition feed-trays. Maximum range was less than hoped for, but it was an improvement on the maximum AA range possessed by earlier classes of destroyers.

Completing the AA armament were twelve Oerlikon guns of 20-mm calibre, mounted on twin power mounts. They were located on the flag deck, amidships and on the after superstructure. The range of these automatic weapons was 6000 yards, and they fired a high explosive incendiary shell.

Tribals carried a light torpedo armament, for torpedoes ranked as a secondary consideration with the designer, a decision which affected their operational capabilities. *Haida* carried four torpedoes, loaded in a quad mounting amidships, forward of the after superstructure on the main deck. The power-operated pivoted mounting could be trained to port or starboard and set at the training angle as required. The torpedoes were 21-inch-diameter, and had a range of 14,000 yards at 35 knots.

The depth charge armament of *Haida*, her anti-submarine weapons, consisted of two throwers, one to port and the other to starboard, aft of the superstructure (in other words, on each side of the forward edges of X mounting), and a single charge

rail on the stern. That meant that *Haida* carried ten depth charges in position. In addition twenty-two were carried on deck and twenty-four between decks.

*Haida* carried a variety of small arms as of 1943: a gas-operated .303 Vickers machine gun capable of 1000 rounds per minute, two gas-operated Bren guns, thirty-two Lee-Enfield rifles, twenty-six Lanchester machine carbines, some .22 rifles, revolvers and Very pistols. Details for these, and all fighting equipment specifications, are given in Appendix I.

## Design

This powerful armament was mounted in a vessel of 1,870 tons, 355.5 feet in length with a beam of 36.5 ft and a 9 foot draft. Parsons marine steam turbines producing 44,000 shaft horsepower at 350 rpm gave Tribals a speed of 36.5 knots. Hull design was also superb, with a long forecastle and a powerful broadside silhouette. Higher amidships than the Fletcher class of the US Navy, the Tribals were not flush-deckers like the Fletchers but had the step down from the forecastle to the main

Loading torpedoes, 1944.
(HMCS *Haida* Naval Museum 991.074.005)

Top: *Haida*'s wake 1945. The Tribals were designed to reach a speed of 36.5 knots. *Haida*'s record top speed was 40.6 knots. Also note the depth-charge racks in the foreground. (Courtesy David Ernst)

Bottom: This quadruple mounting housed four Mk IX 21-inch torpedoes. The torpedoes had a range of 11,000 yards at 45 knots and carried a warhead of 250 lbs of torpex explosive, the equivalent of 800 lbs of TNT. (Courtesy Jerry Proc)

or upper deck. The designer of the Tribals, A.P. Cole, envisaged a good-looking ship that would inspire her officers and men with pride. "Such a feature is beyond statistical evaluation," writes Martin Brice. One senior Australian naval officer described Tribals as "magnificent in appearance, majestic in movement, and menacing in disposition."

Tribals were good sea ships, especially the later hulls, which were strengthened to counter pounding at high speeds in rough seas. The range of the Tribals was 5,700 miles at an economical speed of 15 knots (3,200 at 20 knots). They carried 524 tons of fuel oil. The nominal ship's company was set at 190, but increased to 219 if the ship was employed as the flotilla or divisional leader. *Haida*'s complement for the Second World War was more than originally designed. *Haida* carried three boats, one 27-foot clinker-built whaler, two 25-foot motor-cutters and twelve or more Carley floats.

## Aboard *Haida*

Here is a ship's tour as of the date of commissioning in 1943. Standing on the fo'c'sle deck at the bow, just aft of the jackstaff and anchor light, the visitor's eyes were drawn beyond the capstan and bow anchor cables to the Tribal's forward guns. Separated from each other by a blast shield, the upper B and lower A gun mounts each housed twin 4.7-inch guns. Ammunition hoists were located nearby, reaching down into the ship. Immediately below the fo'c'sle deck and the gun mountings could be found the upper and lower messdecks, where some 220 ratings took their meals, stowed their belongings and slung their hammocks—each separated by a regulation eighteen inches of airspace. Descending further into the lowest level of the ship, the hold deck housed the ammunition magazine for *Haida*'s forward guns.

Aft of the A and B mountings, the forward superstructure rose from the fo'c'sle deck, crowned by the Tribal's open bridge. From here, the CO, his officers and men were afforded an unobstructed view of the horizon, allowing them to direct their ship to best advantage using a variety of equipment. In addition to being the focal point of command and control, the bridge was also the centre of *Haida*'s communications, both internal and external. Alongside signal lamps and flags for passing messages to other ships stood equipment for *Haida*'s internal broadcast system, including sound-powered telephones and voice-pipes leading to all parts of the destroyer. One level down, B gun deck of the forward superstructure was flanked to port and starboard by a twin 20-mm Oerlikon mounting for AA defence and close-range fire. Located within the superstructure on this level, the wheelhouse, signals office, plotting table, charthouse and D/F office processed information from the bridge and relayed orders to the appropriate parts of the ship. One voicepipe from the bridge also led directly to the Captain's sea cabin, so that he might be called to the bridge quickly in case of emergency at sea. Another level down, the messes of the chief petty officers, petty officers and engine room artificers served as the living quarters for senior NCOs.

Aft of the forward superstructure stood a tripod foremast carrying *Haida*'s fighting lights and a crowsnest, which was reached from B gun deck by means of a narrow ladder. At the base of this mast stood the galley, where three or four cooks would prepare three meals a day for the crew of over 200 men. Rising from the upper deck beyond this, two funnels exhaled smoke from the three boiler rooms below, each providing superheated steam to the Tribal's powerful turbines. On either side of the smokestacks, the ship's motor-cutter and whaler were stowed, ready to be put to sea in order to

# Ship Profile, Legend

1. Fairleads
2. Bollards
3. Anchor Guards
4. Shell Racks
5. Carley Floats
6. Scramble Nets
7. Depth Charge Rack
8. Wind Screen
9. Plot View Platform
10. Signal Lamp
11. Bridge
12. Searchlight
13. Director Control Tower
14. Twin Oerlikons Mk V
15. 271 Radar
16. Motor Boat
17. Whaler
18. Galley Stack
19. Searchlight
20. Dinghy
21. Funnel
22. 21-Inch Quad Torpedo Tubes
23. Torpedo Davit
24. Ladder
25. Depth Charge Thrower

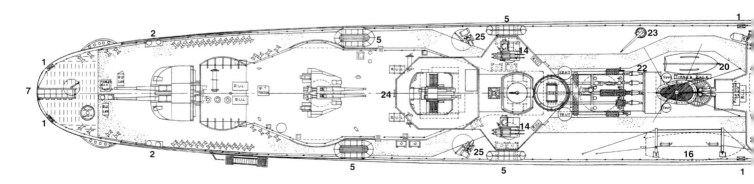

# HMCS HAIDA

# DECK ARRANGEMENT

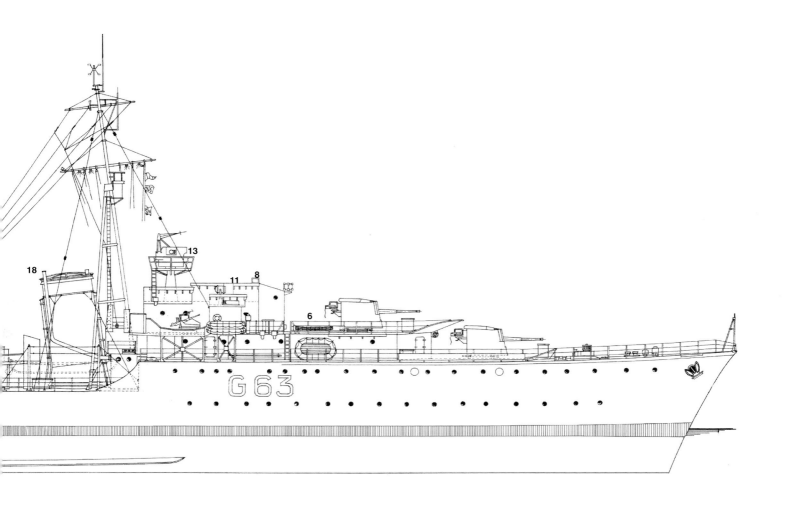

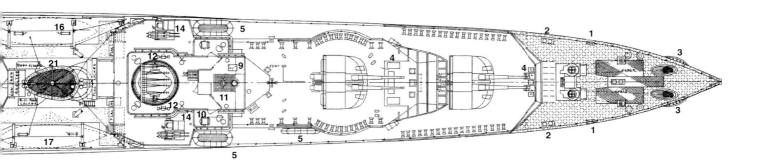

(drawings courtesy Douglas B. Munro)

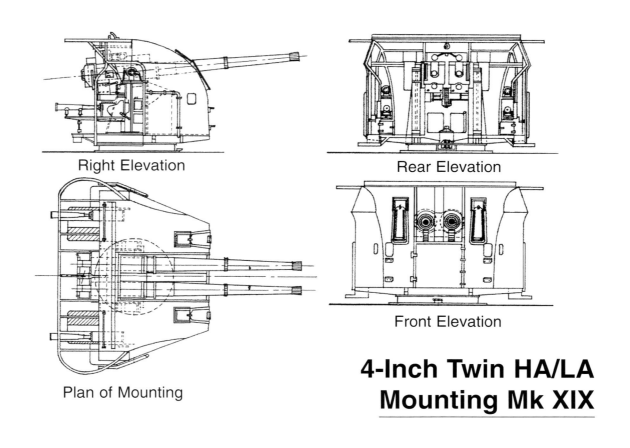

Right Elevation

Rear Elevation

Plan of Mounting

Front Elevation

## 4.7-Inch Twin Mounting

Right Elevation

Rear Elevation

Plan of Mounting

Front Elevation

## 4-Inch Twin HA/LA Mounting Mk XIX

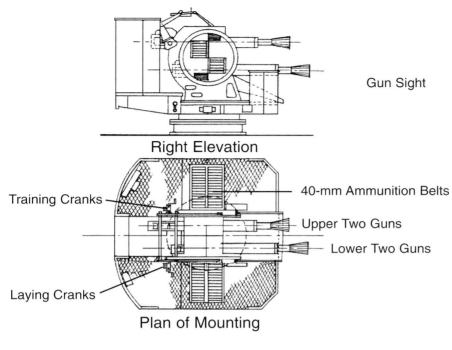

Gun Sight

Right Elevation

Training Cranks

40-mm Ammunition Belts

Upper Two Guns

Lower Two Guns

Laying Cranks

Plan of Mounting

# Quad Pom-Pom Mounting

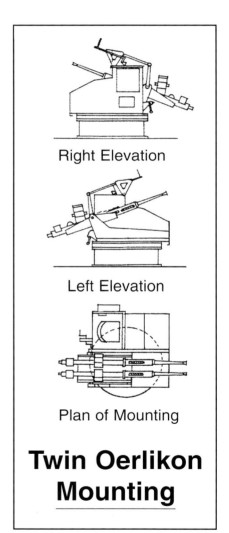

Right Elevation

Left Elevation

Plan of Mounting

# Twin Oerlikon Mounting

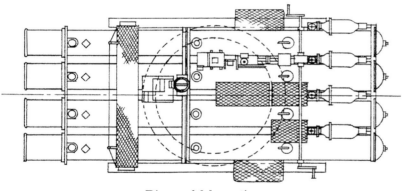

Plan of Mounting

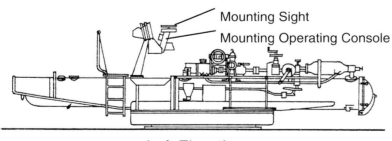

Mounting Sight

Mounting Operating Console

Left Elevation

# 21-Inch Quadruple Torpedo Tubes Mk IX

(drawings courtesy Douglas B. Munro)

recover anyone who fell overboard or to rescue survivors of downed vessels. Between these boats, on a platform amid the two funnels, a quadruple mounting housed four 21-inch torpedoes while overhead a lanyard for hoisting signal flags led back to the mast atop *Haida*'s aft superstructure.

Within this superstructure was located the engineer's workshop, the sickbay and the CO's day cabin, sleeping cabin and pantry. Outside, on the port and starboard sides, two more twin Oerlikons represented the last of *Haida*'s complement of six twin 20-mm gun mounts. Overhead stood the pom-pom gun, searchlight, aft tripod mast, and the twin 4-inch guns of X mounting, which could be used to engage targets in the air and on the surface. There was also an aft conning position, which would be used in an emergency to steer the ship should the wheelhouse be destroyed or rendered inoperable. Immediately beyond the X mounting, a second blast shield sheltered the crew of *Haida*'s 4.7-inch mounting. Below these two mountings, as at the fore of the ship, were crew quarters. These chambers housed *Haida*'s officers and included the wardroom, where officers took their meals, relaxed and entertained guests. Rear ammunition magazines were located at the bottom of the hoist shafts reaching down from X and Y mountings. At the stern of the ship the White Ensign flew from the upper deck, flanked on both sides by single depth charge launchers and located just aft of a rack of six charges, all of which were prepared to carry out attacks against enemy submarines. *Haida* was in all respects ready.

## The Tide of War, 1943

At the time of *Haida*'s commissioning and her first assignment with the British Home Fleet, the tide of the war was flowing in favour of Britain, Canada, the United States and their Allies. The full weight of US naval might was being felt in North Atlantic waters; but in the Battle of the Atlantic, nearing its climax by May 1943, Britain and Canada had provided escort for convoys to such a degree of perfection that the *Kriegsmarine*'s U-boat arm was obliged to shift from its various theatres of operation where concentrated attack on convoys was proving ineffective, and instead to work off Norway, Gibraltar, and West Africa. When German countermeasures were established to deal with airborne ship-locating radar perfected by the British, U-boats were equipped with a more powerful AA armament and were re-assigned to the approaches to the British Isles.

By late 1943 Allied war planners and strategists were making plans to reclaim France, Norway and other nations of Northwest Europe from Nazi occupation. France and Norway were in the minds of most if not all planners because, in German hands, they were so damaging to the maritime activities of the Allies. Since 4 June 1940, the last possible day to rescue British and French troops from Dunkirk, the entire coast of western Europe, from the Norwegian seas south to Spain, had lain under the Swastika. The RN and RCN and their associates had kept the long watch off the Western Approaches to the British Isles, safeguarding the arrival and departure of shipping upon which the defences of the Home Islands and the hopes for the liberation of the Continent rested. Now the time had come to assert the offensive and to carry the war to the enemy.

With French ports on the English Channel and Bay of Biscay in German hands the strategic situation had swung wildly in the enemy's favour. Le Havre, Cherbourg, St-Malo, Brest, Lorient, and Bordeaux became bases for German naval activity. Some bases were U-boat lairs, others minesweeper stations. Still others were nests from which destroyers or fast patrol boats could steal out to prey on Allied shipping or raid English shores if undetected and unanswered. Similarly, German naval units could sow defensive minefields or provide convoy for vessels along the continental shore, thus reinforcing the bases of their Atlantic Wall and strengthening their defences against the Allied invasion that German High Command knew must one day come.

To counter German measures the Admiralty had shifted their convoys away from the English Channel and had re-routed them north of the Irish Sea. Liverpool and Greenock in the Clyde assumed new strategic and commercial significance, and Liverpool had become the operational headquarters of Western Approaches Command. Liverpool took up Plymouth's old role. Even so, Plymouth, Portsmouth and the Nore (at the entrance to the Thames estuary) constituted the new levers from which to exert pressure on German seapower. Taking orders from the Admiralty, and guided by Liverpool's flexible response to the U-boat arm's attempts to grapple with Allied seaborne trade, destroyer flotillas from these bases commenced a campaign to destroy the surface and submarine units of the enemy.

The Admiralty established special U-boat hunting groups to work with intelligence sources to track and destroy U-boats transiting certain areas. Most famous was the support group led by Captain F.J. "Johnnie" Walker, RN. Through dint of experience and Walker's hard-driving character and aggressive spirit, hunting tactics were brought to a high degree of effectiveness.

Fast motor gunboats (MGBs), slower motor-launches (MLs), and improved motor torpedo boats (MTBs), were being deployed to deal with enemy E-boats or undertake forays into enemy inshore waters. These forces were called Light Coastal Forces. They played a prominent role in the struggle for the narrow seas. Canadian units were conspicuous in these close and desperate encounters with the Germans. Young and adventurous commanders found this fast-moving naval warfare entirely to their satisfaction, and the historical record of their exploits is a tale of derring-do, high risk and casualties.

The main prop for the support and escort groups and destroyer flotillas was RAF Coastal Command. Aerial reconnaissance coupled with signals intelligence identified U-boats and could often lead to a kill. Walker's unit in the Western Approaches racked up splendid records. They often found themselves operating in conjunction with Plymouth Command. But make no mistake: this naval war could not be won without the supremacy of the air and co-ordinated intelligence.

## The Royal Canadian Navy

Even more, the naval war could not have been won without highly professional officers and men. The RCN was exemplary in the quality of its personnel, although the training of many of the lower deck was incomplete or hurried. A solid core of the officers, especially those who served on the Tribals, were career professionals who had trained with or served in the RN. Many were members of the Royal Canadian Navy Volunteer Reserve (RCNVR), and the Royal Canadian Naval Reserve (RCNR). Many of them were lawyers, accountants, and not a few of them were medical doctors. An analysis of the complement of *Haida* shows that most of the officers were in their early to mid twenties. Apart from the senior warrant officers, the oldest of whom was forty, most of the ratings were in their early twenties, and a goodly number at the age of eighteen. On her first tour of duty, *Haida* had 17 officers and 258 men, a total of 275.

Prior to December 1939 the RCN had faced many difficulties. Not least had been the inter-war cutbacks and near strangulation begun in 1922. The rise of Hitler and the rearmament of Germany had

HAIDA

Officers and men of HMCS *Haida*, 22 May 1944. Note that the censors have blocked out the destroyer's radar and communications antennae. (NAC PA-176124)

changed Canadian isolationism and naval neglect. Already Canada's foreign policy concerns had been fixed on Japan's immense naval and military build-up and imperial aggressions in Asia. Canadian eyes were beginning, in 1935, to watch Italy's aggrandizements with alarm. But a navy is not acquired overnight, and following the British lead on the outbreak of war, the Canadian government began to arm merchantmen, to take up ships from trade, to build corvettes and minesweepers, and to buy or order Tribals. In a way, it was a just-in-time navy. Long neglected by the State, the RCN was springing to life and thrown into a war not of its choosing.

But this was not an infant navy. It carried with it a great and abiding affinity for the Royal Navy and for the Navy's traditions and heroes. The RCN was the child of the RN. Its naval bases, Halifax and Esquimalt, had been British bases and headquarters of British squadrons and commands. RCN ships wore the White Ensign, emblem of triumph and tragedy at sea. The officers and senior men were steeped in the traditions of British naval heroism, and of undefeated sea supremacy. When HMCS *Rainbow* had sailed from Esquimalt in 1914 to bring the German cruiser *Leipzig* to account off San Francisco, Ottawa had sent the ship and crew this telling message: "Remember the Spirit of Nelson! All of Canada is Watching!"

## *Haida*'s First Commander

Commander Henry G. DeWolf, RCN, was Canada's Nelson. He was otherwise known as Harry DeWolf, and even more affectionately as "Hard-over Harry," owing to his ship-handling propensities. "We saw him as a mild-mannered sandy-haired man, 42 years of age, of medium build, inconspicuous appearance, embarrassingly observant glance, and a very few words." So wrote a member of the lower deck, William Pugsley. "His facial expression seldom relaxed, but when it did as he told a rating, with the faintest of smiles, that some routine request was granted, the guy went away walking on air. With defaulters, he was stern but never harsh. Any man got a very long rope."

Canada's most famous sailor had an official bearing. He often questioned people's abilities when they erred. He commanded everyone's respect. A cool and steady hand, he was as decisive as he was patient, and as detached as he was friendly. "This quiet, almost self-effacing officer, his burberry flapping about him as he stood perched atop the bridge superstructure," says Pugsley, "brought the ship through the harbor with all the casualness of a high-school kid parking a ten-year-old jalopy....Somehow the Captain always managed to stop the ship dead in the right

Six officers aboard *Haida*, 1944. L to R: Lt Hal B. Bolus, Lt Murray Heslam, Surgeon Lt-Cdr Samuel MacDonald, Lt Raymond Phillips, Lt James Flavelle, Lt Phil P. Frewer. (HMCS *Haida* Naval Museum 991.005.001)

spot. We tried to be quick with our lines and fenders, so our performance might match the smartness of his."

DeWolf had the Nelson touch: the desire to "engage the enemy more closely." Pugsley takes up the story:

> If he was cool in these matters, he was no less so in action. On one
> Channel patrol, so a Signalman who'd been on the bridge told me, one of
> our Rear-Admirals had come along for the ride. Most of the night had
> been spent fighting a group of German destroyers, and dawn was now
> approaching, at which time our ships generally sought the protection of
> home waters.
>
> "Don't you think we should go back now, Harry?" suggested the
> Admiral, "it's beginning to get light."
>
> "Not till I've had one more run, and finished off that b——d," replied
> the Captain quietly. They did both. It was this kind of thing that made
> the Limey ratings term the personnel in our Tribal destroyers "white sav-
> ages."

DeWolf brought to *Haida* great professional training and education. Equally important, he brought to his command a restless zeal and a will to bring the enemy to account. His was a hand of steel in a velvet glove. And when a fight was on he would bring it to the enemy. Every time *Haida* destroyed an enemy vessel he carved a notch in the handrail, or dodger, on the bridge. It has been said many times that *Haida* was a lucky ship, a fortunate one. No one doubts that, for in a hot naval war such as that being fought in the English Channel on a nightly basis the odds of not coming home at dawn were considerable. One cruiser and two destroyers working in the same sort of duty as *Haida* failed to return, and many others were damaged, some seriously, in encounters with the enemy or, in fact, from "friendly fire." In DeWolf there was something of extraordinary human dimensions: true leadership, knowledge of calculated risk, and professional seamanship. Fred Ware, one of the commissioning crew, stated, "There was an aura about him. You knew you could trust him." Hard-over Harry was a specialist in navigation. He was also expert in the use of *Haida*'s main armament and torpedoes, and in certain circumstances he regarded guns as the more effective weapon. DeWolf was the man who made *Haida* famous.

The faces in the photographs tell all. The men of *Haida*, the lower deck, were young, the average age twenty-one. They came from the cities, towns and farms of Canada, and the ship's list for her initial commission shows that they represented the nation as a whole. They were of English, Scots, Welsh, Irish and French blood, and most were Canadian-born. They had enlisted in Canada, gone through training in Nova Scotia, and had been sent to Chatham, England, and then north to join *Haida*. The older ones were leading seamen and the still older ones petty officers with skilled trades or other abilities. All were seamen with seamen's qualifications and graduates of a school of hard knocks and discipline. The photos show Canadian manhood of those days in its prime, and

they also reveal the teamwork and fraternity which the lower deck fostered and the Service naturally encouraged. In their previous walks of life these lads had never had to yield to the kind of military-unit discipline required to make *Haida* function as a fighting ship. Soon the pride of belonging took hold. John Leslie Taylor, a seaman on *Haida*, recounted in 1977:

> The memories for me are do deeply cherished that I don't think I want them to be disturbed. I was so young then, by God I was young, weren't we all so young, not even 18 when I first went into action on *Haida*, and came back through the [Plymouth] Sound with the Battle Flag flying. Prouder of my ship, its Captain and all its crew than anyone aboard could know, and a friend amongst strangers. I suppose we all felt alike then, the excitement, the bold courage of those night sweeps along the French coast and the growing truth that we were part of something special, the kind of thing that happens only once in every life ... I named my house *Haida*.

The war would transform John Leslie Taylor as it would transform so many. And *Haida*'s progressions through time and toil would change the lives of all who sailed in her.

Wherever the White Ensign flew during the war – with the North Atlantic convoys, on the hard reach to Murmansk, in the North Sea, the English Channel, the Mediterranean and the Far East – the fighting ships and the fighting men of the Royal Canadian Navy were well represented. For Canada's emergence as a Maritime power was a significant and striking factor in the fight to maintain liberty and democracy.

Within the compass of these grim years, the Great Dominion created, from small beginnings, a Navy that won the admiration of the United Nations.

This is a book about one of the most famous ships of that fighting Navy – H.M.C.S. HAIDA, of the 10th Destroyer Flotilla in the Plymouth Command. In the records of many swift offensive forays off the enemy-occupied coast of France, she inscribed a name that will live as long as the White Ensign endures.

A.V. Alexander

Tribute to HMCS *Haida* by First Lord of the Admiralty, A.V. Alexander, 1946, for William Sclater's book. (Courtesy Barry Gough)

# CHAPTER 2

## HAIDA ON THE MURMANSK RUN:
## OCTOBER – DECEMBER 1943

FOLLOWING THREE WEEKS OF EXERCISES, *Haida* stood ready for her first operational assignment as part of the 17th Destroyer Flotilla based at Scapa Flow. Two operations, codenamed FQ and FR, were to be undertaken concurrently between 14 and 22 October. The object was to allow both missions to be protected by the same covering force. A task force of heavy units from the Home Fleet was to be accompanied by a screen of six destroyers, of which H.G. DeWolf aboard *Haida* was to be Senior Officer. Included in the destroyer screen were HMS *Vigilant*, *Hardy* and *Janus*, USS *Corry* and one of *Haida*'s sister Tribals, *Iroquois*.

FQ was bound for Spitzbergen, a handful of Norwegian islands lying some 450 miles north of the North Cape and occupied by Allied forces. Five weeks before, on 8 September, the islands had been harried by a German task force composed of

the battleship *Tirpitz*, the battle cruiser *Scharnhorst*, nine destroyers and a battalion of the 349th Grenadier Regiment. The attack had destroyed the Allied coal and supply dumps at Barentsburg and put the water and electrical works out of service. Operation FQ was designed as a resupply expedition to the beleaguered Norwegian garrison of some eighty men stationed on the island. *Haida* and the covering force would undertake to provide distant support to a group of Soviet minesweepers and anti-submarine vessels then making their way towards Murmansk as part of Operation FR.

Murmansk, located at the head of the Kola Inlet on the Barents Sea, was the only port in northern Russia which remained free of ice year round. This was due to its location at the far end of the North Atlantic Drift, a warm water current which passes up the coast of Norway and into the Arctic Ocean. The Soviets based vessels of their Arctic fleet near Murmansk at Polyarnoe. There the Russian minesweepers of Operation FR were bound. Murmansk was also highly prized by the Soviets due to its railway links to Leningrad and southern Russia, a route which in the past had allowed material from Great Britain and the United States to reach the embattled Soviet armies on the Eastern Front. To the east and south by way of Barents Sea and Beloje More, or White Sea, lay the port of Archangel, less open in all seasons, and also having rail lines to Leningrad and to Moscow.

As of October 1943, no Allied convoys to the Soviet Union had been sent via Murmansk since the previous winter. The British government had suspended Arctic convoys. During summer, Arctic convoys were exposed to the *Luftwaffe* based in occupied Norway.

Although threat of German attack had discouraged the passage of slow Allied merchant vessels to Murmansk throughout the summer of 1943, the Allies remained confident that any strong covering force, such as provided for Operations FQ and FR, would allow convoys to reach Spitzbergen and Murmansk in safety. Neither operation encountered German resistance. What the officers and men of *Haida* did encounter was miserable weather, a common occurrence in these northern waters. It was a discouraging first look at the dismal seas that would be their home for the next few months. The Canadian Tribal returned to Scapa Flow on 22 October, thus completing her first operational assignment.

Even as *Haida* passed through the Switha Gate, Scapa Flow, plans were underway for the resumption of Arctic convoys for the 1943-44 winter season. The first convoys to the Soviet Union had been sent late in the summer of 1941, arriving in Archangel loaded with tanks, trucks, aircraft and other supplies. These convoys, sent in response to Operation Barbarossa, the German invasion of Russia in June 1941, represented a desperate attempt on the part of the British to prevent the collapse of the Soviet Union under the weight of the German offensive. By the end of 1941, eight British convoys had arrived in Russia, despite numerous dangers inherent in the Arctic passage. The Arctic Run fast acquired a reputation as the most dangerous and certainly the most miserable of the Allied convoy routes.

The passage, as the ship's company of *Haida* knew, crossed one of the most hazardous stretches of water in the world, an area constantly hit by severe Arctic storms. Merchantmen and warships had to contend with gale-driven waves accompanied by rain, sleet, and snow—regular occurrences in these cheerless seas. With much of the route falling above the Arctic Circle, the high latitudes resulted in almost perpetual darkness during winter months, broken only by a few hours of twilight each day. This was the black-out route. Station-keeping was a difficult task, as ships were required to make their way through the darkness without the aid of navigation lights.

On their route to Murmansk or Archangel, Allied convoys passed through a narrow corridor bounded by Arctic pack-ice on one side and German-occupied Norway on the other. Depending on the time of the year, this corridor could be as narrow as 80 miles. The rugged, fjord-dominated coast of Norway provided lairs from which U-boats and surface vessels of the *Kriegsmarine* could spring. Norway also afforded several excellent airfields, and from these the *Luftwaffe* could fly sorties to prey on passing Allied convoys. The *Luftwaffe* had five reconnaissance units in Norway, based at Trondheim, Tromsö, Stavanger and elsewhere. Each unit had a *Blohm Voss 138* flying boat, and ten to twelve aircraft, six or seven being serviceable at any one time. The Bv 138s (and others) were equipped with radar allowing range detection up to 105 miles. Dogged by poor communications, for radio transmission in northern Norway could be poor and no direct link existed between the *Luftwaffe* and *Kriegsmarine*, coordinated attack on convoys often occurred by happenstance.

Such was the state of affairs on 27 June 1942, when convoy PQ-17 departed from Iceland for Murmansk. Summertime spelled trouble for convoys. Onboard the thirty-five merchant vessels which sailed for the Soviet Union were 156,492 tons of tanks, trucks, aircraft and other materials. On 4 July, the Admiralty received ULTRA decrypts deciphered by Bletchley Park. This intelligence led the First Sea Lord, Admiral of the Fleet Sir Dudley Pound, to infer that the German battleship *Tirpitz* had put to sea to attack PQ-17. Pound considered the possibility of dispersing the convoy. He knew the merchant ships would be left defenceless against U-boats and aircraft. Rather than leave the final decision to the Commander-in-Chief (C-in-C) of the Home Fleet, who was at sea onboard HMS *Duke of York* providing distant cover to the convoy, Pound took it upon himself to order the dispersal of PQ-17. To that point in time PQ-17 had been attacked by U-boats but had suffered no losses. At 20:00 on 4 July, an attack by twenty German torpedo-bombers was fought off with a loss of two Allied merchant vessels. At 21:23 on 4 July, the Admiralty gave the order for the convoy to disperse. This was followed by a second fateful signal at 21:36, "convoy is to scatter."

In fact, the German battleship was still anchored in Altenfjord, Norway. Pound's order to scatter the convoy allowed aircraft and U-boats based in Norway to launch a massive attack against the vulnerable merchant vessels. Over 200 German aircraft, including 130 bombers, 43 torpedo-bombers and 29 reconnaissance aircraft were sent to prey on the convoy. Thirteen merchant vessels and one rescue ship were destroyed by air attack. A further ten vessels were lost to U-boats. As for the cargo, some 430 tanks, 210 aircraft and 3,350 vehicles found their way to the seabed of the Barents Sea. Of 156,492 tons of war materials onboard the convoy vessels, only 51,176 tons arrived in Murmansk.

By the time of *Haida*'s arrival in Scapa Flow, PQ-17 stood in the memories of Allied sailors as an example of the perils facing Arctic convoys. As of September 1943, however, urgent negotiations between the British and Soviets were underway regarding the resumption of the Arctic convoys.

Churchill informed Stalin that the British intended to send one convoy of thirty-five ships every month from November 1943 to February 1944. Shortly afterwards, London's War Ministry increased this number to forty ships per convoy. This drew a sharp response from Vice-Admiral Sir Bruce Fraser, C-in-C Home Fleet, who contended that station-keeping would be impossible during winter months, given such large formations. Facing severe weather and persistent darkness, merchant vessels could easily become separated from the escorts and be exposed to U-boat attacks. Therefore, the Admiralty decided that each convoy would be divided into two groups that would sail at two-week intervals.

News that convoys were to be resumed meant that the officers and men of *Haida* could look forward to weeks of blowing sleet and snow driven by Arctic storms. Long hours of perpetual darkness would be accompanied by constant work parties to prevent ice from building up on the upper deck and superstructure. If ice were left to accumulate, it could cause the destroyer to become top-heavy and even capsize. With bad weather and the constant threat of a German attack serving as the likely forecast for the weeks ahead, the memory of PQ-17 stood as an example of the worst case scenario.

### Resuming the Arctic Convoys

First of the renewed convoys, designated RA-54A, would involve the return of thirteen merchant vessels from the Soviet Union and a close escort of nine destroyers, two minesweepers and a corvette. Meanwhile, Operation FS would provide distant cover for the convoy by heavy units of the Home Fleet. These ships would require a protective screen of destroyers. For this purpose *Haida* put to sea from Scapa Flow on 29 October in company with the destroyers HMS *Onslow* and *Venus*, USS *Capps* and *Hobson*, and the Norwegian destroyer *Stord*. Two days later, having been delayed by fog, RA-54A sailed from Archangel bound for Loch Ewe, the rendezvous in northwest Scotland, and arrived safely on 14 November.

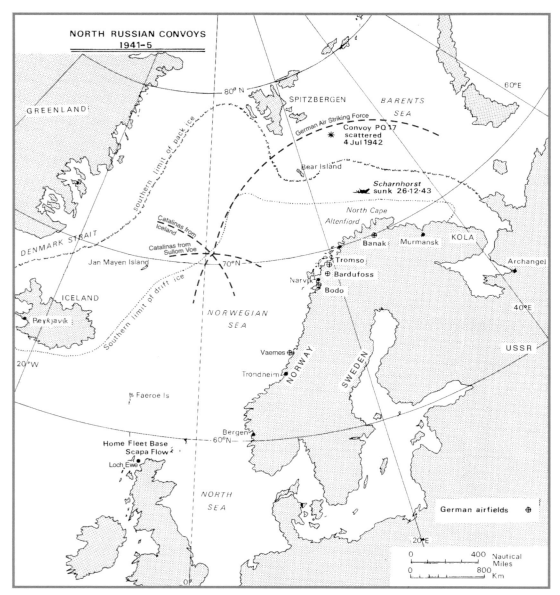

Theatre of Operations Convoys to North Russia

Meanwhile, in home waters of Britain and the Barents Sea, the strategic situation had been altered drastically by Operation Source. On 22 September 1943, four British X-craft midget submarines, armed with high explosive, had penetrated the defences guarding Altenfjord. Cutting their way through protective netting, crews of two X-craft had been able to plant explosive charges underneath the *Tirpitz*. The battleship was out of action indefinitely.

Also in late September, the Germans ordered the pocket battleship *Lützow* from Norway to the Baltic for refit. With the removal of these two capital ships, the strategic situation in the Arctic had been changed entirely within the space of a week. Aside from U-boats based in Bergen and Trondheim and six destroyers based in Altenfjord, the Germans were now left with but a single capital ship in Norway, the *Scharnhorst*. This 32,000-ton vessel mounted nine 11-inch guns as its main armament, along with twelve 5.9-inch guns, fourteen 4.1-inch guns and numerous anti-aircraft and close range weapons. It was powerful enough to "inflict more damage in the two hours of twilight than a whole U-boat flotilla could inflict in six months," wrote the historian Fritz-Otto Busch.

British naval intelligence anxiously followed the progress of German operations in these northern seas. Coordinating information supplied from Iceland; Allied agents in Norway; direction-finding signals and radio traffic from U-boats; and above all, ENIGMA traffic of German transmission (which became ULTRA communications in British hands and used as British SIGINT); the British had the upper hand in naval operations. They comprehended, for instance, that the Germans knew of positions of convoys as reported by the *Luftwaffe* reconnaissance units or as reported by U-boats. Coupled with radar, good gunnery and excellent

tactics, sigint gave the Home Fleet—and all its units, including *Haida*—a superb advantage in the safe passage of the Arctic convoys and in the destruction of the *Scharnhorst*. The events unfold slowly and reach a climax on Boxing Day 1943.

The first outward convoy for the 1943-44 season, designated JW-54A, included eighteen freighters and one transport. Departing Loch Ewe on 15 November, the convoy was accompanied by heavy units of the Home Fleet and a close escort formed by *Haida*, *Iroquois* and *Huron*, and British destroyers *Onslow*, *Onslaught*, *Orwell*, *Impulsive*, *Inconstant* and *Whitehall*.

*Haida* acted under the orders of Captain (D), 17th Destroyer Flotilla in *Onslow*. During this operation *Haida* was senior officer of a division which included *Iroquois* and *Huron*. The destroyers were joined by the corvette *Heather* and the minesweeper *Hussar*. Big guns were provided by the cruisers HMS *Kent*, *Jamaica* and *Bermuda*, sent to cover the convoy as it made its way past the coast of Norway. The British battleship *Anson* and the American cruiser *Tuscaloosa*, reinforcements for the Home Fleet, were detailed to provide distant cover to JW-54A in event of an attack by the *Scharnhorst*. The Allies considered it likely that convoy JW-54A, fully loaded with war materials, would lure *Scharnhorst* to sea. But *Scharnhorst* remained anchored in Altenfjord. JW-54A passed unmolested.

Arriving in Kola Inlet on 24 November, *Haida* proceeded to Vaenga Bay Pier and berthed alongside *Huron*. Crews of the Allied escorts were given shore leave. What they found may be described as discouraging. Vaenga Bay is located a few miles from the port of Murmansk. In the past Allied ships had been required to dock there because the Russians would not allow them to make use of Polyarnoe naval base. Along the shore stood dishevelled buildings housing survivors of

The German battleship *Scharnhorst*. (Imperial War Museum, courtesy Ed Stewart)

torpedoed ships. Nearby were Russian-operated hospitals which tended to sick and wounded servicemen. With frozen bodies stacked outside awaiting burial serving as brutal testimony to the standard of treatment provided by the Russians, it is not surprising that many Allied servicemen came to view being sent to one of these hospitals as a death sentence. Meanwhile, British doctors in Murmansk were forbidden to interfere with the care of patients, owing to professional jealousy on the part of the Russians.

Upon learning of conditions endured by patients sent to the Russian hospitals, a seaman, Andrew Gillespie, chose to wait until the ship was well underway on its return to Scapa Flow before presenting himself at the Sick Bay for treatment of appendicitis. Had he done so while in harbour, there would have been no choice but to put him ashore for treatment. In order to avoid what he considered certain death ashore, the twenty-two-year-old rating did not seek medical attention until two days after the symptoms appeared. By that time, *Haida* was safely away from the Russian hospitals and escorting return convoy RA-54B to Great Britain. It was soon apparent that the operation could not wait and would have to be performed at sea. Shortly afterwards, the ship's medical officer, Surgeon Lieutenant-Commander S.A. MacDonald, RCNVR, along with the sick berth petty officer, the leading writer and the paymaster performed the appendectomy on the dining table of the captain's day cabin. The operation was a success and after twelve days the patient was discharged from sick bay and returned to his mess.

Meanwhile, RA-54B, consisting of eight freighters, was making its way from Murmansk to Loch Ewe. On one occasion tracer fire and an illuminated sky from searchlights were observed in the fading distance and numerous German radio transmissions were overheard. *Haida* continued her station-keeping. The convoy arrived safely in Loch Ewe on 9 December, and *Haida* once more returned to the desolate harbour of Scapa Flow. Next day, after refuelling, she put to sea, this time escorting a second group of reinforcements northward to hard-pressed Spitzbergen.

With the safe return of RA-54B, the Germans had again failed to interfere with the Allied convoys to Russia. Admiral Fraser, C-in-C Home Fleet, unwisely assumed this was because the enemy was unaware that the convoys had been resumed. Unknown to the British, the Germans had been receiving reports since mid-November that the Russian convoys had been reopened and yet had made no move to deploy *Scharnhorst*.

The C-in-C of the German Navy, *Grossadmiral* Karl Dönitz, had Hitler's consent to deploy surface units against enemy convoys when and where he chose. Fully aware that the British and American arms unloaded at Murmansk and Archangel were being used within two weeks of their arrival to fight German armies on the Eastern Front, at a conference with Hitler on 18-19 December, Dönitz outlined his plan to launch a surface attack against the next convoy on its way to Murmansk. The Führer reluctantly agreed. The next convoy was scheduled to depart Loch Ewe on 20 December.

## Convoy JW-55B, Loch Ewe to Murmansk

Convoy JW-55B's nineteen freighters had a close escort of destroyers and smaller vessels commanded by Captain J.A. McCoy onboard the destroyer HMS *Onslow*. The remainder of the close escort included *Haida*, *Iroquois* and *Huron*, along with the British destroyers *Onslaught*, *Orwell*, *Impulsive*, *Obdurate*, *Whitehall* and *Wrestler*. Also included in the escort were the corvettes *Oxslip* and *Honeysuckle* and the minesweeper *Gleaner*.

While JW-55B was making its way towards Murmansk, a second convoy, RA-55A, began the return passage from the Soviet Union with twenty-two freighters in ballast. The two convoys were predicted to make their way past the North Cape at approximately the same time. The plan called for Allied covering forces to provide distant support to both convoys concurrently. Force 1 would depart from the Kola Inlet at 01:00 on 23 December, and included the British cruisers *Belfast*, *Sheffield* and *Norfolk* under the command of Vice-Admiral R.L. Burnett. Its job was to provide close cruiser cover to JW-55B and RA-55A. Meanwhile, Force 2 under Admiral Fraser, would sail from Akureyri, Iceland, with the battleship *Duke of York*, the cruiser *Jamaica* and four destroyers. Fraser had been led to believe that the lack of enemy interference thus far had been due to ignorance on the part of the Germans that the convoys had been resumed. Reasoning that once the enemy learned of the passage of convoys to Russia they would launch a full attack, Fraser decided that convoys JW-55B and RA-55A would receive full support from heavy units of the Home Fleet. Ironically, by attempting to lull the British into relaxing their guard, the German plan had the opposite effect.

*Haida* and the close escort of JW-55B departed Scapa Flow as scheduled at 17:00 on 20 December. Two days later, as *Haida* and the escorts were off the Faroe Islands en route to join the convoy, a lone aircraft was sighted making its

Top: HMS *Norfolk*, one of the three cruisers commanded by Vice-Admiral Burnett at North Cape.
(Imperial War Museum, courtesy Ed Stewart)

Bottom: The battleship HMS *Duke of York*, flagship of Admiral Fraser at the Battle of North Cape.
(Imperial War Museum, courtesy Ed Stewart)

way westward. It was a German meteorological flight, and although the pilot was able to observe both the Allied convoy and the escort vessels, he mistakenly reported the sighting as a formation of forty troop transports. As a result, *Admiral* Otto Schniewind, Flag Officer Group North, headquartered in Kiel, ordered his U-boats to return to the entrance of Altenfjord to guard against what he suspected was an Allied invasion force. The following day Schniewind sent a second flight of aircraft to confirm the identity of the Allied ships.

At 11:35 on 23 December, the close escort of JW-55B sighted two enemy planes thought to be Dornier 217s on the port bow of the convoy. *Haida* and *Iroquois* opened fire. They damaged the aircraft, though not severely, and these planes continued their surveillance, taking cover in the clouds whenever fire was opened on them. At

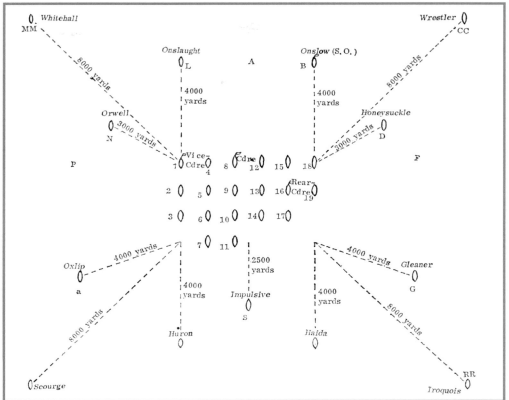

The Sailing Disposition of JW-55B

1. *Fort Nakasley*
2. *Ocean Valour*
3. *John H. Abel*
4. *Bernard N. Baker*
5. *Fort Vercheres*
6. *Cardinal Gibbons*
7. *John Wanamaker*
8. *Fort Kullyspell*
9. *Norlys*
10. *Brockholst Livingstone*
11. *John Vining*
12. *Thomas V. Walters*
13. *British Statesman*
14. *Ocean Messenger*
15. *Harold Winslow*
16. *Ocean Pride*
17. *Ocean Gypsy*
18. *Ocean Viceroy*
19. *Will Rogers*

11:45 McCoy reported to the Senior British Naval Officer in Murmansk, SBNO North Russia, the details of this encounter, indicating that JW-55B was being shadowed. To that point in time, the A/S escort scheduled to cover the convoy from 09:15 to darkness, a Catalina from No. 19 Group, had not arrived. Not until 13:30 did this plane appear, taking up a position ahead of the convoy. Later, two aircraft were sighted, one a Dornier 217 and the other a Bv 138 flying boat. The latter was seen approaching the convoy on the starboard side, flying low. Once within range, the guns of *Haida* and *Huron* opened a brisk fire, forcing the enemy to turn away.

German reconnaissance units identified the Allied ships as a convoy and reported the position, approximately 300 miles southeast of Jan Mayen Island. Soon the convoy would be nearing the coast of Norway and well within quick striking range of *Scharnhorst*. The Germans were also encouraged to learn that no covering force of Allied cruisers or battleships had been sighted by reconnaissance aircraft. *Scharnhorst* in Altenfjord was brought to three hours' notice for steam. Unknown to the Germans, while their reconnaissance aircraft were shadowing the convoy on 23 December, Force 1, consisting of the British cruisers *Belfast*, *Sheffield* and *Norfolk* had sailed from the Kola Inlet, heading west to provide cover for the convoy as it neared Bear Island. Meanwhile, Admiral Fraser in *Duke of York* sailed from Akureyri leading the cruiser *Jamaica* and four destroyers of Force 2.

On Christmas Eve, *Haida* and convoy JW-55B were shadowed by German forces as they made their way eastward, now 240 miles east of Jan

Mayen Island. German aircraft were joined by the *Eisenbart* Group of U-boats. At one point *U601* and *U716* had to be driven away by the Allied escorts. Meanwhile, *Duke of York* was still 400 miles behind the convoy as it neared the most exposed leg. In order to close, Fraser broke radio silence and signalled the convoy to reverse course for three hours while he increased the speed of Force 2 from 15 to 19 knots. Although the convoy was unable to comply with the order, Captain McCoy onboard *Onslow* ordered a reduction in speed. Soon the gap between the convoy and *Duke of York* was reduced by 100 miles. Meanwhile the weather was deteriorating rapidly and in the evening of 24 December the Germans lost contact with convoy JW-55B.

On Christmas Day, in a southwesterly gale, the convoy continued through blowing snow and thirty-foot waves. *Haida* and the other destroyers were forced to reduce speed to 7 knots in order to allow the stragglers to rejoin the convoy. While the reduction in speed was necessary it was unsettling because such slow speeds left the destroyers open to torpedo attacks by U-boats. Meanwhile, Fraser had ordered four destroyers to detach from the close escort of convoy RA-55B, which had not yet been detected by the Germans, in order to reinforce JW-55B. This brought the escort of the outbound convoy to a strength of fourteen destroyers. "Christmas Day was spent at sea under unusual conditions," wrote Commander DeWolf, "in the Arctic, in bad weather and almost constant darkness escorting a straggling convoy, shadowed and reported by enemy aircraft and with the *Scharnhorst* and an unknown number of U-boats in the vicinity."

### The Fate of *Scharnhorst*

The Germans in Altenfjord, meanwhile, spent Christmas Day making ready for the imminent departure of *Scharnhorst* (*Kapitänzursee* Fritz Hintze). At 12:15 Schniewind ordered the battleship to be ready to sail on an hour's notice. The final decision now lay with Dönitz. By this point the C-in-C had been made aware that British cruisers were within range to provide cover for the Allied convoy. The *Duke of York* remained undetected by the Germans as she steamed eastward. Although three German direction-finding stations had intercepted the signal sent by Fraser on 24 December, it had been misinterpreted as having originated from a merchant vessel which had fallen behind the convoy. Dönitz remained confident that these British cruisers would be no match for the superior speed and heavy armament of *Scharnhorst*. As such, at 14:15 on 25 December, the order was given for *Scharnhorst* to attack the convoy. Shortly after 19:00 the battleship, accompanied by five destroyers, departed Altenfjord under the command of *Konteradmiral* Erich Bey.

As the battle group was steaming out of the Altenfjord, a signal was sent to a nearby German patrol vessel to alert it to the passage of *Scharnhorst*. The battle group was soon clear of land, and heavy seas had the destroyers rolling badly. Shortly before midnight, Bey reported to Schniewind that the battle group had entered the area of operation but that his destroyers were experiencing difficulties in the severe weather.

Unknown to the Germans, their stream of radio traffic was being monitored by British Intelligence and deciphered by ULTRA. By 02:17 on 26 December, the Admiralty had in its possession a decrypt alerting them to the possibility that *Scharnhorst* had put to sea at 18:00 on Christmas Day. Within an hour the Admiralty had relayed it to Fraser, who by 03:39 had closed to within 220 miles of the convoy.

At 04:01, Fraser ordered the convoy and escort forces to report their position. At this moment,

*Haida* and JW-55B were 50 miles south of Bear Island, heading easterly at 8 knots. Force 1, led by Burnett onboard *Belfast*, was 150 miles east of the convoy. At 06:28 Fraser ordered JW-55B to alter course northwards, away from the incoming German battle group. By this time, the rear of the convoy had become scattered, and the change in course aggravated this situation. Not until the weather began to improve at around 08:00 were *Haida* and the escort destroyers able to begin rounding up straggling freighters. At that time *Belfast*, *Sheffield* and *Norfolk* were closing rapidly with the convoy.

At 08:40, *Belfast*'s radar reported contact at a range of 35,000 yards on a bearing of 295 degrees. This proved to be *Scharnhorst*, alone now after having detached destroyers at 07:00 to search for the convoy. The German ship was running directly towards Force 1. Burnett responded by ordering his cruisers to alter course and close with the enemy. At 09:21 the cruiser *Sheffield* signalled: "Enemy in sight bearing 222 degrees."

This signal was followed by a hail of gunfire and starshell from the British cruisers. Seen from the bridge of *Haida*, the action at first appeared to have broken out along the starboard wing of the convoy. The flashes of gunfire were coming from the covering force as it engaged the German battleship. At the same time, *Haida* and the escort destroyers were ordered to remain with the convoy and stay clear. The furious exchange of starshell and tracer rounds continued on the horizon until approximately 09:30, when *Scharnhorst* altered course to 150 degrees and increased speed to 30 knots in order to break off the attack. Before this could be done, the British cruisers scored a hit which destroyed the forward radar antenna of the enemy vessel, meaning that *Scharnhorst* (using aft radar) had to steam away from the convoy in order to maintain radar contact with the enemy.

As *Scharnhorst* broke away, *Haida* continued rounding up the stragglers. At the same time, Burnett attempted to maneuver his cruisers so that they would block the way to the convoy should *Scharnhorst* return. Arctic dawn broke at 11:00, providing a dim twilight over the next two hours as the convoy regrouped and Force 1 searched for the enemy. At 11:37, radar contact was made by *Norfolk* but lost soon thereafter. Then at 12:05, *Belfast* detected a radar echo at 30,500 yards and for the second time the cruisers altered course to close with the enemy. Again, it was *Sheffield* who first sighted the enemy, and the British cruisers opened fire at 12:21. *Scharnhorst* returned fire, scoring two hits on *Norfolk*, damaging her radar equipment and killing one officer and six men.

The latest count from *Haida*'s bridge indicated that seventeen of the nineteen merchant vessels of JW-55B were accounted for. Before a second count could be carried out, *Haida* received a signal at 12:27 ordering her to prepare for a torpedo attack against *Scharnhorst*. Before the attack could be carried out, the enemy again disengaged, this time heading southeast, away from the cruisers. For the second time *Haida* was denied the opportunity to engage the enemy.

Turning away, *Scharnhorst* was now on a collision course with *Duke of York* and Force 2. Burnett's cruisers continued to shadow in order to keep radar contact. The trap was set. Force 2 was now able to close rapidly with the enemy until at 16:17 the type 273Q radar high up on the foremast of *Duke of York* detected a contact at 22.75 miles. Closing with the contact, *Belfast* and *Duke of York* put up starshell at 16:47. The brilliant light revealed the silhouette of the enemy. Moments later the sighting was followed by the crashing gunfire of ten 14-inch guns from the British battleship. Turning away from the sudden attack, Bey now saw escape to Altenfjord as the only hope of saving his ship. For the next two hours the two sides exchanged fire as *Scharnhorst* slowly pulled away from her attackers.

The chase continued in this manner until 16:20, when a hit to the rear of the ship caused *Scharnhorst* to lose speed rapidly. The Allies were now able to close and the destroyers of Force 2 were detached to carry out a torpedo attack. Eleven torpedoes were fired, three of which caused serious damage to the enemy. Meanwhile, the guns of *Duke of York* and the cruisers pounded *Scharnhorst* for twenty minutes, bringing the great ship to a standstill. The German vessel was con-

sumed in flames, yet her guns had not been silenced and her colours were still flying. At 19:45, a second torpedo attack was ordered and the Allies closed in and fired at the motionless battleship, scoring several hits. *Scharnhorst* capsized to starboard and went down, taking with her all but thirty-six of her 2,000 officers and men. *Scharnhorst* sank at approximately 72°16'N 28°41'E, about 60 miles northwest of North Cape.

"There is no doubt that, despite its shortcomings, British radar is still far superior to any yet encountered in German ships, and that this technical superiority and the correct employment of

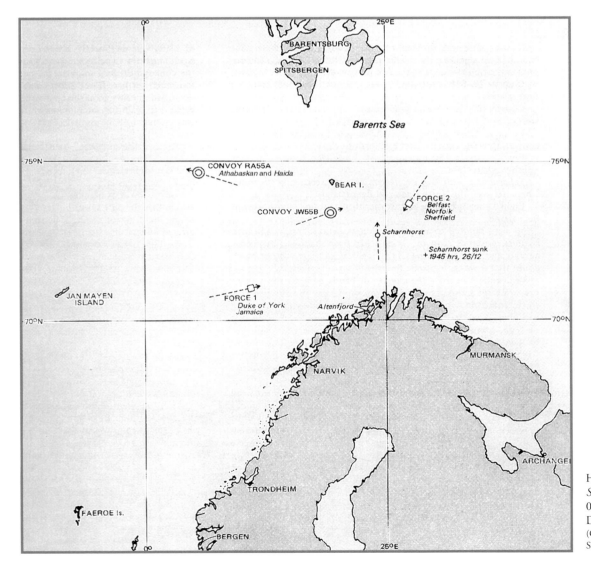

Hunt for *Scharnhorst* at 04:00, 26 December 1943. (Courtesy Ed Stewart)

the gear enabled the Home Fleet to find, fix, fight and finish off the *Scharnhorst.*" So wrote Admiral Fraser, soon to be decorated as Fraser of North Cape. He gave credit to the plotting arrangements conducted by Burnett in the *Belfast*'s charthouse. "In general," he concluded, "the speed of wireless communication and the exceptional performance of radar reflects the greatest credit on the personnel concerned, and in this night battle contributed in great measure to its success."

Convoy JW-55B continued its course to Murmansk, shadowed the entire way by U-boats. Upon *Haida*'s arrival in the Kola Inlet, at noon on 28 December, she proceeded to Vaenga Bay where the escort destroyers were docked alongside the jubilant cruisers of Force 1. While in harbour, the Allied ships were attacked by German aircraft. The attack was fought off by a furious round of anti-aircraft fire and the Allies returned to their belated Christmas dinners. On New Year's Eve 1943 *Haida*, now refuelled, weighed anchor and steamed out of the Kola Inlet escorting RA-55B bound for Loch Ewe.

*Haida*'s role as a fleet and convoy escort contributed to the loss of *Scharnhorst*. She stood her station with the Home Fleet. The Allies held the defence of the convoy to be their first priority, and it was due to the vigilance of the escort vessels that JW-55B arrived safely at its destination. With *Haida* and the other escort destroyers available to guard the convoy, *Duke of York* and the cruisers had been able to run down and destroy the enemy battle cruiser before it could return to Altenfjord. The officers and men of *Haida* had successfully completed another duty. The destruction of *Scharnhorst* marked a turning point in the war to control Arctic waters, and the men onboard *Haida* could be proud of their performance throughout the operation. It was an appropriate introduction to the war for a destroyer that was to become the most famous ship of the Royal Canadian Navy. And so ended the last sortie of the German raider *Scharnhorst.*

As for *Haida* during the three months ending 31 December 1943 she steamed 15,404 miles, had spent 65 days at sea and 27 in harbour.

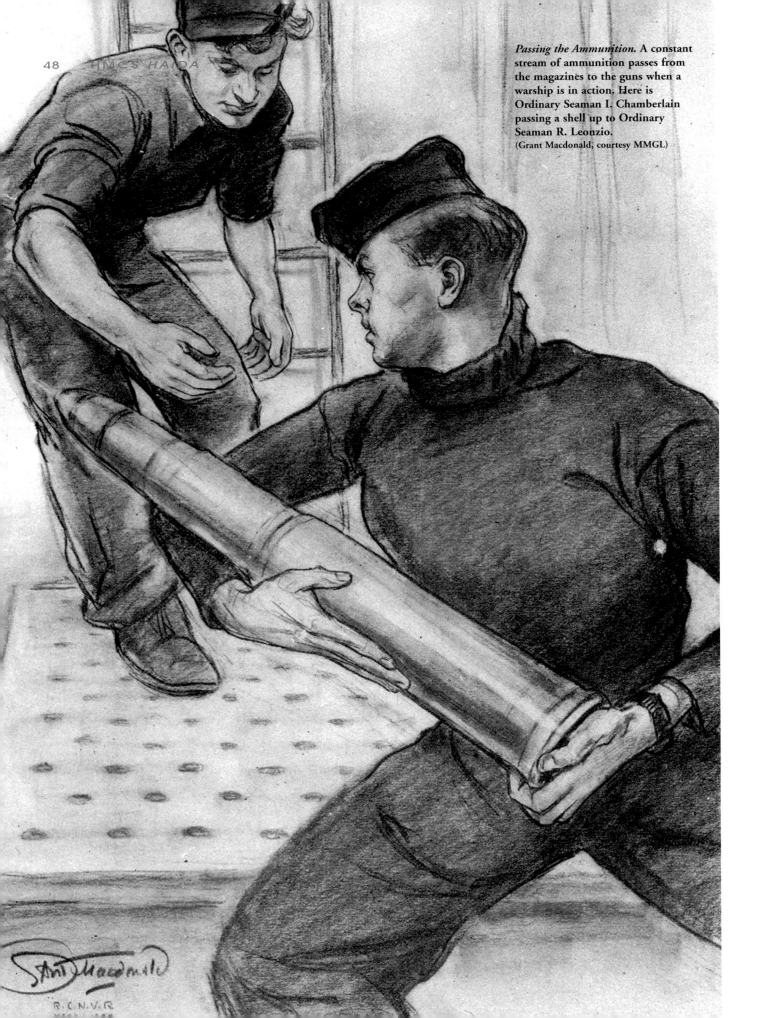

*Passing the Ammunition.* A constant stream of ammunition passes from the magazines to the guns when a warship is in action. Here is Ordinary Seaman I. Chamberlain passing a shell up to Ordinary Seaman R. Leonzio. (Grant Macdonald, courtesy MMGL)

# CHAPTER 3

## PLYMOUTH COMMAND: JANUARY – APRIL 1944

FOLLOWING THE SINKING of *Scharnhorst*, the Admiralty redeployed a number of warships from convoy escort duty in the Arctic Ocean. At 12:00 on 7 January 1944 *Haida* was detached from the escort of convoy RA-55B and arrived in Scapa Flow later that day. By 10 January she had set course for Plymouth, Devon.

*Haida* sailed south with *Iroquois*. The Canadian pair arrived at the seagate of Plymouth on 12 January. For the next nine months *Haida* called Plymouth home. This famous seaport, from which Sir Francis Drake had set forth to harry the Spanish Armada and from which Pilgrims had sailed for the New World, was the centre of gravity for the growing naval power being exercised by British, Canadian, US and other Allied naval forces in the English Channel and Western Approaches.

*Haida* and *Iroquois* were soon joined by *Athabaskan* and other Tribals. On 17 and 18 January *Haida* and *Iroquois* and HMS *Meteor* provided cover for the British battleship *King George V*, back from the Azores with Churchill aboard. *Huron*, the fourth Canadian Tribal based in Plymouth, would not arrive from Scapa Flow until February, as she was still required to escort two convoys to the Soviet Union. In the meantime, her place was filled by HMS *Tartar*.

The destroyers were being gathered at this watch-post of the English Channel at the request of Vice-Admiral Sir Ralph Leatham, C-in-C Plymouth Command. Since August 1943 Leatham, formerly in charge at Malta, had been pressing London for the formation of an offensive strike force for the Western Channel based in Plymouth. That his request had been met was largely the

*Haida* (left) and *Iroquois* shortly after their arrival in Plymouth from Scapa Flow, January 1944. On the far right, behind *Iroquois*, is a Hunt class destroyer.
(Courtesy Michael Whitby, NAC PA-180145)

Opposite: *HMCS Athabaskan*, "unlucky lady," *Haida*'s famous running-mate. February 1944, in Plymouth, wearing Western Approaches Special Forces camouflage.
(Courtesy Gilbert A. Milne)

result of a recent shift in Allied policy towards the English Channel. Allied forces in this area had been limited to a defensive role and the German Navy had taken full advantage of this situation, conducting operations out of the occupied Channel ports after the fall of France in June 1940. With the invasion of Europe steadily approaching, Allied operations in the English Channel began to take on an increasingly offensive nature. Admiralty planners recognized that German surface units in this area would pose a significant threat to the troop transports and supply ships required to support an Allied campaign in Northwest Europe. By January 1944, Allied air power had succeeded in winning control over the Channel during daylight hours. At night, German convoys still ran free along the coast of Brittany, and the surface forces of the *Kriegsmarine* continued to operate against the Allies. It fell to Plymouth Command to intercept and destroy enemy forces and shipping in the Channel. Leatham decided to conduct a series of offensive patrols.

## Lessons Learned:
## Patrolling the English Channel

Patrols fell into two categories and were designated by the Admiralty as either "Tunnel" or "Hostile" operations. Both were to be carried out under cover of darkness

in order to avoid detection by German aircraft and shore batteries.

Tunnel operations consisted of offensive sweeps along the coast of Brittany, with *Haida* and other Tribals accompanied by a cruiser of the Royal Navy, *Bellona* or *Black Prince*. Together, the destroyers and the cruiser were designated as either Force 26 or Force 28. The objective of such patrols was to engage and destroy enemy convoys and escort vessels.

The second type of patrol was designated as Hostile. Here the Tribals were to act as a covering force for Allied motor torpedo boats (MTBs), which in turn screened any fast British minelayers sent to mine enemy convoy routes or approaches to harbours along the coast of France. By means of a strike against German shipping and naval forces, Plymouth Command intended to secure the Western Approaches to the English Channel in preparation for the invasion.

When *Haida* arrived at Plymouth on 12 January, Tunnel patrols had been carried out since September. To date, such operations had met with decidedly unfortunate results. German forces had proven remarkably adept at countering Allied efforts in the Channel, wisely choosing to avoid contact with an equal or superior force. Unlike the Royal Navy, destroyers of the *Kriegsmarine* had permission to turn away from an engagement if it suited them and disappear in the safety of the countless islands, rocks and shoals of the Channel. Before they broke for the cover protection of shore

batteries, islands, or French harbours, the Germans usually availed themselves of the opportunity to fire a full complement of torpedoes at any enemy ships they encountered. Such tactics had frustrated British attempts to draw the enemy into a decisive battle; for in order to avoid approaching torpedoes it was necessary to steer off course, thus allowing the German vessels to gain a great deal of distance in their run for home. On one notable occasion in October 1943, this German tactic had proved to be much more than an inconvenience, and had resulted in disaster for the British forces.

On the night of 22 October 1943, a British force of eight warships consisting of the cruiser *Charybdis*, Captain G.A.W. Voelcker (SO), accompanied by the fleet destroyers *Rocket* and *Grenville* and the smaller Hunt class destroyers *Limbourne*, *Melbreak*, *Talybont*, *Wensleydale* and *Stevenstone*, had set out from Plymouth to conduct a sweep of the Channel in the hope of intercepting a German convoy and destroying the blockade runner *Münsterland*. The German 4th Torpedo Boat (TB) Flotilla, Commander Franz Kohlauf (SO), and comprising *T-23*, *T-22*, *T-25*, *T-26* and *T-27*, were providing distant escort. At 00:45 the Hunts began to pick up German radio transmissions, indicating that the enemy was nearby. At 01:17 and again at 01:30, the Hunts failed to inform the other Allied ships that the Germans were altering course. At 01:30, *Charybdis* detected five radar echoes at 14,000 yards. Even so, five minutes passed before the presence of the enemy was reported. By this time the contacts had closed to within 8,800 yards. At 01:45 *Charybdis* opened fire with starshell, revealing incoming German torpedoes. Too late to avoid the attack, *Charybdis* and *Limbourne* were struck by torpedoes. *Charybdis* was hit by a second torpedo and went down at 02:30. An unsuccessful attempt was made to tow *Limbourne* to Plymouth. The destroyer was sunk by Allied torpedoes in order to prevent her from being captured by the Germans. After losing a cruiser and a destroyer, the six remaining Allied ships set course for Plymouth. At no point on the night of 22-23 October did forces taking part in this Tunnel operation make contact with the five German torpedo boats which had attacked them. The enemy with stealth and speed had claimed two further victims. The *Münsterland* carried on as a blockade runner until the night of 20-21 January 1944 when, in trying to avoid shelling by British long-range batteries near Dover, went ashore in fog near Cap Blanc Nez and was destroyed.

The disastrous outcome of the operation of 22-23 October could be blamed on inexperience and lack of cohesion. Vice-Admiral Leatham recognized that sending out a force consisting of three distinct types of ship, each with different capabilities and armament, made it very difficult for them to function as a cohesive unit. The ships taking part in the operation had never before been to sea together. Moreover, the SO had no previous experience on Tunnel operations. The operation was later described by the destroyer captain Roger Hill as "the classic balzup of the war," although it did have the effect of drawing the Admiralty's attention to Leatham's urgent request for the creation of a homogenous force of Tribal class destroyers. Hindsight makes for perfect vision.

## Night Exercises: Training in the Tribals

Leatham now had the fast, heavily-gunned Tribals he had requested. While newly-arrived Tribals would require time for training, especially in night-fighting, hard-pressed Plymouth Command faced a multitude of operational demands and a shortage of destroyers. Time was not available for the sort of training that would bring the effectiveness of the British and Canadian destroyers up to a level comparable to that of their German opponents. Plymouth Command was forced to ignore the lessons of the *Charybdis* and dispatch the Tribals on their first mission within days of their arrival in Plymouth and without the necessary training.

On 19 January, *Haida*, three sister Tribals and three Hunt class destroyers were sent to conduct a Tunnel operation. The mission was characterized by a lack of organization. The Allied ships were probably lucky that they did not come into contact with the enemy that night. It might be argued they were fortunate not to sink any of their own ships when the two subdivisions of the Allied patrol lost contact with each other somewhere off the French coast. Upon their return to Plymouth, DeWolf stated in his report of action that "it is strongly recommended that the Plymouth forces exercise night encounters."

Time for training exercises was not made available to the Tribals until February. In the interim, in the last week of January, *Haida* was given new radar equipment that greatly improved the ship's overall night-fighting capabilities. This was Type 271Q, a 10-centimetre surface warning radar which provided early warning of approaching enemy vessels. Meanwhile, the Tribals of the 10th DF had already been equipped with Type 285P gunnery radar, then the standard fire control radar for destroyers. This set was capable of directing the ship's main armament to within 3 to 4 degrees bearing and 100 yards range on a 15,000-yard scale. In addition to radar, *Haida* was also fitted with so-called "Headache" equipment, allowing it to monitor German radio transmissions while at sea, and IFF (Identification Friend or Foe) equipment to determine the identity of unknown ships.

From 30 January to 4 February day and night exercises were carried out by *Haida* and other ships off Plymouth. At this time an attempt was made to form Force 26, to consist of the cruisers *Black Prince* and *Bellona* and all available Tribals. However, the organization of Force 26 was interrupted by the departure of *Black Prince* and three Tribals for operations elsewhere. For example, on 4 February *Haida*, *Iroquois* and *Athabaskan* sailed for Scapa Flow at 08;30 arriving 22:30 on 5 February. Gales prevailed for some days but day and night exercises and encounters, as well as A/S exercises were carried out in addition to normal screening duties.

Next came Operation Posthorn. On 10 and 11 February *Haida*, *Iroquois* and *Athabaskan* provided a destroyer screen for the British battleship *Anson*, the French battleship *Richelieu* and the British cruisers *Belfast* and *Nigeria*. This force of heavy units from the Home Fleet had been brought together to protect the aircraft carrier HMS *Furious* then conducting air strikes against German convoys off the Norwegian coast. None of the Allied ships in the covering force encountered the enemy. Nor were RAF units able to locate any worthwhile targets along the Norwegian coast. Instead, a successful attack was carried out against a secondary target, SS *Emsland*, a German merchant ship. The Tribals returned to Scapa Flow, where they refuelled, and then made for Plymouth, arriving on 15 February 1944. This northern enterprise consumed eleven days. "Day and night maneuvers using W/T rapid procedure were exercised on passage," reported DeWolf.

## The Formation of Force 26

While the Tribals were taking part in Operation Posthorn, the organization of Plymouth Command had undergone changes. The Admiralty intended to put some firepower into the hunt for German surface ships in the Channel and on the coast of Brittany. Thus reorganized and reshaped, Force 26 was to consist of *Bellona* and its "spear throwers," as one sailor called them—the destroyers of the 10th DF. On 9

*Joan Jeffrey (Boyd).* "I was a Wren Motor Transport Driver—the best job during the war—always had a vehicle."
(Grant Macdonald, courtesy MMGL)

Top: *Haida* and *Athabaskan* conducting high speed maneuvers in the English Channel. (NAC PA-151742)

Bottom: L to R: *Haida, Huron, Tartar* and *Black Prince* exercising in the English Channel February 1944. (NAC PA-201840)

February, *Haida* and *Athabaskan*, together with the destroyers *Ashanti* and *Tartar*, had been formed into the 10th Destroyer Flotilla. *Iroquois* was not included in the new formation as she was scheduled to depart for Halifax on 18 February for refit. She would be replaced by *Huron*, which arrived in Plymouth that same day from Scapa Flow. The flotilla was led by *Tartar*'s hard-fighting and well respected Commanding Officer, Commander St. John Tyrwhitt, son of the famous First World War naval hero, Admiral of the Fleet Sir Reginald Tyrwhitt. St. John Tyrwhitt had served as a destroyer commander in the Mediterranean since 1940 and was well known to Leatham.

Between 18-29 February, the destroyers of the 10th DF practised gunnery, torpedo attacks, anti-aircraft defence, and towing evolutions. The Tribals also took part in a number of exercises to increase their efficiency as a night-fighting unit.

These night-fighting exercises were conducted as a competition between two sub-divisions of the 10th DF. Under cover of darkness, the two groups would make their way separately into the Channel. Then each sub-division would seek to locate the other. The force first able to illuminate the other with starshell could take pride in having won the competition, although, in fact, both groups benefited from the training. Night-fighting exercises also allowed ships taking part to practise station keeping in situations of limited or non-existent visibility. In such night operations, it was essential that ships work as a team and maintain their positions. Otherwise, an encounter with the enemy could easily degenerate into a confused mêlée where none of the ships could distinguish friendly ships from those of the enemy. This could have been the result had the two separate sub-divisions of destroyers taking part in the Tunnel operation of 19 January come into contact with an enemy (or each other).

*Haida* and her sister Tribals still had limited operational experience in the Channel compared to their German opponents. What the ships now required was a chance to put their training into practice.

On the night of 25-26 February *Haida* took part in a Tunnel operation along with the ships of Force 28, including the Tribals *Tartar*, *Athabaskan* and *Huron*, and the RN cruiser *Bellona*. The operation was under the command of Captain Walter Norris (*Bellona*). At 01:40, just as Force 26 was about to commence its sweep along the French coast, the radar in *Bellona* lit up with blips at a range of six miles. As more echoes appeared, Norris began to suspect that the contacts denoted a group of German E-boats. He decided to turn to port in order to avoid them. As the Allied ships changed course, more radar contacts began to appear at regular intervals. At this point, Norris was preparing to illuminate the area with starshell. At precisely this juncture, a more experienced radar operator took over and realized that the suspected E-boats were in fact a formation of low-flying aircraft, which turned out to be friendly.

Later that same night, at 03:22, *Tartar*'s radar detected another contact eight miles distant. The echo was assumed to be an enemy surface vessel. Five minutes after the contact, *Bellona* put up starshell, revealing what appeared to be a German destroyer. *Bellona* and *Tartar* opened fire, but as the destroyers closed with the "enemy" they realized that they had in fact been firing on a group of small islands, which the navigator had thought to be another three miles distant. The shore bombardment was promptly called off. Force 26 decided to call it a night and set course for Plymouth.

The errors of 26 February had been the result of a lack of experience. The misinterpretation of radar contacts is not surprising given that the equipment was new and the most experienced operators could not be on duty all the time. The months to follow would provide the 10th DF with ample opportunity to gain experience in the Channel. The invasion of Europe was quickly approaching and the pace of Allied operations in the Channel had been stepped up accordingly. Over the course of March and April, *Haida* took part in nineteen Tunnel and Hostile operations, including one which, although it did not result in an encounter with the enemy, was destined to have a major impact on the tactical doctrine employed by the 10th DF in Channel operations.

On the night of March 1, as the Allied ships made ready to leave Plymouth for a Tunnel operation, *Bellona* experienced technical difficulties with her radar that kept the ship in harbour. Accordingly, Commander Tyrwhitt onboard *Tartar* became Senior Officer. The 10th DF set out to conduct a Channel sweep without the big starshell capability of a cruiser.

Shortly before midnight, radar onboard *Tartar* showed eight echoes, which were interpreted as a formation of enemy E-boats. These small *Schnellbooote*, as they were called by the Germans, posed a significant threat to Allied warships in the Channel. They were capable of speeds of 39 to 45 knots and were mounted with forward-firing torpedo tubes. Without further investigation, Tyrwhitt took evasive action and altered course so as to avoid contact. At 02:26, radar again detected several echoes, and shortly afterwards *Haida*'s Headache operator intercepted a close-range German radio transmission which indicated that torpedoes had been fired. Once more, Tyrwhitt immediately ordered the flotilla to perform a 90-degree turn and increase speed to 28 knots in order to avoid the suspected incoming torpedoes. On a third occasion, at 02:42, radar contact was again established, this time by *Haida*, and once more a German transmission was intercepted indicating that torpedoes had been fired. Tyrwhitt again responded by taking evasive action, this time firing starshell over the suspected contact. This revealed nothing. Tyrwhitt now assumed that his location must be obvious to enemy units in the area. Accordingly, he ordered the 10th DF to set course at 28 knots for Plymouth.

Tyrwhitt's action was met with criticism from Vice-Admiral Leatham. Leatham agreed with Tyrwhitt's decision to avoid the eight possible E-boats, but he was opposed to evasive action if it prevented the completion of the Allied mission in the Channel, which was to destroy enemy vessels. Leatham, an adherent to the ancient British naval maxim "engage the enemy more closely," was especially critical of the fact that Tyrwhitt had not investigated the enemy contacts obtained at 02:26

and 02:42. In his report to the Admiralty, Leatham described the overall results of this operation as "disappointing."

Whether or not German vessels had fired torpedoes at the Tribals is unknown. If so, then Tyrwhitt's actions may well have prevented the loss of one or more of the ships to yet another unseen enemy, as had been the case with *Charybdis* and *Limbourne* the previous October. Shortly afterwards Tyrwhitt was reassigned to a position on shore after some four years of service onboard British destroyers. Whether or not his replacement was due to his actions in the early morning of 2 March is uncertain. His replacement by Commander Basil Jones, RN, was a clear message to the commanding officers within the 10th DF that evasive action was not to be undertaken if it prevented the destroyers from completing their mission. This was to have a lasting influence on the 10th DF, as the commanding officers of the Tribals, and in particular those of the RCN, were now determined to adopt more aggressive tactics against the Germans. The change also suited DeWolf's temperament and training.

## The 10th Destroyer Flotilla and Commander Jones

Commander Jones had expected to be assigned to the Atlantic convoy escorts after completing his classes at the Anti-Submarine Tactical School in Londonderry. Therefore, it was a surprise to him when he was called to Plymouth to command the 10th Destroyer Flotilla, and it seems likely that he also interpreted his predecessor's departure as being the result of the indecisive Tunnel operation of 1-2 March. Thus, when he arrived in Plymouth on 15 March, Jones was determined that the 10th DF would be more aggressive in its conduct of patrol operations. To do so, however, it would first be necessary to develop an effective means of countering the hit-and-run tactics of the German Navy.

The Germans, in the habit of avoiding contact with an equal or superior opponent, preferred instead to break contact after firing torpedoes and thus avoid being drawn into a close engagement. To counter these attacks, the Allies were usually forced to increase their speed and turn 90 degrees away from the incoming torpedoes. By turning away, however, the Allies had allowed the enemy to break contact and escape to one of the numerous French ports protected by German shore batteries. Therefore, on future night operations the traditional column or in-line (or line-ahead) formation would be abandoned in favour of a more flexible arrangement. A showdown was approaching—guns versus torpedoes.

In-line formation was useful in night operations as it allowed ships to hold their positions in limited visibility. Unfortunately, this arrangement also had the effect of limiting the destroyers in their movements by tying them to the cruiser, thereby making it very difficult for them to take evasive action while still maintaining contact with the enemy. Jones's new scheme was that in future operations the Tribals would be divided into two groups, with each sub-division running on either side of the cruiser and approximately 1$^1/_2$ miles ahead on an angle of 45 degrees. This formation would enable the Tribals to make use of their high speed and heavy forward armament. Meanwhile, the cruiser would remain at a distance, thus limiting its exposure to German torpedo attacks. From its position to the rear of the formation, the cruiser would use its long-range guns to illuminate the enemy with starshell while the destroyers closed in. In the event of a German torpedo attack, all Allied ships would be provided with greater freedom of movement to take evasive action.

This departure from the line-ahead formation would not have been possible before the destroyers were equipped with radar in January, as the risks of collision or engaging friendly forces would have been considerable during night operations. With new radar systems, it was now possible for the plotting room of each Allied vessel to monitor the position of the others.

The theory behind the new tactics appeared sound; now all that remained was to test their effectiveness against the German Navy. For three months, day in and day out, *Haida* and her sister Tribals had been conducting offensive patrols in the western English Channel. Yet by the end of March they had still not come into contact with the enemy. Meanwhile, as the invasion of Europe drew steadily nearer, the 10th

Commander Basil Jones, DSO, DSC, RN, took command of the 10th Destroyer Flotilla on 15 March 1944 and made it into an efficient fighting unit of immense value. (Courtesy Michael Whitby)

HMCS *Haida*, Plymouth, England, February 1944. (Courtesy Michael Whitby, NAC PA-115055)

DF was increasingly called upon to provide security for landing exercises and to take part in shore bombardment practice in the south of England. In March, *Haida*, in company with sister Tribals, conducted security patrols in support of the Assault Exercises Fox and Muskrat II. The object was to protect the landing craft from German attacks while they were in the training area. The ship also formed part of a gunfire support force, along with cruisers of the Royal Navy in Exercise Beaver on 30 March 1944.

In compiling his month-end report, DeWolf observed that for the period 1 to 31 March the ship had steamed 4014 miles. Twenty-four days had been spent at sea and seven in harbour. During that month the engine room was shut down for only two days. The health of the ship's company was generally good. "Conduct has shown general improvement both ashore and on board and leave breaking has been considerably reduced." Since being based at Plymouth, the ship had steamed 12,885 miles and spent fifty-nine days at sea and thirty-two in harbour. *Haida* was a workhorse.

In April, the pace of invasion preparations was stepped up yet again, and *Haida*, *Huron* and *Tartar* were sent to take part in a combined assault exercise known as Trousers, where the ships were once again tasked with providing seaward security for the operation. In addition to their contribution to the invasion exercises, the Tribals continued to train for night encounters, and carried out regular patrol operations in the Channel. In short, March and April were two very busy months for *Haida*.

Since January, *Haida* and the ships of the 10th Destroyer Flotilla had been conducting offensive patrols in the English Channel off the coast of France. Although the Tribals had keenly sought a chance to engage the enemy, the opportunity unfortunately had never presented itself. Long hours of training had been provided, new radar systems had been installed, and aggressive night-fighting tactics had been developed. The 10th Destroyer Flotilla was now in all respects ready to engage the enemy. On the night of 25-26 April 1944, three months of tireless patrolling in the English Channel paid off.

# CHAPTER 4

## WITH BATTLE ENSIGN FLYING: 26 APRIL 1944

●

*Without fail, [wrote William H. Pugsley] around mid-afternoon, you heard the Quarter-Master's shrill summons. 'Hands to stations for leaving harbour, cable party to muster on the foc'sle.' You spied the Captain ambling for'ard along the upper deck, a huge pair of binoculars over one shoulder. Another operation was in sight.*

*We moved swiftly away from the buoy and headed for the harbour gates. With us were HMS Tartar, another Tribal, and the Polish destroyer, Blyskawica. The boys didn't try to pronounce this name—which meant lightning, I'm told. To us she was the Bottle of Whiskey.*

*Outside the gates we formed up in line abreast and started south. At "X" Gun we tested our communications, then settled down around the turret to while away the hours. One man arrived with a large saucepan of eggnog. You'd never have known it was made with egg powder. The brew was delicious, even if the dark specks on top turned out to be not cinnamon but plain soot.*

*We were on our way to the vicinity of Lorient, the great French naval base in the Bay of Biscay, but none of us ratings knew that then. Many captains, once the ship is at sea, address the men over the loudspeaker system and give them an outline of what's cooking. The Captain of the Haida never did this.*

*...No sooner had we left Plymouth than we had 'buzzes,' one after the other. 'Straight goods, I tell you, we're on our way to the Azores right now ... Hey, fellows,*

*it's Spain ... buzz, buzz ... We'll be in Gibraltar in two days: I heard one of the offi-*
*cers ... There's been another uprising, and we're going to Palestine!'*

*I know these things sound mad now, but at the time and under the circum-*
*stances—three destroyers racing south across a silver sea—anything seemed possi-*
*ble, even Palestine! Actually there was a time when we were under orders, subse-*
*quently cancelled, to be ready to leave for Archangel, but this was almost the one*
*place no "buzz" ever mentioned.*

*The gun's crew and men off watch sat around "X" Gun and yarned. There was*
*plenty of talk about; for so much had happened since the ship commissioned nearly*
*a year before. They talked about how they'd travelled down in a big draft from*
*Chatham to join the ship, the sea trials, the long months working up the previous*
*winter at Scapa, then the practices out of Plymouth with other destroyers as a*
*night-fighting unit.*

*There were tedious uneventful patrols in the Channel, and then one night in the*
*last week of April ...*

In preparation for the imminent invasion of Normandy, Plymouth Command was faced with the task of securing the west flank of the Allied Channel crossing. As of April 1944, air power had extended Allied control over the English Channel during daylight. By night, however, the *Kriegsmarine* had consistently frustrated Allied efforts in this area and had continued to conduct operations off the French coast.

German destroyers went out at night, escorting coastal convoys or on their own. DeWolf recalled:

> The only way we would know that they moved was from intelligence from one of the ports where they had put in, photographic intelligence. They would be in Le Havre one day and in another port the next day. When we knew they were trying to move, we would do a patrol and try to intercept them at night. We always went out at night. On two or three occasions, we did intercept them. However, there were a great many times we saw nothing.

On 23 April, Allied aerial reconnaissance and naval intelligence had established that three German Elbing class destroyers in the port of St-Malo were preparing to leave, destined for Brest. It was also known from long observation that German convoys in that area of the Channel often ran along a course which passed some five miles north of Île de Vierge. These German convoys were usually small and sailed at irregular intervals under cover of darkness. Hoping to intercept the three Elbings, Plymouth Command decided to send Force 26 to conduct a sweep of that area.

## Force 26 Against German Coastal Convoys

*Haida*, along with the cruiser *Black Prince* and the Tribals *Huron, Ashanti* and *Athabaskan*, was to take part in the Tunnel operation on the night of 25-26 April. Force 26 was to pass Plymouth Gate at 21:15 on 25 April and steam south to a position off the Île de Batz by 01:30 the following day. From there, the ships were to conduct a sweep to the east until 03:30. If by that time they had not encountered the enemy, Force 26 was to set course for Plymouth and arrive at a position twenty miles off the south of

Three Tribals (*Haida* at right) and HMS *Black Prince* (second from left) maneuver at high speed March 1944.
(NAC PA-180526)

England by daybreak, so that they would be within range of friendly air cover at first light.

Along with the cruiser and destroyers of Force 26, three MTBs of Force 114 were to depart from their base at Dartmouth at 18:15 on the 25th and make their way to the far eastern end of the patrol line. There the MTBs were to act as spotters for Force 26, remaining undetected and reporting any enemy surface vessels to the strike force. The patrol would also be joined between 23:30 and 00:10 by a Halifax aircraft from Coastal Command. The Halifax was to conduct a radar search of the patrol line and alert Force 26 to the presence of enemy vessels.

In accordance with instructions, shortly after 21:00 on 25 April, Force 26 cleared Plymouth Gate and by 21:14 had set a course of 190 degrees heading for the Île de Batz, there to begin the patrol. A speed of 21 knots was ordered and gradually increased to 25 knots. It was a dark, moonless night with visibility limited to two miles, but the weather was clear and a 12-15 knot wind was blowing from the NNW. By 01:00 of 26 April, the Île de Batz light was seen on a bearing of 123 degrees, and by 01:25 Force 26 had closed to within eighteen miles of the French coast. It was at this point that the Allied ships were detected by German coastal radar. Shortly afterwards an enemy shore battery opened fire. Over the next half-hour, the ships of Force 26 were able to observe a series of flashes as the German guns fired some ten salvoes in their direction. Enemy fire was inaccurate, with the shells falling far enough away that no explosions could be heard.

Meanwhile, off the coast near Morlaix, three Elbing class destroyers of the German 4th Torpedo Boat Flotilla (TBF), *T-29*, *T-24* and *T-27*, had just completed laying a field of contact mines. These ships had originally been designed by the Germans as torpedo boats and minelayers. Later models, however, including *T-22* to *T-36*, had been upgraded with heavier armament and served in

*T-27*, a German Elbing
class destroyer of the 4th
Torpedo Boat Flotilla.
(Courtesy Ed Stewart)

the Channel as light destroyers. These Elbings carried four 4.1-inch guns, four 37-mm AA guns and nine 20-mm guns, and mounted six 21-inch torpedoes. The three destroyers were under the command of *Korvettenkapitän* Franz Kohlauf onboard *T-29*. Kohlauf, we now know, was the same German officer who had directed the lethal attack against the *Charybdis* and *Limbourne* on 23 October 1943.

On the night of 25 April, the German 4th TBF had orders to lay a minefield near Morlaix and to provide long-range protection to a German convoy that was making its way towards Brest. At 01:30, shortly after Force 26 was detected by German coastal radar, Kohlauf received a message detailing the location and course of the Allied patrol. Assuming that the Allies would continue south to intercept the convoy, Kohlauf continued on his westerly course for Île de Batz. He could not have known that just moments after he received the message from coastal radar, the Allied force had changed course to 070 degrees to begin their eastward patrol of the Channel. The 4th TBF and Force 26 were now on a collision course.

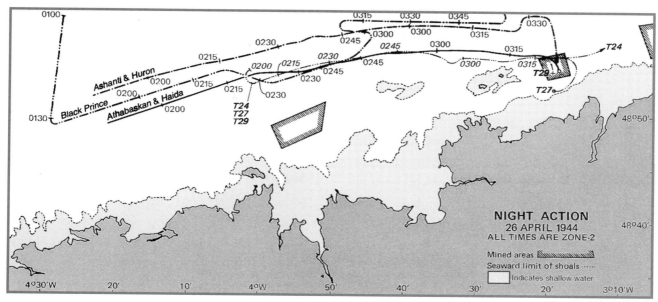

*(Canadian Military History)*

Force 26, commanded by Captain D.M. Lees (SO) in *Black Prince*, was making its way along the patrol line with the Tribals deployed approximately one-and-a-half miles ahead of the cruiser in two pairs, one off either bow of *Black Prince* on an angle of 45 degrees. The cruiser was designated as the first sub-division; the second was composed of *Haida* and *Athabaskan*, led by Commander DeWolf. The third sub-division was led by Lieutenant-Commander J.R. Barnes in *Ashanti*, followed by *Huron*.

At 02:00, the 272 radar onboard *Black Prince* showed four unknown echoes at a range of 21,000 yards. Two minutes later this contact was confirmed by *Haida*'s 271 radar, which reported an object at 17,600 yards moving at 20 knots along a course of 225 degrees. A second signal, at 02:03, revealed the contact on a bearing of 065 at 16,000 yards. The radar onboard *Huron* confirmed this signal, and the order was given to increase speed in pursuit of the unknown vessels. By 02:14, Force 26 was moving at 30 knots and *Black Prince* signalled to Plymouth that it was in pursuit of "Four unknown, bearing 081, eight miles my position."

Kohlauf had not been informed that Force 26 had changed course until 02:01. By that time, the Allied ships were only eleven miles from his position and the German commander correctly assumed that Allied radar had already detected his ships. With the opportunity to launch a surprise attack against the Allies now ruined, Kohlauf decided to avoid contact and attempt to draw the Allies away from the German convoy to the south. At 02:02, he decided to make an about turn and immediately altered course 90 degrees. By the time *Black Prince* made her 02:14 signal to Plymouth, the Germans had completed their turn away from Force 26 and were moving in line-ahead formation on a course of 080 at 30 knots.

At 02:19, Force 26 had closed to within 13,000 yards of the enemy. Captain Lees onboard *Black Prince* now gave the order to open fire with starshell from extreme range. The shells burst in the distance, flooding the area with light but revealing no enemy. "She opened fire rather early," recollected DeWolf, "at very long range, so that we had to open fire beyond our effective gun range which made for a long chase. We were shooting but I don't think we were getting any hits."

DeWolf then signalled the cruiser, calling for more starshell to port of the illuminated area. At 02:23, *Huron* also opened fire with starshell, and at 02:26, three or four enemy ships were sighted at a range of 10,900 yards on a bearing of 095. The enemy ships, which appeared to be destroyers, were dropping smoke floats in order to conceal their movements. DeWolf immediately gave the order to engage. Within thirty seconds, the guns of A and B mountings opened fire, and moments later the guns of the cruiser and the other Tribals were also firing.

Two minutes after the guns of Force 26 went to work, the enemy ships returned fire with high explosive rounds and starshell. Their fire was inaccurate, and the starshells burst far to port of the Allied formation. Meanwhile, the flash of German guns was of great assistance to Force 26 as it allowed the Canadian and British ships to gain an accurate position of the enemy, which would otherwise have been concealed by the smoke screen. The Tribals were also assisted by Type 285 gunnery radar, which was able to determine accurately the distance to the enemy ships. The Germans, on the other hand, were at a disadvantage as the Tribals were using flashless cordite as the propellant, which kept muzzle flash to a minimum and made it very difficult for the German gunners to obtain an accurate position of the Allied ships.

By 02:31, *Haida* was nearing the enemy smoke screen, and suddenly there was an explosion on board one of the German destroyers. Although it is unknown which Allied ship scored the hit, both *Haida* and *Ashanti* reported the explosion. Meanwhile, German reports state that at around this time *T-27*, at the rear of the German formation, was straddled by shells and received two hits on its after canopy, one to the port 37-mm mount and one hit in the forward engine room. The damage

was serious enough that at 02:36, Kohlauf ordered *T-27* to detach from the flotilla and break away from the engagement. Two minutes later, *T-24* also received a hit that disabled its radio communications equipment.

In spite of this, the German guns were now achieving greater accuracy, and a number of enemy shells were reported to be landing near *Black Prince*. Then, at 02:48, the cruiser's B turret jammed and was no longer able to fire starshell over the enemy position. In consequence, the Tribals were forced to take turns providing illumination while engaging the enemy. At 02:50, *Haida*'s radar indicated that three enemy ships were now at a range of 7,300 yards on a bearing of 090 degrees. The radar did not indicate that, at approximately this time, the commander of the damaged *T-27* was able to comply with Kohlauf's order and break away from the engagement. Before disengaging, however, *T-27* availed itself of the opportunity to fire a parting shot at Force 26.

At 02:54, the Headache operator onboard *Ashanti* reported a German radio transmission indicating that the enemy had fired torpedoes. Before this point in the engagement, the angle between the Allied and German ships had been too acute for the latter to release their torpedoes. After breaking away from the German formation, *T-27* was able to move southeast past Force 26, and as it passed it fired a spread of six torpedoes at the cruiser. The torpedoes were sighted from the bridge of *Black Prince*, and the cruiser turned sharply to port in order to avoid the attack. The Tribals continued to pursue the remaining German destroyers at speeds of up to 32 knots. Although the torpedoes missed their mark, the attack had forced *Black Prince* to become separated from the Tribals, and the cruiser would not be able make up the time needed to rejoin the engagement. *Black Prince* was left to follow the destroyers at a distance, and command of Force 26 devolved to DeWolf onboard *Haida*.

### *Haida* Leads the Chase

A long stern chase ensued, during which the Tribals steadily overhauled the Elbings. At 03:02, two enemy destroyers were sighted at the windward edge of the smoke screen. As the two German ships immediately changed course, turning back towards the smoke, it was thought that the enemy might have been attempting to maneuver for a better angle to fire torpedoes. By this time the Allies were able to recognize the two German vessels as Elbing class destroyers. Shortly after the two destroyers were identified, however, a third unidentified vessel was sighted off the *Haida*'s port side.

Sweeping past *Haida* at high speed and throwing a four- to five-foot bow wave, was a suspected German E-boat. It was in fact a British MTB, returning from operations on the hostile shore. *Haida* immediately signalled *Ashanti* and *Athabaskan*, inquiring whether they had also sighted the unknown vessel. *Ashanti* replied in the negative, and it was now appreciated by the ship's company that *Haida* could have just passed within four hundred yards of a German torpedo moving along the surface.

The Tribals continued their chase, closing steadily on the two remaining Elbings. The enemy was now altering course every few minutes, probably in the hope of throwing the Allied destroyers off their trail. By 03:10 *Haida*, leading the chase, had closed to within two-and-a-half miles of the enemy. Meanwhile, all four Tribals, using their main armament, were directing continuous fire on the enemy destroyers. At 03:12, *Athabaskan* signalled to *Haida* that it had run out of starshell. Meanwhile, the Elbings were laying smoke floats at regular intervals. Although it was becoming very difficult to follow the enemy's many changes in course, the fast Tribals were steadily closing on their prey.

At 03:24, as *Haida* was nearing a gap in the German smoke screen, one of the enemy destroyers came into view on a bearing of 140 degrees two miles distant. It was *T-29*, which at about 03:20 had received a hit which put its rudder out of service, causing the Elbing to veer off towards the Allied formation. The sighting lasted only a moment, however, as the light of the starshell faded and *Haida*'s B gun, which had been firing starshell, became temporarily jammed. If the gun could not be cleared quickly enough, *Haida* was in danger of losing sight of the enemy ship. In response, a sharp turn to port was quickly ordered, allowing the X gun to put up a starshell. The shell ignited directly over the target, silhouetting the enemy destroyer. The Elbing was now close enough for the shape of the hull to be distinguished clearly, and it was soon apparent that *T-29* was heading into a British minefield. Determined that the Elbing would not be allowed to escape, DeWolf ordered the second sub-division to alter course 090 degrees to starboard. At the same time as the order was given to pursue the enemy into the minefield, the guns of *Haida* and *Athabaskan* opened fire from close range.

Shells crashed through the Elbing's hull about ten feet below the upper deck. A second salvo landed below deck and a third impacted below the bridge. The after funnel, both boiler rooms, the engine room, Numbers 3 and 4 guns, and the bridge of *T-29* were all hit by the storm of Allied shells. Fires broke out in numerous places in the Elbing. *T-29*'s rudder was no longer functioning. The ship had been forced to reduce speed. Nevertheless, the Germans gallantly continued to serve their guns, and the Canadians responded with a barrage of heavy gunfire. By 03:30, the main deck of *T-29* was on fire from stem to stern. The hiss of steam escaping from the Elbing was loud enough to be heard by the crews of *Haida* and *Athabaskan* two miles away.

Meanwhile, following a brief search for the third German destroyer, *T-24*, Lieutenant-Commander Barnes in *Ashanti* gave the order at 03:29 for the third sub-division to alter course to 175 degrees in order to join *Haida* and *Athabaskan* against the crippled *T-29*. Unfortunately, Barnes failed to signal the second sub-division to inform them of his change in plans. Furthermore, during the turn, *Huron* and *Ashanti* lost contact with each other, resulting in much confusion when the third sub-division arrived to join the fight against *T-29*.

*Haida* and *Athabaskan* were now preparing to close and finish off Kohlauf's stricken destroyer. As they advanced, the two ships were met by a shelling from *T-29*'s close-range weapons, still being manned despite the fact that the Elbing was now a blazing wreck. The Tribals responded with close-range fire from their own 4.7-inch guns and Oerlikons, and in the exchange one of the shells from *Haida* hit a German life raft, destroying it and killing its occupants. The Tribals now prepared to fire torpedoes in order to sink the enemy destroyer.

*Athabaskan* attacked first, firing a spread of torpedoes from 3,000 yards, all of which missed their mark. Before *Haida* could close to deliver her attack, however, the hulls of two approaching ships suddenly loomed out of the darkness ahead, forcing DeWolf to call off the attack. They were *Ashanti* and *Huron*, which had just returned from the unsuccessful pursuit of *T-24*. Having failed to alert the second sub-division to their approach, the two Tribals caused a great deal of confusion as there were now four Allied destroyers circling the doomed Elbing. Lieutenant-Commander John Stubbs, DSO, RCN, of *Athabaskan*, himself a great

and gallant skipper, and a superb ship handler, described the scene in his action report:

> We passed the Elbing at a range of 2,000 yards. It was hard to miss at this range and we pounded her heavily with main armament and close range weapons. Although by this time burning fiercely, the Elbing maintained a constant fire of close range weapons as we were circling her. *Huron* and *Ashanti* joined and there was a certain amount of cross fire although this was unavoidable. Fighting lights had to be switched on on several occasions to avoid collision.

This cross-fire was, in fact, serious enough that after the battle, DeWolf returned to his day cabin to find that his golf clubs had been hit by bullets—with British markings on them.

At 03:35, the Allies scored a direct hit on one of *T-29*'s unfired torpedo tubes. The result was a massive explosion which stopped the Elbing in the water. *Haida* again closed with *T-29* and this time was able to let go all four torpedoes to no effect. *Haida* and *Athabaskan* now cleared the way for the third sub-division to make their attacks. At 03:47 *Huron* fired two torpedoes from approximately 2,000 yards and *Ashanti* followed with a spread of four torpedoes fired from 800 yards. Both attacks missed their mark. Shortly afterwards, *Huron* completed the Tribals' unfortunate torpedo performance by firing her remaining two from approximately 2,000 yards, again missing the target. The torpedoes presumably passed underneath the Elbing without detonating. Nevertheless, the Tribals continued to engage the enemy with their heavy armament and close-range weapons. At 03:48, *Haida* signalled *Ashanti* inquiring as to the condition of the Elbing, to which the latter replied, "Finished for keeps."

*T-29* had by this point absorbed tremendous punishment and was burning furiously. The German destroyer was still on an even keel, however, and was showing no signs of sinking. At 03:50, *Haida* closed for another attack and obtained several hits, then cleared the way for the others do likewise. At 03:54, *Ashanti* and *Huron* closed in and at this point DeWolf signalled to *Athabaskan*, asking for a report as to whether the enemy was sinking yet. Minutes later, at 04:00, he received his answer when *T-29* began to list to port, the first indication that the ship could in fact be sunk. At 04:03, DeWolf signalled Plymouth to report that the Elbing was going down. The Tribals prepared to rejoin *Black Prince* and return to Plymouth. They did not remain to pick up survivors.

As the destroyers were pulling away, the ships maneuvered to reform in their original positions. After losing contact with *Ashanti* when they had changed course at 03:29, *Huron* had wound up at the head of the 3rd sub-division and found herself now astern of *Haida* and *Athabaskan*. The smoke and general confusion of the battle had further aggravated this situation and now, as the Tribals were preparing to disengage, there was some doubt as to the relative position of each destroyer.

At 04:13, the order was given for the Tribals to alter course together 090 degrees to starboard. Two minutes later, this order was revoked, and as *Huron* turned to resume her original course, a destroyer was seen approaching from the port side. It seemed that the incoming Tribal had not received the latest signal, and *Huron* quickly altered course to starboard in the hope of clearing the way for the approaching destroyer. It was too late. At 04:15, *Ashanti* struck *Huron* amidships, splitting her bow away from the stem to a depth of nineteen feet. At 04:20 *Ashanti* signalled to *Haida*: "Have been in a collision with *Huron*."

The fires of *T-29* were slowly fading as the Elbing disappeared beneath the waves. It had taken an hour and ten minutes to effect the destruction of tough *T-29*. At 04:22, *Haida* signalled to Plymouth that the Elbing had sunk. Course was set for Plymouth, speed 25 knots. At daybreak, the destroyers rejoined *Black Prince* and Force 26 proceeded toward home. At 07:20, as the ships were approaching Plymouth, *Black Prince* signalled to the Tribals: "Force 26 will wear battle ensigns on entering harbour."

## Return to Plymouth with Battle Honours

At 08:21, Force 26 passed Plymouth Gate with the White Ensign flying from their yards. On the way to the Devonport Docks they were met by numerous salutes from the other ships docked in Plymouth Harbour. It was a proud day for HMCS *Haida* and for Canada as the Canadian Tribals and their companions made their way across the harbour. The destruction of *T-29* marked the first occasion in which an enemy surface vessel had been sunk by the Royal Canadian Navy. First blood had gone to *Haida*, *Athabaskan* and *Huron*—a fine flotilla victory.

When Force 26 arrived at the docks, ambulances were waiting to disembark the wounded. Onboard *Haida*, two men had been wounded, although not seriously. Lieutenant D.F. McElgunn, RCNVR, had received leg wounds and was sent ashore. As for the ship, she had received numerous splinter holes through the hull and X gun deck, while the sick bay and the cutter had been hit by close-range fire. There was also the previously mentioned damage to the captain's day cabin and personal effects.

The other ships of Force 26 had come through the fight in reasonably good shape as well. The forward guns of the *Black Prince* had jammed badly, but the crew had suffered no casualties. The

*Athabaskan* received some minor damage from close-range weapons fire, one rating onboard was wounded by shrapnel, and the "Sick Berth Attendant, who was sitting in the Sick Bay waiting for casualties, received a bullet through the seat of his trousers, with a resultant scar on his business end."

The most serious damage to the Allied ships had been caused by the collision of *Huron* and *Ashanti*, both of which required time in drydock for repairs. Onboard *Huron*, the motor-cutter had been destroyed, the guard rails and stanchions bent, and the bulkhead between the No. 1 and No. 2 boilers had buckled. Altogether, it was estimated that the damage would require ten days to repair. Furthermore, *Huron* had been attacked at close range by the guns of the *T-29* and both the bridge and stokers' mess had been hit by close-range fire. One gunner had been killed and four others wounded when the feed-rail of the pom-pom gun they were operating had been shot away. As for *Ashanti*, the bow had been split open, and it was estimated the damage would require three weeks to repair. In fact, the repairs were not completed until mid-May, during which time the 10th DF was reduced to two Tribals, as HMS *Tartar* was currently undergoing a refit.

The damage on the German side had been much more severe. Of the two ships which had escaped, *T-24* got away with its communications equipment destroyed, three men killed, and eleven wounded. Meanwhile, *T-27* had suffered severe damage to its engines and after guns and one of its magazines had been flooded. Among the crew, eleven had been killed and three wounded. As for *T-29*, it had been sunk with great difficulty by the Allied destroyers, with a loss of 135 out of a crew of 206 men. Among them was *Korvettenkapitän* Kohlauf, commander of the flotilla, who, for his actions on the night of 25-26 April, received a posthumous Knight's Cross. Of the survivors from *T-29*, many were wounded.

The defeat had cost the Germans one of the few destroyers available for the defence of the Channel, a loss which the *Kriegsmarine* could ill afford with the threat of an Allied invasion looming in the near future. The two Elbings which escaped from the encounter, *T-24* and *T-27*, had fled to St-Malo, although both required repairs which, at this stage of the war, were only available in Brest, 120 miles to the west. The destroyers would thus be forced to put to sea again before all repairs could

RAF photograph of *Haida* making good speed off the coast of England, 1944. (Courtesy Ken Macpherson, NAC PA-115058)

be completed. Furthermore, the loss of *T-29* along with many of its crew had a serious impact on the morale of the 4th TBF, made worse by the loss of the flotilla's gallant commanding officer.

As for the 10th Destroyer Flotilla, the battle represented its first engagement after three months of uneventful patrolling in the English Channel. That the encounter had resulted in a victory became a source of great pride for the Tribals, especially the Canadians, who felt that they had performed at least as well as their Royal Navy counterparts. Although the action was met by some criticism from the Admiralty, especially where the use of torpedoes and the collision between *Ashanti* and *Huron* were concerned, Vice-Admiral Leatham of Plymouth Command expressed almost complete approval of the action. The Tribals of the 10th DF had been preparing for this battle since January, and the long hours of training and the development of an improved night fighting formation had paid off. On a technical note, DeWolf reported that *Haida* had approached to within a mile of the French Coast and that in such tight circumstances the electronic fixing gear, Q.H.3, was invaluable in keeping an accurate navigational plot.

From a gunnery point of view, the main armament guns and close-range weapons had suffered no failures other than a few minor jams and stoppages, which were immediately cleared. Gunfire had been opened at a radar range of 10,000 yards but enemy smoke had obscured any splashes or night tracer. *Haida* had employed night tracer fitted to 4.7-inch ammunition, and the value of it, commented the gunnery officer in his report of 27 April, was well demonstrated. He noted: "It was invaluable for spotting as splashers were generally unobserved or indistinguishable from those of other ships." *Haida* was perfecting the tactics of night fighting.

Following the return to Plymouth, the crews were set to work repairing the damage and replenishing stores and ammunition. For *Haida* and *Athabaskan*, the stay in port would prove to be brief. *Huron* and *Ashanti*, on the other hand, would remain in drydock until mid May.

With *Ashanti* and *Huron* undergoing repairs and *Tartar* away for refit, the only Tribals available to the 10th DF were *Haida* and *Athabaskan*. Thus, it fell to the tired officers and men of the two destroyers to continue operations in the Channel, despite the fact that all were badly in need of rest. Nevertheless, the Canadians worked through the day of 26 April making minor repairs and replenishing stocks of ammunition. That night, *Haida* and *Athabaskan* set out from Plymouth to conduct Exercise Tiger in the Channel. Orders were given to darken the ship and the Tribals made speed as required to close the enemy's suspected location. Action stations were sounded at 02:00 when radar detected a contact directly ahead, eight miles distant. The two Tribals closed in and fired starshell from a range of four miles. The descending light revealed what appeared to be a formation of German E-boats, but before the main armament could be brought to bear the enemy escaped into a bank of fog and visual contact was lost, sufficient to call off the chase. The following morning, the 27th, at 08:00, *Haida* and *Athabaskan* returned to Plymouth.

Meanwhile, the two damaged Elbings that had escaped from the 10th DF on 26 April were preparing to steal out of St-Malo to make their way to repair facilities at Brest. Sailing on the night of 28-29 April, the Germans unknowingly headed toward their second encounter with the Canadian Tribals.

*Two Generations of Sailing Men.*
**Leading Stoker G. Eden; Ordinary
Seaman H.G. Richmond.**
(Grant Macdonald, courtesy MMGL)

# CHAPTER 5

## TRAGIC LOSS OF A FRIEND,
## HMCS *ATHABASKAN*: 29 APRIL 1944

●

SOUTHWEST ENGLAND was fast becoming an American zone of military occupation and training, in preparation for the invasion of France. At the same time, Commanders-in-Chief at Plymouth, Portsmouth and the Nore (for control of the Thames Estuary) ran training programs for their forces. What was intended was the largest combined operation in history, and for this purpose Slapton Sands in Start Bay, Devon, had been requisitioned by the British Cabinet. Overall naval administration was headed by Admiral Sir Bertram Ramsay, famous for the Dunkirk evacuation, but commands such as Plymouth retained their autonomy and responsibilities.

Ramsay and others knew that the training of the assault forces would take time and that there might be disasters along the way. On 27 April, for instance, while he and Field Marshal Bernard

Montgomery were observing the final rehearsal at Slapton Sands, the naval bombardment was not followed up by the arrival of the assault forces. The problem had been a failure in communications.

At 00:20 on the 28th nine E-boats out of Cherbourg—six from the 5th Flotilla and three from the 9th—eluded British naval patrols and escorts, intercepted a force of LCTs, and sank two LCTs and damaged a third. This encounter took place fifteen miles off Portland Bill in Lyme Bay.

What in fact happened was a disaster for the Allies, one kept secret for many years. The E-boats sank the American *LST 507*, *LST 537* and torpedoed the *LST 289* with a loss of at least 197 sailors and 441 soldiers. The escort was to have consisted of the destroyer HMS *Scimitar* and corvette HMS *Azalea*. But owing to damage sustained, *Scimitar* was in Plymouth for repairs. The British had given no communication to their American counterparts that the invasion trial was underprotected.

That very evening, on 27-28 April, *Haida* and *Athabaskan* had been at sea as covering force for a D-Day rehearsal named Exercise Tiger. The night passed uneventfully until 02:00 on the 28th, when radar sets in *Haida* and *Athabaskan* picked up echoes at a range of eight miles. DeWolf ordered an increase in speed in order to close the enemy. At four miles, the Tribals fired starshell and these revealed what appeared to be German E-boats. Whether these were among those which pounced on the LCTs has not been determined. As the main guns of the Canadian pair were being directed on the target, the German E-boats, two in number, made their escape and disappeared from visual contact into a fog bank. No other action ensued and the Tribals returned to Plymouth at 08:00.

After standing down for twenty-four hours, and with Plymouth Command in a high state of concern, *Haida* and *Athabaskan* were ordered to two hours' notice for steam at 15:00 on 28 April. This was a sure indication of another night operation. The sisters were moored to the buoy named Canada House. There had been much visiting between the ships, as their crews had become fast friends. As the ships prepared to slip and proceed, there was an omen that did not bode well for *Athabaskan*. Ginger, the ship's cat, had jumped repeatedly over to *Haida* and was in turn gently thrown back. As the ships separated the cat made one last attempt to jump but was restrained by a sailor. One Athabaskan was heard to remark: "That's not a good sign."

Operation Hostile XXVI was scheduled for the night of 28-29 April. These British mine-laying missions were part of Operation Neptune and the Normandy invasion. Hostile XXVI was to be conducted by the 10th Mine Laying Flotilla, consisting of eight mine-layers which were to be screened by the British Motor Torpedo Boats *MTB 677* (SO) and *MTB 717* of the 52nd MTB Flotilla. *Haida* and *Athabaskan* were to be the support force. The minefield in question was to be sown in an eight-mile pentagon with the base point being 16.7 miles northeast of Île de Batz. *Haida* and *Athabaskan* were to steam northwest, patrolling a box from 49°10'N to 49°5'N, and from 04°W to 4°10'W. This deployment would allow the Tribals to intercept any enemy heading north. Laying the minefield was to be completed at 03:30 after which *Haida* and *Athabaskan* were to return to Plymouth at 03:45 at 20 knots.

Plymouth Command determined that it was too dangerous for their ships to be near the French coast at daylight. Accordingly, all patrols had 10th DF vessels back on the English side of the Channel by then. Daylight in April, at that latitude, came an hour or more before sunrise.

In keeping with their instructions, the Tribals arrived at their patrol position at 02:00, went to action stations, and began "snaking" the patrol line at 16 knots.

### Hunting the E-Boats *T-24* and *T-27*

Meanwhile, the German Elbing class destroyers *T-24* and *T-27* had left St-Malo under cover of darkness. They were ghosting along the coast towards Brest to repair the damage suffered during the action of 26 April. Their run had to be a coastal passage from east to west, a transit exposed to the 10th DF's surveillance positions. Plymouth's coastal radar intermittently followed these proceedings and advised accordingly. Why the German vessels did not maintain radio silence is puzzling. Their radio messages were being intercepted and decrypted in Plymouth. As the vessels skirted the French coast, the captain of *T-27* issued orders to "head for the coast and avoid combat" if the enemy was encountered. *T-27* could make only

24 knots due to the damage suffered during the previous engagement.

Plymouth continued to monitor these transmissions. At 03:07 HQ Plymouth signalled: "Support Force to Steer SW at Full Speed for 20 miles." This message was received in *Haida*'s plot at 03:22. Her course was altered to 205 degrees and then at 03:43 course was shifted to 190 degrees. DeWolf's intention was to "prevent the enemy getting past to the westward."

At 03:59 *Athabaskan* obtained a radar contact bearing 133 degrees at fourteen miles. *Haida*'s 271Q radar confirmed this at 04:02. Course was altered to the east to close. *Haida*'s plot established that the Germans were steering 280 degrees, speed 24 knots. At 04:11 *Athabaskan* reported "three echoes" which *Haida*'s 271Q radar again confirmed, with the third echo being smaller.

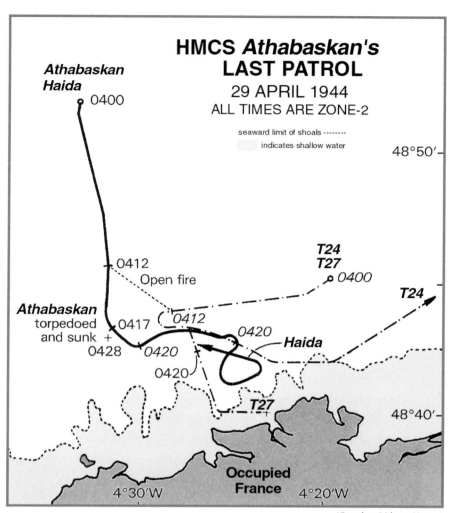

(*Canadian Military History*)

At 04:12 DeWolf as SO gave the order to engage the enemy. *Haida* and *Athabaskan* opened fire with starshell at 7,300 yards. The enemy saw only *Athabaskan*'s gun flashes because *Haida* had changed to using flashless cordite that same day. Two minutes later DeWolf signalled Plymouth:"2 Enemy Destroyers bearing 115 distance 4 miles course 260 speed unknown bearing 014 Île de Vierge 6 miles."

When they were illuminated by starshell, the two German destroyers were taken by surprise. They reacted quickly, and began to turn away to the south, in keeping with their instructions. The Germans made effective use of smoke, and spot-ting by the Tribals was extremely difficult from the start. *Haida*'s radar continued to track the enemy. German tactics were to turn and fire torpedoes

when engaged. *T-27* fired six torpedoes on the wrong bearing, actually at *T-24*, which had to take evasive action. *T-24*'s after torpedoes were also fired on the wrong bearing. The three from the forward mounting however were fired on the correct bearing.

Alerted to the close-range torpedo shot by the Headache operator, DeWolf ordered a 30-degree turn to port at 04:17 in order to comb the oncoming torpedoes. *Haida* came to her new course. The port lookout and *Haida*'s torpedo control officer reported a torpedo passing close down the port side, a near miss. *Athabaskan* lay four hundred yards astern.

For some reason *Athabaskan* was tardy in commencing her turn, and as she did, torpedo No. 3 from *T-24* struck the ship at an oblique angle on the port side of the wardroom and the 4-inch mag-azine. *T-24*'s other torpedoes passed harmlessly astern. Lieutenant Robin Hayward, *Athabaskan*'s navigating officer, recalled that:

> There were two definite explosions, one
> light, one heavy almost simultaneously.
> The explosion caused the propeller
> shafts to snap, the Pom Pom to be
> thrown into the air and the whole of
> the after superstructure to be set on fire.
> The only survivor from Y gun reported
> the stern broke off between Y gun
> ammunition hoists and the Wardroom
> hatch.

Such damage could only be consistent with the explosion of a torpedo. The blast also wrecked X gun, the after twin 4-inch mounting, and Y gun, the after twin 4.7-inch mounting, killing most of the guns' crew. *Athabaskan* sheered off to port and began to slow. At 04:17 *Athabaskan* signalled *Haida*: "Hit aft." At 04:19 *Haida* altered course 90 degrees and began to lay a protective smokescreen around her stricken sister.

Even while *Haida* was maneuvering to lay smoke, her guns kept firing, scoring their first hit on *T-24* at 04:18 and another at 04:20. At 04:22 *T-27* was observed broad on *Haida*'s starboard bow, and fire was shifted to this German vessel. *T-24* disappeared in smoke to the east. DeWolf altered course to keep *T-24* ahead and *T-27* on the starboard bow. This way he could engage both targets simultaneously.

*Haida*'s gunnery was superb. Hit after hit punished the fleeing *T-27*. A fire broke out behind the forward gun, blinding the bridge. Ablaze, *T-27* was run hard ashore. The crew, under orders, abandoned ship by jumping from the fo'c'sle while still being hit by *Haida*'s salvoes. A gunner in *T-27*, Wilhelm Zerter, wrote in his diary that the crew members, wet and cold, took refuge on the nearby rocks and hung on for dear life. From their dismal perch they watched the bridge of *T-27* burn furiously and then fade out. When daylight came some of the survivors used lifeboats and brought all the rest to shore. *T-27* lost 17 crew members and had four injured out of a crew of 180.

We now retrace the events aboard *Athabaskan*. DeWolf's recollection, published 1985, is as follows:

> I stopped the turn [90 to port] about
> half way around because the bearing of
> the [enemy] ships had dropped aft and I
> wanted to keep all guns bearing. It was
> during that turn that *Athabaskan* was
> hit. There was no indication to us that
> she had been hit by a torpedo. He just
> said, "I've been hit and stopped." I
> thought perhaps gunfire had hit her.
> Later on, I thought it might have been a
> mine, but anyhow, we exchanged a few
> signals and I told him to get ready to be
> towed, that we'd come back for her. We
> were five miles away when she blew
> up. There was a tremendous explosion
> that we all saw, even though she was
> five miles astern. It lit up the sky. There
> was no such explosion when the torpe-do hit her. Certainly, I didn't see one.
> And yet MTBs fifty miles away in the
> Channel reported seeing two explosions
> and the times corresponded with the
> time she was hit and the time she blew
> up. That's all in the history. So I don't
> know what happened in the first
> instance. Possibly our guns were going
> off at the same moment the torpedo hit
> and I didn't notice it. On the other
> hand, she was close on my port beam
> somewhere and I think I would have
> noticed it. I've never solved that one.

## The Loss of *Athabaskan*

Stopped and on fire, *Athabaskan* had but ten minutes to live. The torpedo from *T-24* had crippled her. She began to settle heavily by the stern. Preparations were made up forward to rig for a tow from *Haida*. The portable 70-ton pump was being muscled aft to control the flooding. As the flooding increased, *Athabaskan*'s CO, Lieutenant-Commander Stubbs, ordered: "Stand by to Abandon Ship."

Lieutenant Hayward recalled:

The Captain said he was going down to his cabin for a moment. On his way back, he looked into the Charthouse where Paymaster Lieutenant T.J. Brandson was putting C.Bs [Confidential Books] and charts into weighted bags....the torpedo struck between Nos. 1 and 2 Boiler Rooms on the port side. This caused a terrific explosion throwing half of the boiler rooms into the air. A blanket of oil [probably the galley stove oil] followed the debris of red-hot shrapnel falling everywhere and put out all the fires except for a small one on the midship Oerlikon gun deck. The after half of the ship sank immediately while the forward half rolled slowly over to port and as soon as the mast touched the water, the after end commenced to sink, the bows lifted into the air and she sank in a vertical position....Almost all those on the port side were instantly killed, while those on the starboard side were badly burnt or blown over the side.

*Athabaskan* assumed a "sprout" position. At 04:27 she sank stern first in position 48°43' N 4°32'W in 240 feet of water.

At the time of DeWolf's signal to Plymouth, *Haida* was directing a barrage of fire from her A and B mounts onto the grounded Elbing. One of the German survivors of *T-27* later recalled watching salvoes from the Canadian destroyer "walk" up and down the length of his stricken ship. At 04:35, with the enemy aground and burning fiercely, DeWolf order a cease-fire.

*T-27* lay on the rocks, a shattered and fiery ruin, and would play no further role in the encounter that night. The days to follow would prove, however, that the Elbing may have been down, but it certainly was not out of the picture. The Germans had not given up hope that their grounded ship might be repaired. In the days that followed, a salvage operation was mounted to raise *T-27*; the effort was soon beset by Allied attacks aimed at preventing the rescue. The first Allied attacks came from the air, but were met with indecisive results and two attacking planes were lost to German Flak guns. For a while, it looked as if the Elbing might be saved until a difficult night attack by three British MTBs under Lieutenant-Commander J.N. Cartwright succeeded in destroying much of the grounded ship with a well-directed torpedo fired in shallow water.

*Haida*'s gunnery had been superb. The gunnery officer, in his report of the action dated 1 May, recounted the techniques of training guns on the enemy:

Shortly after *Athabaskan* was hit and stopped the leading ship which had been hit turned and made off to the Eastwards under cover of smoke. The rear ship suddenly came into view at this time and fire was shifted to her. During the chase which ensued repeated hits were observed both visually and by Radar. At times the target was completely obliterated by smoke. Blind fire was then used, the Director Layer laying on what he thought was the horizon and the Rate Officer training by Remote Tube in the Director. Hits were also observed during these periods of Blind Fire. They appeared as bright red flashes through the smoke and could not be mistaken for enemy gunfire flashes as he was using flashless cordite throughout the action. Finally a large fire broke out on the target and thenceforth this served as an excellent point of aim despite smoke.

After breaking away from the attack on *T-27*, *Haida* set a course for the site of *Athabaskan's* sinking. Contact had been lost with *T-24* at 14,000 yards, and DeWolf reasoned that the best course of action would be to rescue the survivors. Accordingly, he signalled Plymouth that one German destroyer had escaped to the east, and he requested fighter aircraft cover at daylight.

*Haida* approached the area, firing starshell to illuminate the scene and to ensure that *Athabaskan* was not still floating and a danger to shipping. Clusters of blinking lights from the crew's new-issue lifejackets dotted the area. At 04:57 *Haida* stopped amidst the survivors. While the guns remained manned, every available officer and man concentrated on saving their chums.

Tension and frustration on *Haida's* bridge was enormous. Tension due to the fact, known only to Commander DeWolf and one other officer, that they were very close to a German minefield. Frustration because a gentle breeze was blowing the ship downwind, making it difficult for those swimming on the starboard side to keep up. Many of those on the port side swam away believing the ship to be German, as they did not know how the battle had gone and feared *Haida* had been sunk. This was quickly dispelled when shouts were heard in English.

In an unselfish and hazardous action, which would have left *Haida* helpless had they gone down, DeWolf ordered the serviceable motor-cutter, the whaler and all twelve Carley floats to be dropped. The motor-cutter and the whaler were to be unmanned; but at the last minute Leading Seaman William McClure, Able Seaman Jack Hannam and Stoker William Cummings jumped into the motor-cutter. Cummings started the engine and the boat began to pick up survivors. At 04:48 C-in-C Plymouth ordered the Senior Officer of the 52nd MTB Flotilla to "proceed immediately with *MTB 717* to rescue the survivors of *Athabaskan* in approximate position 020 Île de Vierge 8 [miles]."

DeWolf, meanwhile, said that *Haida* would remain for fifteen minutes. In fact, *Haida* remained for eighteen minutes. During this period some forty-one Athabaskans were pulled aboard, many badly injured. *Athabaskan's* Captain Stubbs, hands burned and badly damaged, was in a raft. He could have been picked up, recounted Lieutenant J.W. Scott, one of those taken into *Haida*, "if he had wanted the *Haida* to stay." "It was the action of a very brave and gallant gentleman," recounted Lieutenant-Commander Sclater. Stubbs shouted "Get away *Haida*! Get clear!"

DeWolf now had to make a particularly weighty decision: to stay and face an enemy torpedo, mine or an aircraft attack (a certainty in daylight), or to pull away from those awaiting rescue in the water. Plymouth Command expected all its vessels back on the English side of the Channel by dawn. He lingered as long as he dared. A countdown was made on *Haida's* bridge: ten minutes, five and so on. At 05:15 DeWolf reasoned, "We lost one ship we cannot afford to lose two." He then made what he said was the most difficult decision in his life: "We are now going slow ahead."

*Survivors.* When a ship picks up survivors of a stricken vessel they are first given blankets and a hot drink. Among those pictured in these drawings are Seamen Yard, Walsh, Hart, Hooper, Gauthier, Denny and Marentette.
(Grant Macdonald, courtesy MMGL)

As *Haida* was gaining way two sailors who were on the scramble net aiding the survivors were pulled off the net, miraculously escaping the churning propellers. Shipmates in the motor-cutter rescued them. At 05:16 *Haida* went to 31 knots. *Haida* signalled C-in-C Plymouth and the SO of the 52nd MTB Flotilla, Lieutenant Clayton: "Survivors of *Athabaskan* in position 020 Île de Vierge 5.5 [miles]." C-in-C Plymouth recalled the MTBs at 05:37, as the belief was they could not arrive until well after sunrise and would be exposed to enemy attack.

As *Haida* was racing north, rescue of the remaining Athabaskans came from another quarter. *T-24* had been ordered to the area accompanied by two minesweepers. They arrived at 07:15 and began to pick up survivors. Meanwhile, *Haida*'s motor-cutter had picked up six Athabaskans and the two Haidas. They were attempting to take a survivor-laden Carley float in tow when one of the minesweepers gave chase. The motor-cutter's cranky engine was coaxed into life (assisted by a well-delivered blow with a hammer) and the motor-cutter began to flee. Fortunately, the boat was in the German minefield which *Haida* had narrowly avoided, and when the minesweeper realized its precarious position, gave up the pursuit and turned back to the men in the water. In all *Haida* had rescued forty-seven, including six in the motor-cutter. The Germans picked up eighty-five men (who would become prisoners of war) and two dead (one was buried at sea and the other at Brest). One hundred and twenty-eight Athabaskans had died, and of these ninety-one were buried in Brittany, most in Plouescat, about thirty miles north of Morlaix. Thirty-eight were lost at sea. (Almost a year later eighty-five Athabaskan prisoners of war were liberated).

Aboard *Haida* shell casings littered decks covered in oil. The wounded and injured had been taken to the wardroom. Many of the badly injured were put in officers' cabins, with one very serious case in the Captain's day cabin. He did not survive. All hands were alert as the ship raced north. No rafts or boats existed aboard, a precarious state of affairs should *Haida* be stopped in the water by a German torpedo. Plymouth sent the destroyers HMS *Offa* and HMS *Orwell* to meet *Haida* and give her protection. *Haida* met *Offa* at 06:35 and *Orwell* at 06:50. As they passed Eddystone Light, thirteen miles SW of Plymouth, the routine signal "Have you any casualties or survivors?" was answered in the affirmative.

*Haida* secured alongside No. 1 wharf at 09:09 and landed the survivors to waiting ambulances at 09:30. Shortly thereafter, C-in-C Plymouth, Vice-Admiral Leatham, arrived. A couple of days later, "For gallantry in action with enemy destroyers," DeWolf was awarded the Distinguished Service Order in recognition of the fact that, in two actions, DeWolf had destroyed two enemy destroyers, a feat no one else in Plymouth Command had accomplished.

Then followed an example of unselfish kinship and patriotic camaraderie. The Haidas were exhausted and "out on their feet," after having been in action, coupled with the strain of the loss of their sister ship. In keeping with their doctrine of "always

Opposite top: *Haida's* company alongside the ship on the morning of 29 April, 1944, before *Athabaskan's* sinking. (Courtesy Ed Stewart)

Opposite bottom: A wounded Athabaskan being carried in a stretcher down *Haida's* gangplank to a waiting ambulance. (Courtesy Ed Stewart)

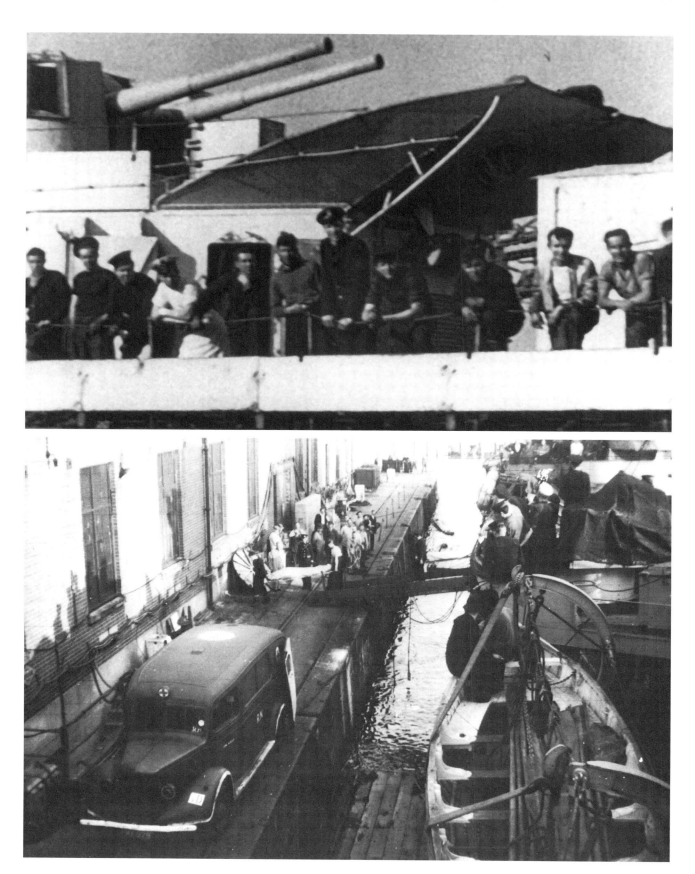

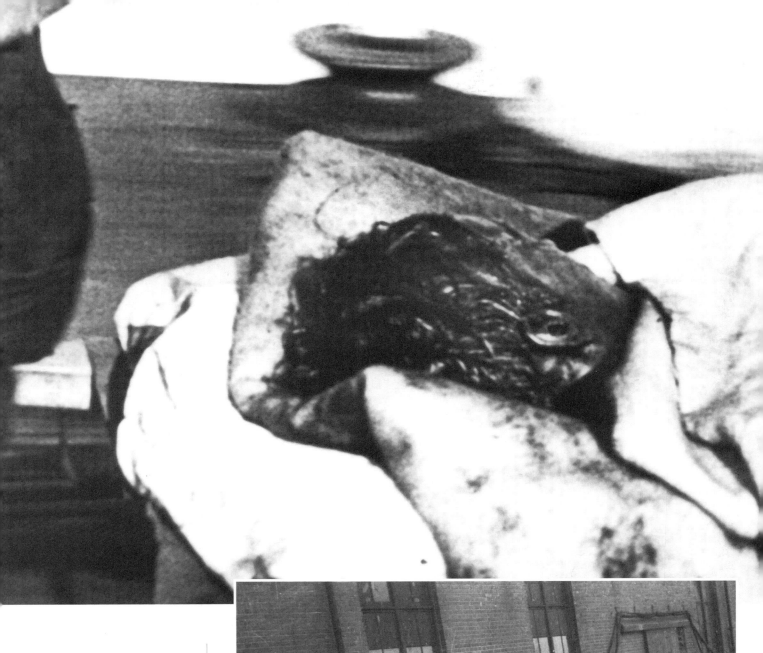

Above: A survivor from *Athabaskan*, his hair soaked with fuel oil, lies on *Haida*'s deck.
(Courtesy Ed Stewart)

Right: A badly burned survivor of HMCS *Athabaskan* is being carried off *Haida* on a stretcher.
(Courtesy Ed Stewart)

Above: A group of *Haida*'s crew on the morning of 29 April, 1944.  (Courtesy Ed Stewart)

Below: Survivors from HMCS *Athabaskan* watch as their wounded are disembarked from *Haida*.  (Courtesy Ed Stewart)

be ready" *Haida* had made arrangements for the ammunition barge to come alongside at noon to commence the backbreaking task of re-ammunitioning the ship. As *Haida* made her solitary approach up harbour, the crew of the *Huron* watched and resolved to take action. Although shore leave had been granted for that afternoon, a call for volunteers resulted in the entire ship's company stepping forward. Two officers and fifty ratings went over to *Haida* and set to work. When the exhausted crew of the *Haida* stepped out on deck after their noon meal, they could not

Commander DeWolf and Vice-Admiral Ralph Leatham in Plymouth after the loss of *Athabaskan*. DeWolf was awarded the Distinguished Service Order for his actions on the night of 29 April 1944. (NAC PA-180348)

believe what they were seeing. The Hurons commanded the Haidas not to lift a hand. As the Hurons stowed the ammunition, the Haidas reaped the reward of a much-needed rest.

Another saga was unfolding in the English Channel. When *Haida*'s motor-cutter eluded the German minesweeper, it continued heading north. There had been discussion among the crew as to what direction to steer, and north was the compromise. Later in the morning two aircraft were seen approaching. The Very pistol was fired and a flare put up. Two German Me 109s buzzed the boat and left. The boat's engine remained cranky, cutting out frequently. Stoker Cummings finally got it running smoothly and they continued on their 100-mile voyage, unaware that friendly aircraft were looking for them. *Haida* had reported

them and a search had begun, although a twenty-five-foot boat is very difficult to spot in miles of ocean. Later that evening the boat's crew again heard the sound of aircraft and huddled inside the boat's canopy to avoid the mistake with the Me 109s. These however were RAF Spitfires that were looking for them. The aircraft radioed their find, and were relieved as escorts by a Lancaster bomber. *Haida*'s boat approached England with a four-engine bomber providing cover overhead. An Air Sea Rescue launch from Falmouth towed them to Penzance. There the Athabaskans were hospitalized. The next day the five Haidas were re-united with their ship. In recognition of his tenacity and his determination in keeping the engine running, Cummings was awarded a Mention in Despatches.

Top: L to R: Stoker William
Cummings, Leading Seaman
William McClure and Able
Seaman Jack Hannam in
*Haida*'s motor-cutter in
Penzance, England. Six
Athabaskans were rescued by
these men, including Able
Seaman Jean F.A. Audet, Able
Seaman Stanley J. Buck,
Chief Petty Officer Charles T.
Burgess, Petty Officer George
W. Caswell, Signalman
Thomas J. Eady, and
Signalman Guy J. Norris.
(NAC PA-152033)

Bottom: L to R: Leading
Seaman William McClure,
Stoker William Cummings
and Able Seaman Jack
Hannam after their return to
England.
(Courtesy Ed Stewart)

## A Tribute to "AthaB"

By month's end new totals were available, *Haida* had been at sea on seventeen days during the month of April and had steamed 2,853 miles. "The health and behaviour of the ship's company have been satisfactory," reported DeWolf.

Each year, on the Sunday closest to 29th April, a commemoration is held aboard *Haida*. This is known as *Athabaskan* Sunday. The event is hosted by the Friends of HMCS *Haida* and the *Haida* Association; respectively, the volunteer organization dedicated to the preservation of the ship as a Canadian naval museum, and those former officers and men who served in her. *Athabaskan* Sunday is not about *Haida*, it is about her famous fighting companion, sometimes called Unlucky Lady. In the tragedy as told in this chapter, *Haida* rescued many but not all the survivors of *Athabaskan* in grave circumstances of fear and foreboding. Many Athabaskans were lost at sea and a goodly number were rescued by German vessels and made prisoners of war. It will always be a matter of gnawing regret that *Haida* could not have remained longer and taken aboard each and every Athabaskan. Naval fighting experience had shown the folly of lingering too long in cases such as this, and an even greater tragedy was likely averted by *Haida*'s departure from the scene. At the time, disappointment and despair existed among the Athabaskans because of the apparently callous action of steaming away while Canadian sailors awaited rescue. The weight of history and the passage of the years do not make any easier the loss of the Athabaskans, and to this day their memory is ennobled by shipmates and comrades in arms. One day there will be no *Athabaskan* survivors to attend the service, for the passage of time takes all away in like measure. Similarly, before long, no survivors of *Haida*'s complement will be present. But this story of heroism and tragedy, one as poignant as exists in the long and brilliant career of the Royal Canadian Navy, will not die; events of epic proportions, although they may fade in public memory, do not escape the notice of future generations and have an imperishable life. The Athabaskans and their ship deserve that, and the Haidas and their ship intend to maintain the same.

# CHAPTER 6

NORMANDY AND AFTER:
"ONE ENEMY DESTROYER BEACHED
OFF ÎLE DE BATZ" 9 JUNE 1944

ON 10-11 MAY, the three Tribals were sent to provide an escort to the battleship HMS *Howe* as she made her way from Plymouth to the Smalls. This was followed by three Hostile patrols in support of Allied minelaying operations between 15 and 20 May. Further patrols were carried out off Cherbourg on the nights of 20-21 and 22-23 May in company with Allied Coastal Forces. On none of these operations did the 10th DF come into contact with the *Kriegsmarine*. *Ashanti* returned to service in mid-May, raising the strength of the 10th Destroyer Flotilla to four Tribals, with further reinforcements arriving later in May in the form of two British and two Polish destroyers. HMS *Eskimo* was the only Tribal of the four, but the J class destroyer HMS *Javelin*, and the Polish destroyers ORP *Blyskawica* and ORP *Piorun* were comparable vessels in size and mounted similar armament to the Tribal class. Their arrival was welcomed by the 10th DF, as D-Day was now fast approaching.

## New Electronic Detectors

For three days in May *Haida* was in Scottish waters to test a new means of military deception that scientists, particularly Dr. Joan Curran, were perfecting. Curran called it "Moonshine," which Anthony Cave-Brown defines in his *Bodyguard of Lies* (1975) as "an electronic device used to amplify and return the pulses of German radar and thus simulate large numbers of approaching ships and aircraft." Moonshine, when used with what the British called "Window" and the Americans "Chaff," could perplex and confuse the enemy, so Curran theorized. Tests were required. For this purpose *Haida* was detailed, along with a number

of minesweepers, to work in conjunction with Lancaster and Stirling aircraft. The destroyer and minesweepers would sail into the Firth of Forth trailing naval balloons in which radar reflectors were mounted internally. At a prearranged time, from a specific altitude, the bombers would drop bundles of Window. The tests revealed what the scientists had hoped: the search radar of the Lancaster was made to literally "moonshine" on the balloons. The resulting impressions on the scientists' screens showed a sizeable armada approaching the enemy's intended shore. In addition, noise amplifiers were mounted on the vessels, and the exercise demonstrated that anchor and chain noise and the sound of approaching landing craft could be deployed from ships.

These electronic counter-measures now had to be implemented. At 01:00 on D-Day, operators in Allied naval units off the coast of France near Calais turned on their Moonshine apparatus, and when a German aircraft probed them, the echoes created seemed to be the approach of the invasion fleet, although this location was far distant from Normandy.

## Operation Neptune

The success of Operation Overlord, the invasion of Normandy, depended largely on the ability of the Allies to transport vast quantities of men and materiel across the Channel. This required an armada of troop transports and cargo vessels, which were gathered as part of Operation Neptune, the naval component of Overlord. These slow-moving convoy vessels would in turn require protection from attacks by the *Kriegsmarine* and *Luftwaffe*.

The German Navy still had a force of two hundred and thirty surface vessels stationed in French harbours along the English Channel and the Bay of Biscay, including some fifty E-boats, sixty R-boats, and sixteen destroyers. In the operational area described in this account, German operational strength at that time was three destroyers, five torpedo boats and forty-one E-boats. In addition, a hundred and thirty U-boats were stationed in the Bay of Biscay and along the Norwegian coast. While these U-boats could be deployed only with great difficulty amid the shallow depths and unpredictable cross-tides of the Channel, they posed a significant threat should the Germans decide to mount a determined offensive against the convoys.

The Admiralty did not underestimate the enemy. The armies in Europe would require constant resupply from Great Britain. If the Germans were successful in disrupting the vital convoys,

the entire Allied effort in Normandy would be compromised. Therefore, in order to counter the threat of a German naval offensive in the Channel, both flanks of Neptune would have to be protected by a screen of warships. In the western Channel this task fell to Plymouth Command.

In response to an Allied invasion, the Germans would likely use the sixteen destroyers at Brest, Cherbourg and Bay of Biscay ports to do everything in their power to attack the invasion convoys as they crossed the English Channel. As the tragedy of 28 April showed, when E-boats jumped LCTs off Portland Bill, the Germans could profit by doing so again. Meanwhile, U-boats would probably be used only as a last resort by the Germans. Therefore, while smaller Allied vessels patrolled the Channel searching for U-boats, the more powerful destroyers would guard the convoys against the threat of German surface attacks. To this end, *Haida* and the 10th DF were to conduct a series of covering patrols to the west of the invasion convoys.

Opposite: *Haida*'s first Commander, Henry DeWolf, DSO, DSC, RCN, better known as "Hard-over Harry" for his shiphandling techniques. Sadly, Vice-Admiral DeWolf (Ret) passed away in January 2001, during the production of this book. (Grant Macdonald, courtesy MMGL)

ORP *Blyskawica* and other ships of the 10th Destroyer Flotilla in the English Channel. (Courtesy Michael Whitby, NAC PA-180512)

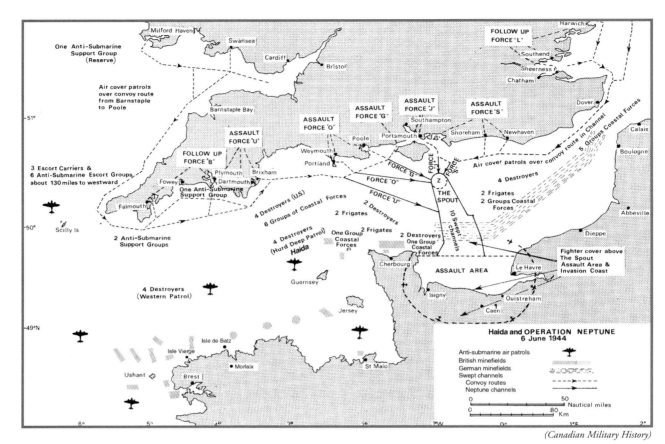

*(Canadian Military History)*

DeWolf, in his report of proceedings for June 1944, described *Haida*'s work at the time of the Normandy invasion:

> The Flotilla's invasion role was that of Covering Force in the western Channel to protect the invasion convoy routes from attack by enemy surface vessels. The Flotilla continued to operate directly under the orders of Commander-in-Chief, Plymouth and in effect little change of routine resulted directly from the invasion. With the arrival in the Channel of the numerous A/S Escort Groups, to counter the U-boat threat, the scope of the Flotilla's patrol was extended to provide cover for those groups operating near the enemy coast.

On the night of 5-6 June *Haida* deployed in Hurd Deep, a stretch of deep water located north of the Channel Islands. Approximately seventy miles to the east, invasion convoys steamed towards the Normandy beaches. As the 10th DF proceeded along the patrol line, countless numbers of Allied aircraft and gliders passed overhead, making their way towards France. The ship, DeWolf wrote, "witnessed the inspiring sight of the vast air armada of transports and gliders passing a few hundred feet overhead, on their way to open the invasion." At 01:00 and 02:00 the ship's log noted the passing of airborne transports overhead, and at 06:45 "60 bombers b[earing] 090... presumably friendly." By 09:00 large flights of bombers were observed northward bound, missions accomplished. Throughout the day the destroyers patrolled Hurd Deep, returning to Plymouth for fuel at 16:00. Meanwhile seven battleships, twenty-three cruisers and one hundred and four destroyers had been stationed off the beaches to provide gunfire support as troops were landed. The 10th DF maintained their patrols in the Channel.

Meanwhile, Commander-in-Chief, Plymouth, Vice-Admiral Leatham, had been alerted by Allied Intelligence that the *Kriegsmarine* was preparing to strike against the invasion convoys.

*Admiral* Theodor Krancke, the German commander of *Marineoberkommando West*, had ordered three destroyers of the 8th Destroyer Flotilla to make their way north from the Gironde Basin towards Brest. Under the command of the Senior Officer, *Kapitän zur See* Baron Theodor von Bechtolsheim, two of these destroyers, *Z-32* and *Z-24*, were of the powerful Narvik class. These 2,600-ton destroyers mounted five 5.9-inch guns, eight 21-inch torpedoes, and good anti-aircraft armament, and were capable of a speed of 38 knots. The third destroyer ordered from Gironde was the *ZH-1*, a captured Dutch vessel formerly known as *Gerard Callenburgh*. Commanded by *Korvettenkapitän* Barkow, this destroyer carried five 4.7-inch guns, heavy anti-aircraft armament, and eight torpedo tubes. Scuttled by the Dutch at Rotterdam on 10 May

1940, this ship had been raised by the *Kriegsmarine* two months later, on 14 July, repaired and put back into service.

Upon arrival at Brest, the *Kriegsmarine*'s 8th Destroyer Flotilla was to be joined by the Elbing *T-24*, lone survivor of the German 4th Torpedo Boat Flotilla. To this point, *T-24*, under the command of *Kapitän-Leutnant* Wilhelm Meentzen, had fought the 10th Destroyer Flotilla on two occasions and had succeeded in torpedoing the *Athabaskan* during the second encounter. Von Bechtolsheim was ordered to depart from Gironde early on 6 June. However, the orders Krancke had sent to the 8th Destroyer Flotilla were intercepted by Allied signal intelligence (SIGINT). Shortly afterwards, the message was decrypted by ULTRA and made known to the C-in-C Plymouth. In response, Leatham ordered air strikes against the three German destroyers making their way north in the Bay of Biscay.

Beginning at 20:30 on 6 June, *Z-32*, *Z-24* and *ZH-1* were attacked off St-Nazaire by two formations of rocket-armed Beaufighters, including fourteen planes from 404 Squadron, RCAF. Although the attacks killed three crewmen and wounded

This postwar photograph shows a Narvik class destroyer in British markings. Note the two quadruple torpedo mountings fore and aft of the second funnel.
(Courtesy Michael Whitby, DND PMR 92-707)

twenty-one, they failed to prevent the German 8th Destroyer Flotilla from reaching Brest. The damage inflicted was sufficient to keep von Bechtolsheim in harbour for the next two days during which his destroyers underwent repairs.

Concurrently, on the evening of 6 June, *Haida* and the 10th DF resumed their patrols in the Channel, now running on a westerly course some thirty miles south and southwest of Lizard Point. Later that night at 23:00, the patrol line was shifted twenty miles to the south until 07:00 the following morning. Throughout the day, the 10th DF maintained station in the Channel, with destroyers being detached in pairs to return to Plymouth for fuel while the other six continued patrolling. It was only a matter of time before the German destroyers in Brest would be ordered out. The 10th DF would have to be there waiting for them. Because of its recent success against enemy destroyers, and in view of the weak reaction of the *Luftwaffe* to the invasion, bolder tactics were being adopted by the 10th DF.

In Brest repairs to the damaged German ships were nearing completion and the Germans were preparing to make a run for Cherbourg. On the night of 7-8 June, German E-boats of the 5th and 9th Flotillas based in the latter port had been involved in several attacks against Allied transport and patrol vessels. While the E-boats succeeded in sinking two Allied LCTs and damaging a third before being forced to withdraw, two of their own vessels were mined and sunk upon return to harbour. These E-boat attacks had expended a large number of torpedoes and these weapons were now in short supply at Cherbourg. Fully aware that continued E-boat operations from that port depended on the safe arrival of additional torpedoes, the Germans decided to shift the 8th Destroyer Flotilla from Brest to Cherbourg with each ship sporting four torpedoes on its deck.

Therefore, on 8 June, *Kapitän zur See* von Bechtolsheim received orders detailing the time his destroyers would leave Brest, their course, speed and estimated time of arrival in Cherbourg. Again these orders were sent by radio. Again they were decrypted by ULTRA and word was passed on to Plymouth Command.

To date, the Tribals had done well against the German Elbing class destroyers, and the Elbings had put up a good fight. Now, stronger forces faced the Tribals. Sclater writes: "In the Tribals the chance of an encounter with the German Roeder class ships, as the improved Narviks were called, had been a subject of interesting speculation." These vessels were 470 feet in length, with 5.9-inch guns and engines that made them faster than Tribals. The Tribals could handle the Elbings. Could they deal with the bigger, speedier, more heavily-gunned Narviks?

That same afternoon, 8 June, *Tartar* and *Ashanti* were returning to Plymouth to refuel. While underway, the two Tribals received orders to turn back and head to the patrol area. By 16:30, the 10th DF had been gathered approximately fifty miles south of Penzance awaiting further orders. Shortly afterwards, the destroyers were directed by Plymouth Command to set course south for Île de Vierge, there to conduct a sweep towards Île de Batz. Upon reaching the second island, the 10th DF was to reverse course back towards Île de Vierge and continue patrolling until 04:00 the following morning. Unknown to the destroyer commanders at sea, Leatham had directed the 10th DF into a perfect position to intercept the German destroyers as they made their way to Cherbourg.

By 22:00, the Allies were off Île de Vierge and Commander Jones, commander of the 10th DF, ordered the ships' companies to be in the first degree of readiness as they began their patrol. While conducting their sweep, the eight destroyers of the 10th DF were divided into two divisions. The 19th Division was composed of the veteran Tribals, including *Tartar*, with Jones SO on board, *Ashanti* commanded by Barnes, and *Haida* and *Huron*, commanded by DeWolf and Lieutenant-Commander Rayner respectively. Meanwhile, the less experienced destroyers were grouped together in the 20th Division, which included *Eskimo*, *Javelin* and the Polish destroyers *Blyskawica* and *Piorun*. Led by Commander C.F. Namiesniowski in *Blyskawica*, the 20th Division was to take up station to seaward, approximately two miles to starboard of the 19th in hopes of broadening the front and increasing the chances of encountering the Germans.

For this patrol Jones intended to have his two divisions proceed in a staggered line-ahead, or column open order, until they came into contact with the enemy. Upon encountering units of the *Kriegsmarine*, the 10th DF would then shift into a line-of-bearing facing in the direction of the enemy. Jones hoped that when the Germans turned and let go their spreads of torpedoes, as was their usual practice, the 10th DF would be facing into the attack, thereby exposing only the narrow width of their bows to the Germans. Jones hoped that this would allow his destroyers to comb the tracks of incoming torpedoes while still advancing briskly towards the enemy. Departure from the DF's usual practice of increasing speed and turning ninety degrees away from the deadly German attacks would also prevent the 10th DF from losing contact with the enemy as had previously happened in the process of avoiding torpedoes.

Facing directly towards the enemy would eliminate the opportunity for the Allies to fire their own torpedoes. However, this would be compensated for by allowing them to make use of their substantial forward 4.7-inch mountings. In this way the gun crews would be able to take best advantage of the radar-controlled gunnery so as to inflict maximum damage on an enemy who had deliberately turned himself broadside in order to fire torpedoes.

Success relied on being able to detect the enemy and the ability to move the destroyers into the direction of attack before the Germans had a chance to fire. Here lies the purpose of the staggered line-ahead, or column open order formation, while patrolling. With each destroyer following its next ahead at an oblique angle, the destroyers were able to maintain station with relative ease, despite the limited visibility afforded on night patrols. At the same time the radar equipment on board each ship would be provided with a good arc of coverage to the front.

## The 10th DF Engages the Narviks of 8th DF

At 22:00, 8 June, the 10th DF began its first sweep towards Île de Batz. Proceeding at 20 knots, the Allies meandered along the patrol line, changing course periodically in order to increase their frontage. At 22:36, a message was received from Plymouth ordering the destroyers to shift their patrol line five miles to the north in order to avoid an enemy minefield.

By 01:00 in the early morning of 9 June, the 10th DF had reached a position approximately fifteen miles north of Île de Batz and had turned west, back towards Île de Vierge. By this time, the weather had deteriorated to intermittent rain squalls and the low cloud cover was interfering with radar reception. As a result, the Allies ignored a series of erratic radar echoes being detected ahead.

It was not until fourteen minutes later that *Tartar* established four reliable contacts bearing 241 degrees, distance ten miles. Considering it likely that the enemy would not fire their torpedoes until they had closed to within 10,000 yards,

Jones allowed the 10th DF to continue on its course for several minutes before giving the order to shift to line-of-bearing. At 01:22, both divisions were ordered to execute a turn 35 degrees to starboard followed by a 50-degree turn to port, allowing the rear vessels to steer into their line-of-bearing positions facing the enemy. The 10th DF increased speed and began its advance.

Meanwhile, the Allied destroyers had already been detected by German coastal radar and a message was sent to von Bechtolsheim alerting him to their approach. It is doubtful that this came as much of a surprise to the German commander, as he had already recorded in his diary days earlier that he did not expect his destroyers to reach Cherbourg unmolested. At 01:24 these suspicions were confirmed when the moonlight exposed the Allied destroyers as they turned towards him.

On board *Haida* and her companion vessels, the Headache operators were suddenly flooded with German radio transmissions as the enemy exchanged sighting reports. Moments later, at 01:26, an R/T transmission was overheard in which the German senior officer ordered his ships to turn away from the Allied formation and fire torpedoes. At the same time, *Ashanti* opened fire with two starshell, followed immediately by *Haida* and the other Tribals. From high over the enemy position, the light from the shells exposed four German vessels—three destroyers and one large torpedo boat—turning hard to port at 4,000 yards range. True to form, the Germans were turning away in order to fire torpedoes before running for the safety of the French coast.

*Haida*'s upper deck pitched suddenly from the recoil of the forward guns as they opened fire on the enemy. The main armament of the other three Tribals had also come to life, and a hail of tracer fire could be seen arcing towards the German destroyers. Moments later, as the 19th Division

raced towards the enemy at 27 knots, the tracks of German torpedoes were observed passing through the Allied line. Facing directly towards the enemy, however, the Tribals did not present much of a target and the torpedoes passed by without incident.

The German formation had been thrown into confusion by the sudden attack. Hit by four shells from *Tartar*, *Z-32* turned away to the north after firing its torpedoes. The lone Narvik was now heading towards the Allied 20th Division.

Jones ordered his ship, *Tartar*, to join *Ashanti* in attacking *ZH-1*. This former Dutch destroyer had attempted to escape from the Allies behind the cover of a smoke float, but before she could get away was hit four times by *Tartar* and *Ashanti*. The shell impacts brought *ZH-1* to a halt while also concealing her in a cloud of smoke and steam.

*Haida* had opened fire on *Z-24*, hitting her several times before the enemy became obscured by a smoke screen at 01:31. At this time, *Haida* joined *Huron* in engaging the Elbing *T-24* as the faster Narvik drew out of range. Both Canadian Tribals were now pursuing *T-24* as she fled to the southwest, and although there were several near misses, neither were able to score any hits on the destroyer that had torpedoed *Athabaskan*.

All this time, to the north, von Bechtolsheim in *Z-32* was drawing closer to the four Allied destroyers of the 20th Division. Commander Namiesniowski of *Blyskawica*, however, had not yet been able to deploy his destroyers in a line-of-bearing as ordered. Nevertheless, when *Z-32* was seen approaching from the south, all four destroyers of the 20th Division opened fire, hitting the approaching enemy several times. The German Narvik immediately returned fire. Following this initial exchange the Headache operator on board *Blyskawica* intercepted a transmission indicating that the enemy was about to fire torpedoes. With his destroyers still deployed

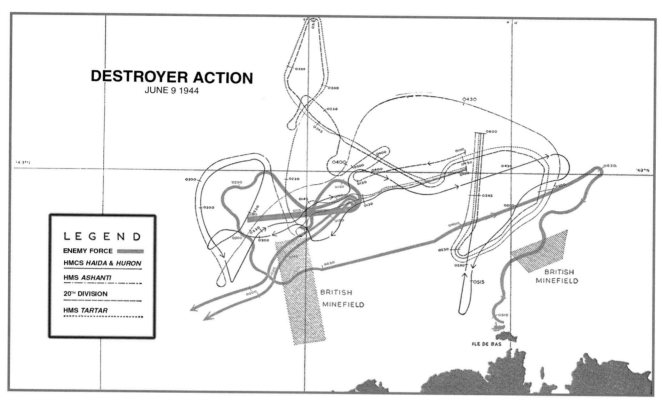

(*Canadian Military History*)

in line-ahead formation, Namiesniowski knew that the 20th Division would present an easy target to the Narvik. Accordingly, he quickly ordered his ship to take evasive action by turning away to starboard and making smoke. The destroyers following him believed the turn was executed in order to carry out a torpedo attack and both *Eskimo* and *Javelin* fired a spread as they followed *Blyskawica*. The attacks missed their mark. By turning away the 20th Division lost contact with the enemy. Von Bechtolsheim was thus able to wheel *Z-32* around and return to the fight with *Tartar* and *Ashanti*.

The Allies' radar failed to detect the approach of *Z-32*, whose crew was soon able to distinguish the silhouette of a destroyer on their starboard beam. It was *Tartar*. *Z-32* opened fire from short range. Jones later described the damage as follows:

Four shells burst about *Tartar*'s bridge, starting a fire abaft her bridge, cutting

leads to her directors, bringing down the trellis foremast and all radar, and cutting torpedo communications to aft.

The wheelhouse was also hit, killing the assistant coxswain; and on the Bridge the P.C.O. and torpedo ratings were killed and a number wounded. As the mast fell over, the call-up buzzer from the aloft look-out position jammed on, and splinters pierced the upper deck of No. 1 Boiler Room causing loss of air and reduction of speed.

Below the bridge in the Action Information Centre, all was in darkness, for the lights had been knocked out and the small compartment swept by shrapnel and filled with smoke. The attack claimed the life of one officer and two ratings, with several others wounded, including Jones. Meanwhile, *Z-32* had turned away and was lost in the smoke from *Tartar*.

With much of the superstructure of the British destroyer on fire and the alarm siren blaring it would not have been exceedingly difficult for the enemy to return for a second attack. The only question was from which direction the Narvik would come. The answer came at 01:38. The Headache operator on board *Ashanti* intercepted this German signal: "I am steering 190 degrees towards the burning destroyer."

Moving into position to intercept the incoming Narvik, *Ashanti* chanced upon *ZH-1*, lost earlier in the smoke. With her main turbine damaged in the initial exchange of fire at the opening of the battle, the German destroyer now lay motionless across *Ashanti*'s port bow. At the same time, *Tartar*, whose damage control was trying to extinguish fires burning on the superstructure, found herself only five hundred yards away from the stern of the enemy destroyer. Her gun crews opened fire with the 4.7-inch guns in local control, raking the enemy from close range. At the same time, *Ashanti* fired a spread of four torpedoes, two of which hit *ZH-1*, blowing off the bow and stern of the ship. With his destroyer under heavy fire and torpedoed in two places, *Korvettenkapitän* Barkow knew that *ZH-1* could not be saved. He ordered the crew to lay scuttling charges and abandon ship. With that done, he is then reported to have shot himself in the head. At 02:35, *ZH-1* blew up. The massive explosion could be heard in ports all along the western Channel.

With *ZH-1* destroyed and the fires on board *Tartar* being brought under control, Jones signalled the 10th DF to reform on his position. At the time of this signal, *Haida* and *Huron* were already speeding to rejoin *Tartar* and *Ashanti*. At 01:46, DeWolf had been forced to break off the chase of *Z-24* and *T-24* when the plot indicated that the enemy was heading directly into Allied minefield QZX-1330. While a few weeks earlier

*Haida* had followed a fleeing Elbing through a minefield without incident, DeWolf was now under orders expressly forbidding him from testing fate a second time. As a result, the two Canadian Tribals were forced to steer around this minefield while the German destroyers sailed through, quite unharmed. By altering course around the obstacle, the Canadians had fallen nine miles behind the enemy. At 02:14 they abandoned the pursuit in order to rejoin *Tartar* and *Ashanti*.

At 02:23, as they proceeded towards the rallying point with *Tartar*, radar equipment on board both *Haida* and *Huron* obtained a contact bearing 032 degrees, range six miles. In view of the fact that the two Tribals had been chasing the enemy to the southwest and this contact was on a bearing of roughly northeast, it seemed likely that the approaching ship was *Tartar*. Under normal circumstances the IFF (Identification Friend or Foe) associated with radar gear on board *Haida* would have been able to confirm the identity of the approaching ship by an exchange of recognition signals. In this case, however, IFF was unable to recognize the unknown ship, possibly because the equipment on board *Tartar* had been destroyed by gunfire from *Z-32*. Therefore, as the silhouette of the ship came into sight at 02:30, *Haida* and *Huron* remained uncertain of her identity. A challenge was issued by signal lamp but was met by a meaningless response. By this time, the main armament of the Canadian Tribals was aiming directly towards the stern of the unknown ship, but DeWolf hesitated to give the order to fire as he still considered it possible that the destroyer was *Tartar*, unable to respond to his signal due to damaged equipment or casualties.

Meanwhile, on board *Z-32*, von Bechtolsheim was equally hesitant to open fire on the source of the unintelligible light signals his ship had just received. The unknown ships had not opened fire

upon receiving a series of German light recognition signals, and therefore he considered it possible that the two vessels were *Z-24* and *T-24* making their way back towards the engagement. Nevertheless, he ordered *Z-32* to drop smoke floats and turn away to the northwest.

The Canadians altered course to follow but *Z-32* quickly disappeared. Moments later they saw the massive explosion which marked the end of *ZH-1*. At 02:47, *Haida* signaled: "What was that explosion?" This was followed by a response from *Ashanti* "Enemy destroyer we have just sunk." Given that *Ashanti* and *Tartar* had been attacking an enemy destroyer at the time *Haida* and *Huron* came into contact with the unknown ship, it was now almost certain that the destroyer to the front was not friendly. This suspicion was confirmed at 02:55, when starshell revealed the outline of a Narvik class destroyer bearing 135 at 6,900 yards range. At once the forward guns of the Tribals opened fire on the German ship, which had by this time worked its way around to an easterly course. Several hits were observed on *Z-32*, which fought back with accurate fire from his main guns. The Tribals continued their pursuit, but before they could close range the Narvik disappeared into minefield QZX-1330.

Again the Tribals were forced to break off their pursuit as the enemy fled into the same Allied minefield which had blocked the pursuit of *Z-24* and *T-24*. Altering course to the northeast at 03:11, *Haida* and *Huron* slowly made their way around QZX-1330 while *Z-32* continued on course, steadily drawing away from the Tribals. By 03:20, the range had opened to 10,000 yards and DeWolf gave the order for *Haida*'s gunners to check their fire. Soon afterwards, the two Tribals rounded the northern boundary of the minefield and at 03:37 came upon the site of the *ZH-1* explosion. Not a trace of the enemy destroyer remained. Large numbers of survivors

*Z-32* grounded on the rocks of Île de Batz on the morning of 9 June 1944. Later that day, the Narvik was destroyed by Allied aircraft.
(Courtesy Michael Whitby, DND CN-6870)

could be seen on rafts or clinging to floats. *Haida* continued to pursue *Z-32*. The enemy was now ten miles to the southeast and radar contact was lost shortly thereafter. For the second time, it appeared that the Germans had frustrated attempts to bring them to battle. Nevertheless, the Canadians continued their pursuit, although the chances of regaining contact with *Z-32* were slight.

Von Bechtolsheim, in the meantime, was preparing to rally the 8th Destroyer Flotilla for a second attack on the Allies. Believing *Z-24* and *T-24* to be only twelve miles from his position, the German Senior Officer felt confident that his force could be rallied off the Channel Islands and from there, force a second confrontation with the Allies before continuing on to Cherbourg or Morlaix. At 04:20, however, *Z-32* received a message from the other two destroyers requesting permission to return to Brest. As it turned out, *Z-24* and *T-24* were actually 25 miles west of *Z-32* and would be unable to rejoin with the Senior Officer before daylight. Furthermore, von Bechtolsheim suspected that his destroyer was still being shadowed by Allied forces to the northwest.

He was correct. At 04:12, *Haida* and *Huron* re-established radar contact with *Z-32* and altered course to 070 in order to parallel the Narvik as she made her way towards Cherbourg. By the time von Bechtolsheim learned that his ship was isolated from the rest of the flotilla at 04:20, the Canadians were slowly closing. Meanwhile, the two British Tribals were approaching from the north in order to block the way to Cherbourg. Whether or not von Bechtolsheim knew that his ship was trapped is uncertain. Nevertheless, at 04:32 he gave the order for *Z-32* to double back towards Brest. At the same time, the radar on board *Haida* indicated that the enemy had reversed course. DeWolf ordered a turn south to intercept. Range was now decreasing rap-idly and by 04:44 *Haida* and *Huron* had closed to within 7,000 yards of *Z-32*.

At 04:45, DeWolf gave the order to illuminate the enemy with starshell and open fire with the main guns. In the storm of incoming shells, von Bechtolsheim thought his ship had come under fire by a pair of Allied cruisers. Turning sharply to port and taking several hits as she went, the Narvik fired a spread of torpedoes at the Allies before altering course south towards Île de Batz. The attack missed its mark, however, as did the 5.9-inch guns on board the Narvik; although several of the German shells missed the Tribals by a margin of only fifty feet. Meanwhile, *Z-32* was constantly being hit by 4.7-inch shells from *Haida* and *Huron*.

Shortly after 05:00, *Haida* or *Huron* scored a hit on *Z-32* which put the port engine of the Narvik out of commission. Another three hits destroyed one of the ship's forward gun mountings. DeWolf, meanwhile, had ordered *Haida*'s rate of fire slowed to between five and six salvoes per minute in order to improve accuracy. Nevertheless, the steady volume of punishing fire directed at *Z-32* was enough to lead von Bechtolsheim to hope that the Allies would soon run out of ammunition. The Narvik had by this time absorbed a tremendous amount of fire and, without some relief, the German commander did not rate his chances of escape as being very good. Then at 05:13, another well-aimed shot from one of the Canadian Tribals shut down the Narvik's starboard engine. With escape now out of the question, von Bechtolsheim ran his burning ship aground on the rocks of Île de Batz.

Minutes later the Tribals closed to within 6,500 yards of the grounded Narvik. Dawn was fast approaching. In the early morning light the crews could see black clouds of smoke forming above *Z-32*. At 05:17, *Haida* signalled to

Plymouth: "One enemy destroyer beached off Île de Batz." At 05:25, a parting shot was fired at *Z-32* which set the entire deck ablaze. *Haida* and *Huron* then turned away to rejoin the 10th Destroyer Flotilla. As they left, *Z-32* was observed to begin firing red and white flares into the sky as a distress signal. Shortly afterwards, the two Tribals lost sight of the Narvik as they proceeded towards their rallying point with the 19th Division. Upon regrouping, the Allied destroyers set course for Plymouth, where they arrived safely at 08:50. Making their way past the breakwater and into the harbour with battle ensigns flying at the peak, the 10th DF was met by cheering crowds along the roads and dockyard.

Upon their return to Plymouth, the ships' companies were congratulated by Vice-Admiral Leatham and the Admiralty; the Tribals had been matched against a force of powerful German Narviks and had snatched a victory. The only serious criticism was of Namiesniowski's decision to turn away from *Z-32*, as both Leatham and the Admiralty concluded that, had the 20th Division not been led away from the battle by *Blyskawica* the entire German force might have been destroyed. When the 20th Division disengaged, *Haida* and the 19th Division had been left on their own against an enemy which clearly outgunned them. Nevertheless, the Tribals had succeeded in destroying two German warships that the enemy could not afford to lose with the Allied invasion of Europe now underway.

It had been a brilliant piece of work, that night of 9 June. When Admiral A.B. Cunningham, then commanding the RN in the Mediterranean heard of it, he called it "a spirited action." And forever after, the episode would remain a noted achievement in the annals of naval warfare.

The day after the battle, *Z-32* was sighted on the rocks of Île de Batz by a flight of Allied aircraft who reported that the Narvik was listing to starboard at an angle of thirty-five degrees with her stern well below the waterline. An RAF photographer captured the moment. Following the departure of the Canadian destroyers, von Bechtolsheim had ordered the crew to abandon ship while scuttling charges were laid. At 05:50, the Senior Officer made his way ashore and the charges were detonated. Later that day, the wreck of the ship was attacked with rockets by Allied aircraft, including Canadian Beaufighters from 404 Squadron. This was followed by an attack by motor torpedo boats on 12 June. Although neither of the attacks were able to sink the ship, *Z-32* was now damaged beyond hope of salvage by the Germans.

Von Bechtolsheim, meanwhile, was transferred to Brest where he took command of *Z-24*. This second Narvik had escaped from the engagement with extensive damage inflicted by *Haida* at the opening of the battle. Her crew could count themselves as fortunate in comparison to the officers and men of *ZH-1*. The former Dutch destroyer had been sunk by *Tartar* and *Ashanti*, with only twenty-seven of the ship's company able to make their way back to the coast of France. Another hundred and forty were taken prisoner by HM Ships *Fame* and *Inconstant* while on anti-submarine patrol.

Of the four German destroyers which had set out for Cherbourg, only *T-24* was able to return to Brest undamaged. Five weeks earlier, this same Elbing had torpedoed *Athabaskan*. The engagement of 9 June marked the third occasion in which *T-24* had come away from an encounter with the 10th DF. But the Elbing's days were numbered, as were those of the Narvik *Z-24* which had also escaped to Brest. On 24 August 1944, *T-24* and *Z-24* were bombed by Allied aircraft off LeVerdon. The attack destroyed the Elbing and inflicted heavy damage upon the Narvik. It was only by means of painstaking effort that the crew of *Z-24* were able to guide their crippled ship back safely to its harbour. Upon their arrival, however, the Narvik rolled over and sank at its mooring.

With the destruction of *Z-32* and *ZH-1* on 9 June, the threat of a surface attack by German destroyers against the west flank of the Allied invasion convoys was greatly diminished, but not removed. The loss of these two powerful destroyers had crippled the *Kriegsmarine* in the western Channel, and following the battle von Bechtolsheim referred to the action of 9 June as evidence that no further possibility existed for the movement of larger German vessels along the coast of Brittany.

The sea lanes to Normandy had been made safe from attack by German destroyers, and the officers and men of the 10th DF were congratulated by the Admiralty for "the spirited action which has caused a potential menace to the main operation to be removed." Even as the 10th Destroyer Flotilla was celebrating the removal of one threat, a second was preparing to make its way south from Norway to take its place.

# CHAPTER 7

## THE KILLING OF *U971*: 24 JUNE 1944

●

*U971*, ONE OF THE CLASS CALLED VII-C, the workhorse of the *Unterseebootwaffe*, was one of forty-four built by Blohm & Voss, Hamburg, and one of five hundred and sixty-eight such commissioned between 1940-45. The type VII-C had come into service as the opportune time of hunting Allied merchantmen was nearly over. This boat faced the final challenge of the Allied anti-submarine campaign in late 1943 and 1944. The most famous type VII-C, *U96*, featured in the movie *Das Boot*. "Medium sized, readily manoeuvrable, reliable and exceptionally seaworthy," wrote U-boat ace Peter Erich Cremer, "this was *the* U-boat of the Second World War and caused the enemy a lot of headaches."

The type VII-C submarine had a range of 8500 miles at 10 knots on the surface, and could make a maximum speed of 17.7 knots on the surface or a submerged speed of 7.6 knots for one hour. This boat carried a maximum of fourteen torpedoes and had four bow tubes and one stern tube. Displacement was 769 tons surfaced, 871 submerged. It could dive to a maximum depth of 722 feet. These boats measured 220.5 feet in length, beam 20.3 feet, draught 15.4 feet, with a height of 31.5 feet. The VII-C could carry twenty-six mines.

Customarily they had a crew of forty-four but late in the war, as in the case of *U971*, they carried a larger crew so as to serve the larger number of AA guns. A VII-C normally sported one 37mm AA and two 20-mm AA guns, sufficient to ward off attack aircraft but often not enough to deal with bombs and rockets.

*Haida*, in company with *Eskimo* (Lieutenant-Commander E.N. Sinclair), was detailed by Plymouth Command to patrol the area around Land's End in support of the 2nd Support Group.

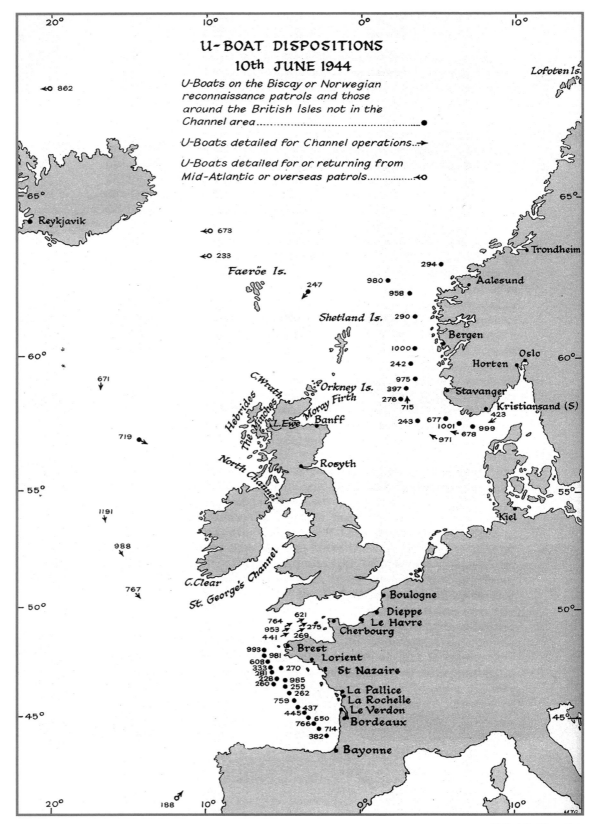

(S. Roskill, *War at Sea*)

Their task was to control the sea lanes and to ensure that German destroyers did not interfere with Allied submarine hunting groups.

*Haida* and *Eskimo* were sent out on the evening of 23 June and the morning of 24 June to conduct sweeps inside the Channel Isles in support of the Light Coastal Forces that had been operating off St-Malo throughout the night. On Saturday 24 June, a flat calm day (race day in Plymouth, officers and men noted), *Haida* and *Eskimo* were occupied in such a manner—zig-zagging in line-abreast at 25 knots—when they received a signal from Captain Frederic John Walker, of the 2nd Support Group. An aircraft had sighted a U-boat on the surface, south of Land's End and just northwest of Ushant, at position 49°00' N, 05°40' W, and had engaged the enemy with rockets and depth charges. *U971* had been obliged to surface to empty holding tanks and clear out foul air. The periscope of another U-boat was sighted in almost the same position and was attacked in the same way. The aircraft was a very long-range Liberator bomber from 311 (Czech) Squadron, RAF Coastal Command (Flying Officer J. Vella).

By the time *Haida* and *Eskimo* had arrived on the scene, the Liberator had lost contact with the target—which was later identified as *U971*. Forcing the submarine to dive in order to escape certain death, the Liberator then dropped smoke floats in order to mark the last known location of the German submarine.

*U971* suffered damage to her flak armament and torpedo tubes. Her acoustic torpedo, the *Zaunkönig* (wren), in the stern tube, could not be made functional and set free. Report of a U-boat *on the surface* was welcome news, "so we roared off to that spot," said DeWolf. "We couldn't talk to the Czech, we couldn't understand him and he couldn't understand us, but we did get the messages he was sending to the Admiralty."

## Cat and Mouse with *U971*

Both *Haida* and *Eskimo* reduced speed to 7 knots in order to facilitate their Asdic search. *Eskimo* was the first ship to detect the submarine, with *Haida* obtaining contact a few minutes later. From 16:34 until 18:30, nine complete depth charge attacks were relentlessly carried out by the two ships, seven by *Eskimo*. Although no visible results from these attacks could be discerned, it

View from *Haida* 24 June 1944 after destruction of *U971* by *Haida* and HMS *Eskimo*. *Eskimo* stands by as a boat from *Haida* goes to rescue the U-boat survivors. (Imperial War Museum A. 25386)

was believed that the submarine was still lurking somewhere in the immediate area. The cat and mouse waiting game had begun. The depth of water here was 250 feet, hardly enough for the U-boat to make a deep dive, and she could only lie quietly on the ocean floor.

For almost one hour after the last depth charge attack, *Haida* lay still in the water, listening for any indication of the submerged U-boat. Meanwhile, *Eskimo* had lost contact with the German submarine, and was quietly conducting a slow speed search. At that moment DeWolf held little optimism about the outcome: "I thought— well, the Channel here is full of wrecks, so we're probably bombarding wrecks on the bottom and we'll go on doing that till we give up, or we've already destroyed the submarine and it's on the bottom."

In the U-boat the situation grew desperate. Her batteries were flat and the torpedoes were damaged. Air quality was poor and probably worsening. At 18:25 *U971*'s commander, *Oberleutnant zur See* Walter Zeplien decided to surface and scuttle. He explained the plan to the crew "while they finished off the last of the boat's beer ration standing knee-deep in rising water in the control room." At his order the ballast tanks were blown. The U-boat began its rise to the surface.

*Haida*'s Asdic officer reported the submarine blowing tanks and coming up rapidly. *Haida* burst into action, and without waiting for back-up from *Eskimo*, launched a full depth charge attack on a suspected contact. Within minutes of the attack, the submarine surfaced seven or eight hundred yards off *Haida*'s port bow. Reaction from *Haida*'s gunners was immediate. The guns were turned quickly around. Gunners in B mounting commenced their unrelenting fire. As DeWolf describes it: "a hit was obtained on the conning tower, with the second salvo. High explosive was used and penetrated the conning tower, starting a fire, the flames being clearly visible through the hole made."

A rating, Al Warner, recalled the scene:

The submarine was almost between us and the *Eskimo*, and she [*Eskimo*] went full astern to back up when the boys opened up with the 20-mm B gun was fully manned at this time, and when the submarine surfaced they depressed the gun to fire at the submarine. We were cruising with the guns elevated at 45 degrees, anti-submarine positions, A gun off to starboard, B gun to port. The sub was so close [200 yards] they had to depress A gun so B wouldn't hit the barrels. That gave *Eskimo* time to back up before we opened fire. The first salvo hit the sub; the second, too. That's all B gun fired. Two salvoes, four hits.

The first guy that came up through the conning tower saw what was comin' at him, so he went back inside! And he was the one that went down with the sub. I understand, also, that when the survivors were picked up and taken aboard our ship, one of them asked if this was the G-63. We said yes. He says, "Well, you have the other ship [*Eskimo*] to thank for your lives." They'd pinpointed us and were goin' to let go their torpedoes, but when they scanned the surface and saw the *Eskimo* they knew that if they torpedoed us, the *Eskimo* was right there; they'd be dead within an hour. They were lookin' out for themselves.

The enemy could offer no resistance. Fire from B mounting and numerous small arms was quickly checked.

The U-boat lay awash. Men were coming up on deck and jumping over the side, says DeWolf. As the U-boat crew began to abandon ship, both *Haida* and *Eskimo* closed for boarding and lowered their whalers in an attempt to reach the stricken submarine before it went down. Any chance of capturing the U-boat intact, or recovering any secret documentary material or the coveted Enigma signals encrypting machine quickly disappeared. The damage done by *Haida*'s excellent gunnery was too great. The submarine turned turtle and quietly slipped beneath the waves of the Channel. Although small explosions were later heard, there can be little doubt that the German submarine was destroyed by *Haida*'s gunfire and not by the scuttling charges set by the crew. She was lost at 19:17, at 49°01'N 05°35'W, northwest of Ushant.

The task of rescuing the German crewmen was begun, with a total of fifty-two of the fifty-three being recovered and taken into *Eskimo*. This number included the U-boat captain, Zeplien, and three of his officers. Of the rest of the crew rescued, six were injured, three seriously. One of the injured, having suffered a wound to his leg believed to have been inflicted by Oerlikon fire, was given an emergency blood transfusion. The action report indicates that the transfusion consisted of "one pint from a German volunteer and three of plasma, without which he would not have survived." Once the whalers were recovered, the ships proceeded to Falmouth, arriving at 03:00 on 25 June 1944. The prisoners were landed and taken into safe-keeping.

Later assessments of the attack on the U-boat contained comments in regards to future anti-submarine work with Tribal class destroyers. The commander of *Eskimo* put it thus: "In spite of this success I am strongly of the opinion that Tribals should not engage in prolonged A/S work. An

escort group should take over at the first possible opportunity. I think it is reasonable to sit on a contact for a short period, but early relief by the proper A/S ships from escort groups is most desirable. Though this success adds to the variety of the 10th Flotilla's bag, and is a feather in our cap, it should not be taken as too strong an encouragement to go after U-boats when so many better equipped vessels are available." In fact, it was rare for Tribals to kill U-boats. Usually it was the other way round.

Comments on the attack gleaned from interviews with German prisoners lend a unique perspective to the events as described. *U971* was a new boat (commissioned 1 April 1944), on its first operational patrol. For many of the crew, this was their initial patrol, with the average age of the crewmen being approximately twenty-one. The patrol had to be cut short due to mechanical problems. *U971* had sailed from Kiel and then on 8 June from Kristiansand on the southern tip of Norway.

*U971* was assailed from the air on several occasions. Passing near the Faroes, 15 June, a British Sunderland attacked the submarine. On the 17th a Sunderland of 228 (RAF) Squadron and a Halifax bomber of 502 (RAF) Squadron had punished *U971*. Again, on the 20th a Leigh-light-equipped Wellington bomber of 407 RCAF Squadron, piloted by F.H. Foster, attacked with depth charges and inflicted damage to three bow torpedo tubes. The U-boat had been attacked southwest of Ireland by Coastal Command aircraft. At the time *Haida* and *Eskimo* encountered *U971* Zeplien had aborted his earlier orders—to attack ships shelling Cherbourg—in favour of seeking shelter in Brest.

Curiously enough, none of the crew interviewed could explain why the German submarine was running on the surface during the daylight hours of 22 or 24 June—the date of *Haida*'s and

*Eskimo*'s attack. The report indicates that "the crew were quite mystified as to why it was necessary—they did not think it was, in fact, necessary at all." This cannot be so, and is an incorrect view based on ignorance of the full details. *U971* was on the surface to clear holding tanks and refresh the air. The reporter in question tended to diminish the perils facing the crew at this urgent hour. How this informant could have been ignorant of the effects of the pounding his submarine had taken in the face of repeated air assaults is a matter of wonder.

German sources have since revealed that during the aerial attack on 24 June conducted by the Liberator from the Czech squadron of RAF Coastal Command, only slight damage was sustained as a result of the depth charging. The net effect, however, was to force the U-boat to dive so as to avoid certain destruction. When *Haida* and *Eskimo* arrived and began laying their depth charge patterns, the situation began to deteriorate rapidly. As a result of their attacks, a moderate amount of water appeared, sloshing around the control room, but repairs were quickly made. Never having experienced depth charging before, the crew was very nervous. After being bombarded for nearly two hours by *Haida* and *Eskimo*, the strain started to take its toll. According to the prisoners, "The captain made up his mind that escape was unlikely, further depth charging too awful to contemplate, and that the only thing to do was to surface and save his crew."

*U971* was one of 785 U-boats lost at sea, and was one of 215, or one-third, lost during their first war patrol. By the time of *U971*'s sortie, one out of two boats sent into the Atlantic failed to return.

Some years after the event, DeWolf was asked if he ever had any communications with the celebrated Captain Johnnie Walker. DeWolf said that at the time Walker was only a few miles off. "We have a submarine here, would you like to take over?" was DeWolf's query to the great submarine hunter. "No," came the reply, "go ahead and get on with it." DeWolf added, with classic understatement, "Frankly, I hadn't much confidence in our ability to sink the bloody thing. We weren't in that kind of game, we hadn't any practice at it."

*Haida* and *Eskimo* returned to normal duties. Upon her return to Plymouth *Haida* received this signal from *Black Prince*: "Elbings, Narviks, and submarines all seem to come alike to you." To this DeWolf replied that it was just recreation for the crew.

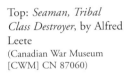

Top: *Seaman, Tribal Class Destroyer*, by Alfred Leete
(Canadian War Museum [CWM] CN 87060)

Right: *The Dead British Sailor, The Morgue, Murmansk*, by Julius Griffith
(CWM CN 82557)

Top: *Cold Day – Scapa
Flow* by Lieutenant
Leonard Frank Brooks
(CWM CN 10091)

Left: *Canadian Tribals at
Anchor at Scapa Flow*
artist unknown
(CWM CN 10247)

Top: *Canadian Tribal Class Destroyers Leaving on Patrol, Plymouth* by C. A. Law (CWM CN 10249)

Right: *HMCS Athabaskan, The Unlucky Lady, 29 April 1944* by Walter W. Pranke (CWM Accession No. 19900153-001)

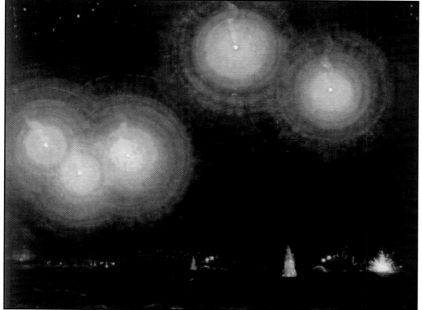

Top: *HMCS Haida Gets an Elbing* by Commander Thomas Harold Beament (CWM CN 10036)

Middle: *HMCS Athabaskan's Last Fight* by Commander Thomas Harold Beament (CWM CN 10034)

Bottom: *HMCS Haida (G-63)* by Douglas Grieve (CWM CN 74005)

*Canadian Tribal Destroyers in Action* by Commander Tony Law
(CWM CN 10248)

Top: *Train Busting –*
*HMCS Crusader in*
*Korea* by David Landry
(CWM CN 86362)

Left: *HMCS Haida,*
*Action at Dawn* by C.G.
Evers

*His Majesty's Canadian Ship Haida, Scapa Flow, Evening* artist unknown
(CWM CN 10276)

# CHAPTER 8

## IN THE BAY OF BISCAY:
## JULY–AUGUST 1944

●

ON 25 JUNE, after *Haida* accompanied *Eskimo* to Falmouth to land prisoners from *U971*, she proceeded to Plymouth. The following day the ship was taken in for repairs and boiler cleaning. The crew was given leave for some well-deserved rest and recreation. Some arranged a visit to a nudist camp. Others found their customary haunts ashore where friendships and liaisons were established, maintained and broken. The WRENS of Plymouth, so important in the communications of Plymouth Command, took a strong liking to *Haida*'s officers, whom they regarded as polite gentlemen. Visits were made to Bristol and to London. Leave was fully enjoyed but was short enough.

On 29 June, *Haida* was shifted to No. 3 Drydock at nearby Devonport in order to replace the main inlet grating that had been fractured dur-

ing high-speed maneuvers in the Channel. Meanwhile, as the ship's company enjoyed its liberty in Plymouth, a contentious issue was developing within the upper ranks of the 10th Destroyer Flotilla.

In late June, Commander Basil Jones was called to the office of the Chief of Staff at Plymouth and informed that, by the end of the month, the Government of Canada would likely authorize the promotion of *Haida*'s Commander DeWolf to Captain. This would place Jones in the uncomfortable position of being out-ranked by one of his RCN subordinates, a difficult situation for the British commander, as "ordinary tact to the Canadians required that they should not be under the command of a Junior Officer," as Jones put it. Jones fully agreed that DeWolf deserved to be made a captain. He likewise felt that his own serv-

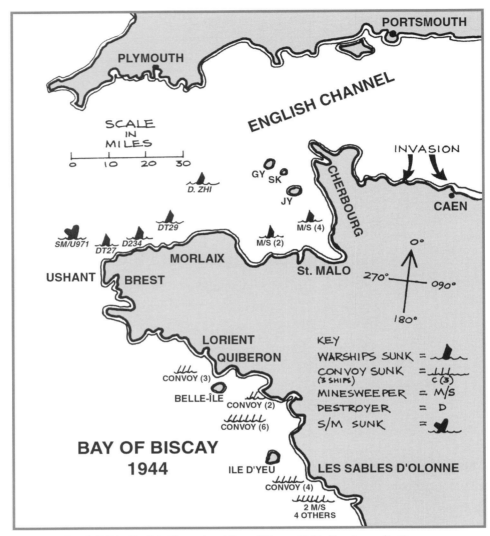

Activities of 10th DF in English Channel and Bay of Biscay, 1944. (See Appendix 6)

ice as a commander and his success in the Channel also merited a promotion. Failing this, Jones expected that he would at least be promoted to the rank of acting captain in order to avoid offending the Canadians of the 10th Destroyer Flotilla. His request was denied, on the grounds that Vice-Admiral Leatham was opposed to the idea of having acting captains under his command.

On Dominion Day of 1944, Commander DeWolf was promoted to the rank of Captain and shortly afterwards Jones raised the question of who was to be the SO of the 10th Destroyer Flotilla. Bringing his concerns to the attention of the C-in-C, Commander Jones was told in no uncertain language that *he* was in command of the Flotilla and that Captain DeWolf remained his subordinate. Although DeWolf never commented on the situation, for many of his fellow Canadians it was taken as an insult that a captain of the RCN should be under the command of an officer of less senior standing with the Royal Navy. The ships' companies of the 10th DF had been working long enough to avoid being overly upset on account of

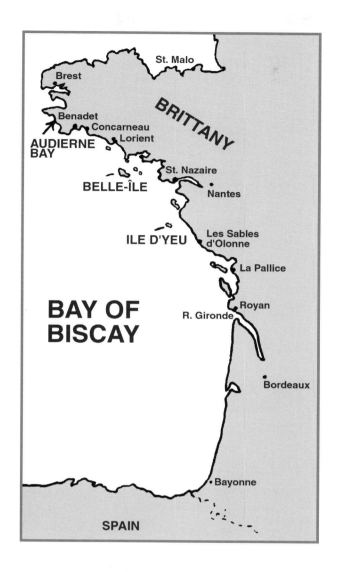

tion, Plymouth Command was tasked with conducting patrols off the Channel Islands in the hope of intercepting the enemy. At night during the patrols men on watch or at their guns watched the French shore for flashes of fire, not knowing whether it was the US Army chasing the Germans or the Germans putting up fierce resistance. All this was a matter of speculation, for before 6 June, nothing of the sort had been seen and the French shore had been cloaked in darkness, save for the fire put up by the German naval batteries.

On the night of 27-28 June, *Huron* and *Eskimo* encountered a formation of three German trawlers and a minesweeper south of the Channel Islands. Opening fire on the surprised enemy, the two Tribals had been able to sink the minesweeper and one trawler before the Germans escaped to the cover of their shore batteries. Subsequent patrols in this area also made contact with the enemy, although the Allies were again frustrated by German coastal guns. The Germans had precious few ships available to them. Admiral Krancke, the German commander of Group West, was forced to admit that the Allied night patrols were rapidly making it impossible for his forces to maintain sea communications with the Channel Islands.

This was the state of affairs when *Haida* returned to service on 11 July. The 10th DF was then preparing to extend its operations southwards into the Bay of Biscay. Since July 1940, Biscay harbours such as Lorient and La Rochelle had been the home ports of the U-boats that had menaced Allied convoys. Throughout 1943 Coastal Command, and RN and RCN escort and support groups had made the Bay of Biscay an increasingly hazardous transit area for U-boats. As of July 1944, the Allies were ready to render the Bay of Biscay as dangerous for the *Kriegsmarine* as the English Channel.

a formality. By the time *Haida* was released from dockyard and put back into service on 11 July, the officers and men focussed on the more immediate concern of fighting the remnants of the *Kriegsmarine* forces based in France.

While *Haida* was undergoing repairs, the US Army had succeeded at great cost in capturing the fortress of Cherbourg, forcing the German Navy to abandon this prized and vital Channel port. It had been expected that the Germans would attempt to escape from the besieged port by making their way west along the coast of Brittany towards Brest and the Bay of Biscay. In order to cut off this evacua-

## Patrolling the Bay of Biscay

Commencing on the night of 12-13 July, *Haida* was to take part in the first of a series of offensive sweeps off the approaches to Lorient. With *Tartar* and *Blyskawica*, the three destroyers would be operating close to the French coast in the hope of intercepting any German convoy or escort vessels that attempted to sail from the heavily defended harbour.

Setting out from Plymouth on 12 July, the Allies made their way south to the Bay of Biscay and began their patrol. The sweep off the approaches to Lorient passed uneventfully. Daybreak found the three destroyers heading westwards, away from the coast of France and back to base. A second patrol was carried out on the night of 14-15 July, with *Haida*, *Tartar* and *Blyskawica* arriving off Lorient at 23:00 and turning towards the coast at midnight. It was a moonless night, with clear visibility and calm seas. The three destroyers proceeded northward along their patrol line, with radar constantly searching the blackness ahead for the echoes which would indicate that enemy ships had ventured out from Lorient.

Off the coast of France, crews of the three destroyers were able to see flares and anti-aircraft fire on the horizon and they presumed that Allied aircraft must be attacking a German position somewhere off in the distance. By 02:09, the patrol had closed to sixteen miles off Lorient, when *Tartar* detected a contact heading towards the harbour entrance. At the time, the destroyers were steaming at 25 knots, but it was soon realized that 35 knots would be required to close with the enemy vessel before it passed safely into the harbour channel. In the circumstances, the Allies wisely but reluctantly gave up the chase and allowed it to pass.

Within ten minutes, however, the radar screen of *Tartar* showed new contacts on a bearing of 051 degrees at a range of thirteen miles, heading on a southerly course right towards the Allied patrol. Moments later *Haida* confirmed this contact. The destroyers prepared to close the approaching vessels. At the present course and speed, it was estimated the Tribals would come into contact with the enemy ships while they were still within range of the German shore batteries. Furthermore, Lorient was known to be surrounded by minefields and it would not pay to engage the enemy in such restricted waters while within range of German artillery. Therefore, the order was given to reduce speed to 15 knots, allowing the enemy to draw away from the shore and beyond the range of the coastal guns.

In the tense moments that followed, officers and men of *Haida* waited as the trio of German vessels closed. It soon became apparent that the enemy was proceeding at a very slow speed and the Allies were forced to alter course to south in order to allow them to draw further out to sea and set the trap. For ten minutes, the plotting rooms of the destroyers carefully tracked the course and speed of the German vessels until 02:55, when the order was given to alter course in succession and resume a northerly course in staggered line-ahead formation. In doing so, the

Opposite Top:
HMCS *Huron* off Plymouth, England, ca July 1944.
(Courtesy Ed Stewart, NAC PA-108169)

Opposite Bottom
HMCS *Haida*, Plymouth, England, 4 July 1944.
(Courtesy Michael Whitby, NAC PA-115045)

Allies expected to pass the enemy to starboard at a range of 4,000 yards, allowing the Tribals to use their main armament to best advantage while remaining out of range of their opponent's close-range weapons.

### Target Practice

The importance of avoiding German guns had been impressed upon Plymouth Command during an earlier engagement on the night of 27-28 June. On that night, *Huron* and *Eskimo* had engaged an enemy minesweeper and three trawlers off St-Malo. Although *Huron* sank the minesweeper and one of the trawlers, dense smoke had concealed one of the German trawlers and allowed her crew to open fire on *Eskimo* from close range with the 3-inch gun, Flak armament, and machine guns. Incredibly, the attack brought the Allied destroyer to a halt, when a single 20-mm bullet in a certain spot caused her to lose power. Having learned their lesson, the Allies planned to maintain a healthy distance from their German opponents on the night of 14-15 July.

By 03:00, the Allies were within 3,000 yards of the enemy and *Tartar* opened fire with starshell, illuminating what appeared to be four German ships off the starboard bow, heading south in line-ahead formation. Following *Tartar*'s lead, *Haida* fired starshell from her X mounting. In its light, two of the enemy vessels were revealed as armed merchant vessels, the third as a trawler, while the fourth vessel at the rear of the enemy line could not be identified. Meanwhile, as the enemy came within sight of the bridge crews, the gunners trained their weapons onto their targets and prepared to open fire. *Haida* took aim at the smaller of the two merchantmen. Within seconds the order was given to commence rapid firing. At the same time, *Tartar* engaged the larger merchant vessel and *Blyskawica* opened fire on the trawler.

Opening fire with her main armament, *Haida* reduced her opponent to a shattered wreck within seven minutes, at which time the order was given to join *Tartar* in engaging the larger of the two merchant vessels. Meanwhile, *Blyskawica* continued firing on the trawler and the unknown vessel at the rear of the German line. The enemy responded with starshell and intermittent bursts of well-directed gunfire which, although resulting in several near-misses, caused no actual damage to the Allied destroyers. Meanwhile, shells from *Haida* and *Tartar* were constantly falling on the second merchantman, and by 03:09 this vessel was also on its way to the ocean floor. The trawler and the unidentified vessel behind it were now subjected to the guns of all three Allied destroyers, and the forward ship found itself on the receiving end of a spread of torpedoes fired by *Tartar*. The torpedoes caused extensive damage and the burning trawler was soon observed to be sinking.

With the two enemy merchantmen and the trawler damaged beyond hope of recovery, *Haida* joined *Blyskawica* in engaging the unknown vessel at the rear of the enemy line. *Tartar* quickly followed suit. Before long this target was at the centre of a barrage of gunfire. Surprisingly, the German ship seemed unaffected despite being caught by several direct hits. It was not until the unknown vessel had received numerous salvoes of 4.7-inch shells that *Haida*'s officer of the watch realized they had been firing on a battle practice target which had been towed to the scene by the German trawler. Built to withstand an enormous amount of damage, the smoking target had become separated from the trawler when its towing chain was shot away and was now drifting aimlessly, indifferent to the bombardment to which it had been subjected.

Once the harmless character of the target was revealed, the Allies directed a final round of gunfire into the one German ship remaining afloat. For five minutes, the destroyers raked the enemy ship with gunfire until 03:35, when it began sinking. The Allies now prepared to disengage, leaving the German survivors to be rescued by their own vessels from Lorient. At 03:40, the destroyers regrouped and a westerly course was ordered as they made towards Plymouth at a speed of 30 knots. Later that day, *Haida*, *Tartar* and *Blyskawica* arrived safely at Plymouth and from there proceeded to refuel and replenish their stores and ammunition.

So ended the events of another dramatic night action, 14-15 July. The one-sided results of this latest engagement seemed to suggest that the enemy had been caught off guard by the extension of the 10th DF patrols into the Bay of Biscay. With the limited surface forces available in the region, there was little the *Kriegsmarine* could do to counter the Allied patrols so long as they remained beyond range of the shore batteries. Therefore, when it became clear that Allied destroyers were conducting patrols off the approaches to Lorient, Admiral Krancke, who could no longer provide escorts to the submarines as they made their way out into the Atlantic, was forced to divert incoming and outgoing U-boats further south towards La Pallice. Should the Allies decide to extend their patrols further south, Krancke knew that his U-boats would be in danger of being entirely cut off from the Atlantic.

## Intercepting Shipping Along the French Coast

With a limited number of escort vessels available in the Bay of Biscay, the Germans were forced to rely almost entirely upon shore batteries to defend German shipping along the coast of France. They were unwilling to risk the few destroyers remaining in Biscay harbours. For escorts, the Germans would have to make do with less powerful minesweepers and trawlers to protect their coastal shipping. Admiral Krancke knew these

vessels would be no match for the Allied destroyers which were now making their way south into the Bay of Biscay.

In late July, *Haida* and *Huron* were detailed to provide an anti-submarine escort for the infantry landing ship HMCS *Prince Henry* as she made her way to Gibraltar and Naples. During the invasion of Normandy, *Prince Henry* had been the senior landing ship of Force J, which ferried the Third Canadian Division to *Juno* Beach. Now she was being sent to the Mediterranean to join the collection of American, British, French, Greek and Polish ships gathering at Naples for Operation Dragoon, an amphibious landing on the French shore between Toulon and Cannes. Since mid-July, *Prince Henry* had been in Southampton preparing for her departure. Setting out on 24 July, she fell in with *Haida* and *Huron* in the waters off Start Point, to the southeast of Plymouth. Steaming west, the three ships continued on towards Land's End and the Scilly Isles. While en route, no enemy forces were encountered, and upon reaching the Isles, *Haida* and *Huron* broke off while *Prince Henry* continued on towards Gibraltar.

Planned as a subsidiary operation to Overlord, this second, smaller invasion was to deliver the American Seventh Army to Southern France—the point of departure for an advance up the valley of the Rhône. For the invasion *Prince Henry* was to sail as the Flagship of "Sitka Unit B", embarking Rear-Admiral T.E. Chandler, USN, and his headquarters staff to direct operations. Also on board *Prince Henry* on August 15, the day of the landings, were thirty-six officers and two hundred and forty-three men of the First Special Service Force, a joint Canadian-American assault force and the predecessor of today's US Army Special Forces.

Meanwhile, planning was underway in Plymouth for the next phase of operations in the

Warriors of the Channel night, *Haida* and *Huron* in the stream at Plymouth, England, ca summer 1944.  (Courtesy Michael Whitby, NAC PA-180480)

Bay of Biscay. The US Army was preparing for an advance on Nantes from St-Lo; and if their move south were successful, the German forces on the Breton peninsula would be isolated from landward resupply. At the same time, the naval forces of Plymouth Command would conduct offensive sweeps off the coast of Brittany as part of Operation Kinetic. These patrols were meant to intercept German supply convoys en route to the Breton ports while also preventing the enemy from evacuating the peninsula by sea. It was also hoped that Operation Kinetic would confine a significant number of U-boats to their pens by blockading the approaches to Brest, Lorient and St-Nazaire.

The first Kinetic operation was scheduled to depart from Plymouth on the night of 30 July. A significant number of Allied vessels would be taking part in the operation. These were to be divided into three groups, thereby allowing sub-divisions to be detached from the patrol for tasks that did not require the attention of the entire force. The first sub-division, Force 26, would provide air support. Force 26 consisted of the escort carrier HMS *Striker* and a screen of three Canadian destroyers: *St. Laurent*, *Chaudière* and *Kootenay*. Meanwhile, the second sub-division, Force 27, would be one of the striking arms, comprised of the British cruiser *Diadem* and the 19th Division of the 10th Destroyer Flotilla, including *Tartar*, *Ashanti* and *Blyskawica*. The third sub-division, Force 28, would include the cruiser HMS *Bellona* and the destroyers of the 20th Division, *Haida*, *Huron* and *Piorun*.

As scheduled, the patrol departed from Plymouth at 18:20 on 30 July, and by 22:00 the following day was in position approximately 105 miles southwest of Ushant. At this time, HMS *Striker* and the destroyers of Force 26 were detached from the patrol while the strike forces carried on towards Île d'Yeu. Shortly afterwards, Force 27 broke away to the southwest. *Haida* and Force 28 sailed northwest in order to conduct sweeps of the German convoy routes between Brest and La Rochelle. Both patrols passed without incident. Dawn of 1 August found the strike forces heading west towards a rallying point far offshore, where they would be free from attacks by the *Luftwaffe*. Remaining over the horizon and far from land throughout the day, Force 27 and 28 waited until after sunset before making their way inshore for a second sweep off the French coast. Once again, the patrol was uneventful. On the following day the Allies set course for Plymouth, arriving on 3 August. It had been a slow start for Operation Kinetic.

Their stay in harbour was brief, reflecting the new importance that recent developments had given to the interception of German shipping along the Bay of Biscay. With Allied land forces advancing into France, naval units in German-occupied harbours along the Bay of Biscay were in danger of being trapped. Meanwhile, the countryside was swarming with *Maquis* of the French resistance. These guerrilla forces were unable to engage the heavily armed *Wehrmacht* directly but they were more than capable of wreaking havoc upon German supply lines. As a result, it was rapidly becoming impossible for the enemy to resupply the garrisons of Brest, Lorient, St-Nazaire, La Rochelle and La Pallice overland. Rather than surrendering these ports, the German soldiers had been ordered to hold their positions at all costs, thereby preventing the Allies from seizing the valuable harbours and using them to transport war materials to the invasion forces. The only way the Germans could hold these ports was to deliver supplies to them by sea. Plymouth Command intended to make this a costly operation for the *Kriegsmarine*.

As a result, on the night of 4 August, *Haida* steamed in company with the cruiser *Diadem,* and the destroyers *Tartar* and *Ashanti* to conduct a sweep from Belle Île to Chausée de Sein. Absent from the patrol was *Huron*, whose officers and men were preparing for passage to Halifax, where they were due for a refit. In her place would be *Iroquois*, recently arrived in Plymouth after five months in Halifax. Having been detached from the 10th DF in February, *Iroquois* had missed taking part in the Channel actions of recent months and was now looking forward to a chance to fight Germans in the Bay of Biscay. Nevertheless, the night of 4-5 August would prove to be a slow start for the newest addition to the Plymouth forces. As planned, the Allies arrived off Belle Île late in the evening of 4 August and began their sweep towards Chausée de Sein. Continuing along their patrol line into the early morning of 5 August, the Allies set course for Plymouth after another uneventful night in the Bay of Biscay. Arriving in harbour later that day, the destroyers parted company with *Diadem* and prepared to embark on another patrol that same evening.

We now come to the events of 5-6 August. On this occasion, the Tribals would be patrolling between Île d'Yeu and Belle Île accompanied by the cruiser *Bellona*, whose captain would act as SO. Departing from Plymouth in the evening of 5 August, the cruiser and the Tribals made their way to the Bay of Biscay under a full moon and scattered clouds.

For this patrol it was decided that Force 26 would adopt a formation similar to that of the night of 26 April while conducting a sweep off the coast of France with the cruiser *Black Prince*. Therefore, upon turning south onto the patrol line, *Haida* and the other Tribals deployed on a line-of-bearing approximately two miles ahead of *Bellona*, with the cruiser aft to provide starshell illumina-tion from her 5.25-inch guns in the event of an encounter with the enemy.

Although this formation was intended to pro-tect the cruiser from torpedo attacks by an enemy encountered to the front, the first radar contacts appeared *astern* of the Allied formation. At 23:55, the Allies were approximately thirty-five miles south of Belle Île when *Tartar*'s radar detected a group of echoes on a bearing of 033 degrees at very long range. Five minutes later, the SO gave the order to alter course northwards and the Allies began trailing the enemy to seaward. Shortly after-wards, the plotting rooms were able to establish that the enemy was zig-zagging along a southerly course at 12 knots. Knowing that if the Germans continued on their present course and speed it would be possible to maneuver between them and the coastline, the Allies held their fire. Force 26 moved in to cut the enemy off from the shelter of their shore batteries.

Shortly after midnight, *Haida* and the destroy-ers crossed the enemy line of advance and altered course northwards, increasing speed to 25 knots. While moving inshore of the Germans had the dis-advantage of silhouetting the Allies in the light of the full moon, it was of more immediate concern that the enemy be prevented from escaping towards the coast of France.

At 00:34, the enemy came within range off the port bow. *Bellona* fired a starshell to illuminate the German position. At the same time, the destroyers altered course to northwest and prepared to open fire. The shell burst low above the horizon, reveal-ing what appeared to be a convoy of six enemy ships at a range of approximately 9,000 yards. Almost simultaneously, *Haida* and her sister Tribals opened fire, their main guns launching a barrage of shells at the enemy. As the destroyers continued to close, the cruiser altered course to port in order to engage the leading enemy ships and prevent the Germans from escaping south-wards. As the Tribals drew abreast of the German line, the order was given to turn to port and advance directly towards the enemy line.

Firing as she went, *Haida* closed on her target, which appeared to be a trawler. For four minutes, the gun crews furiously loaded and reloaded their weapons as the enemy ship was steadily reduced to a flaming wreck. The men serving the guns worked with precision and care. Then, with her first enemy in flames from stem to stern, *Haida* shifted her aim onto a second target, an M-class minesweeper. Within three minutes, this vessel was ablaze and at 00:57 was destroyed by a massive explosion.

The Allies had happened upon a German convoy escorted by minesweepers and trawlers. As the Allies approached, the enemy line seemed to have been thrown into confusion. The Germans were for some unknown reason firing a large number of rocket flares. Although the Allies did not know it at the time, the surprised Germans believed that their convoy had been mistakenly engaged by their own coastal guns. The rockets were meant to be a signal to call-off the bombard-ment, but the flares did little besides adding to the illumination provided by Allied starshell over the German position.

Shortly after 01:00, the Allies crossed the line of enemy ships one by one and, as they did so, *Haida* finished off a merchantman which had already been set afire by gunfire. Upon passing through the enemy line, *Tartar* altered course to starboard and the Tribals circled around to the north of the enemy formation in order to ensure that no German ships were escaping from the encounter by turning back the way they had come.

As they made their way north alongside the enemy, the main armament of the four destroyers repeatedly pounded their opponents with high explosive shells. Following in the wake of her next ahead, *Haida*'s guns raked a German coaster and then a minesweeper, both of which had already been damaged in the encounter. At 01:28, *Haida*'s gunners took aim at another coaster that was spotted lying motionless on the water. As the Canadian destroyer passed alongside at close range, the enemy was subjected to a violent round of gunfire. Then it capsized and sank. Meanwhile, *Tartar* was rounding the northern end of the enemy formation and altering course to the east and then south in order to continue back on the inshore side of the line of burning ships.

Before the Tribals could complete their second pass at the enemy, a signal was received from *Bellona* ordering them to consolidate on her position. The SO of Force 26 was preparing for a sweep along the enemy line in order to ensure that the entire convoy had been destroyed. Upon rejoining *Bellona*, they took up position, and the destroyers fell in astern of the cruiser as she proceeded alongside the burning convoy, finishing off any ships which had become scattered in the initial attack.

As they passed, *Haida* engaged a German ship previously lost in the smoke of the burning convoy. Just as flames were beginning to engulf her target there was an explosion on *Haida*'s quarter-deck. Looking back towards the stern of the ship, the officers and men on the bridge could see flames rising from Y turret. For a moment the scene bore a striking similarity to the night *Athabaskan* had been sunk. It was soon learned that a shell had exploded upon entering the breech of a gun in Y turret. Two men had been killed, eight others wounded, and *Haida*'s Y mount destroyed. The damage control crew was now busily working to extinguish the flames as *Haida* continued firing on the wreckage of the German convoy.

By the time the action was broken off, DeWolf counted eight or nine enemy ships sunk. Of these, Commander Jones was able to identify seven, including the cable and net layer *Hoher Weg*, one merchant vessel, two minesweepers, one trawler, and two coasters. The convoy had been completely destroyed and the force could be well satisfied by its work. Meanwhile, as Force 26 regrouped to continue their sweep, the fires on board *Haida* were brought under control and the ship was ready to continue patrolling towards Belle Île. In spite of the evening's successes, there was still work to do in closing the Bay to German vessels.

At 03:10, Force 26 was proceeding north towards Belle Île when *Tartar*'s radar detected a surface contact almost directly ahead at very long range. Shortly afterwards, the contact could be distinguished as a small group of surface vessels proceeding south at eight knots. As before, the Allies reversed course as the enemy approached in order to avoid detection by the dreaded German radar station and gun batteries on Belle Île and along Quiberon Bay. Turning away would also allow the German vessels to draw clear of the dangerous shoals and small islands of the inshore waters.

For the next forty-five minutes, the Allies maneuvered into position for the attack before closing on the enemy in line-abreast at 25 knots. Once within range, *Bellona* opened fire with starshell, revealing three or four German M-class minesweepers. The enemy immediately responded to the illumination with the familiar tactic of turning away from the encounter and making smoke. At the same time, the destroyers opened fire. The combination of starshell, white smoke, and the light of the full moon proved particularly effective at concealing the German ships and before long the enemy was lost from sight. With the enemy heading back towards Quiberon Bay,

the destroyers altered course to port and decreased speed to 12 knots. Given that visibility was severely limited by the enemy smokescreen, it would not have been wise to follow the Germans into inshore waters as they made for the cover of their shore batteries. Instead, the destroyers formed a line parallel to the coast and commenced firing broadside at the Germans as they fled.

Although the observers were able to catch only glimpses of the enemy, the radar-controlled guns of *Haida* and her companions were able to inflict several hits on the fleeing Germans. Meanwhile, the enemy returned fire and the action became general as each Allied ship engaged their opposite number. Gaining a momentary view of the enemy through the smokescreen, *Haida*'s crew observed the impact of one shell, which caught their opponent amidships, causing flames to break out on the German ship. This was immediately followed by the flash of an explosion above *Haida*'s foredeck, followed by a muffled secondary blast.

### *Haida*'s Guns are Damaged

A second shell had exploded prematurely in *Haida*'s guns, this time putting the A gun mounting out of service. Luckily, the explosive charge detonated in the barrel of the gun and no casualties resulted. With both Y and A mounts now out of action, only B mount was left to engage the enemy, with X firing starshell. Three minutes later, *Haida* scored a second hit on the enemy as he rapidly drew out of range. The enemy returned a starshell, which burst overhead. This was followed by one final volley of shell from the burning German ship, which burst harmlessly over *Haida*. Then it was over. The German starshell fell into the sea. The enemy withdrew behind their smokescreen into Quiberon Bay. It had been a grand, running fight, skilfully fought by both sides.

The German withdrawal had been well-timed, for half-light would bring threat of a *Luftwaffe* attack. As the enemy disappeared from sight, Force 26 regrouped and proceeded quickly out to sea, then back to Plymouth.

Upon her arrival in port, *Haida* disembarked her two men killed in the explosion of Y mount. On 9 August, the two victims of the explosion, Leading Seaman Roy H. Betts and Able Seaman Gordon J. Rowe, were buried at Weston Mills Cemetery in Devonport with full military honours, including a firing party from the RN barracks at Devonport. Able Seaman M. Kerwin received a Conspicuous Gallantry Medal (CGM) for going into the turret to rescue a shipmate. The citation reads: "In action 5th-6th of August a fierce fire occurred at Kerwin's gun as a result of the explosion of a cordite change and the ignition of oil from the damaged hydraulic system. The fire was centered in right gun shield. Kerwin, though blinded and wounded by splinters, went into blazing gun shield and dragged out injured Trainer."

The damage was extensive and upon arrival in harbour the guns of Y mount were hanging over the side of the ship. Forward, A gun mounting had also received serious damage and the ship had to remain in drydock for repairs until 20 August.

For her efforts during the action of 6 August, *Haida* was credited with the sinking of the *M-486* minesweeper and *SG-3C*. Prisoners of war taken by the Allies during the engagement told that the German convoy had been carrying eight to nine hundred special troops who were being evacuated from Bay of Biscay garrisons. Of these, postwar reports indicate that 91 were rescued on 6 August by German escort vessels. The remainder are thought to have gone down with their ships, aside from the few taken prisoner by the Allies. The loss of the convoy had been a disaster for the Germans. It came as a shock to Admiral Krancke that an Allied strike force had been able to advance so far south without being detected by coastal radar. If the Allies could not be detected by radar, there was little hope that the shore batteries could stop them from destroying the convoys, which were now the only means of delivering provisions to the isolated garrisons. Under these circumstances, the German Admiral conceded that it would be impossible to halt the Allies in this area. The Bay of Biscay, which had been under German domination for four long years, now was the parade ground of the 10th DF.

These successive sweeps by the 10th DF, which became more extensive and aggressive with the passage of time, sealed the fate of the German Atlantic Wall. As the US Army continued its remarkable assault against German fortifications, ports and armies, new footholds were being acquired along France's Atlantic shore. On 13 August the US Army reached the River Loire at Nantes. Operation Overlord had reached its conclusion, and now it remained for the Allied Armies in France to complete their tasks, push back the German armies, and carry out the invasion, occupation and defeat of Nazi Germany.

*The Beards Are Losing Out.* Because of the danger of choking when beards became saturated in the oily waters around a shipwreck, they were discouraged in the Navy. Stoker J. Livingstone possessed one of the rare and picturesque adornments. (Grant Macdonald, courtesy MMGL)

## "THE SHIP WHOSE BLAZING GUNS HAVE WRITTEN A NEW AND IMPERISHABLE CHAPTER IN OUR COUNTRY'S HISTORY:" AUGUST–29 SEPTEMBER 1944

FOR TWO WEEKS, *Haida* lay confined in the dockyard undergoing repairs to Y mounting. During this time, the ship's company bid farewell to *Huron* as she departed from Plymouth on 6 August bound for Halifax and a refit—and some rest and recreation for the men. Meanwhile, the 10th DF continued its nighttime patrols in the Bay of Biscay and began extending its coastal sweeps into the hours of daylight. As before, the object of these operations was twofold—to destroy enemy shipping and to provide cover for submarine-hunting groups operating off enemy held ports. On the night of 8 August, *Tartar*, *Ashanti* and *Iroquois* sailed from Plymouth with orders to approach the coast of France at Audierne Bay and remain there until the morning. Daylight revealed three Allied destroyers in Audierne Bay. The Germans opened fire with an angry barrage of heavy artillery, forc-

ing the intruders to withdraw behind the cover of smoke. The *Luftwaffe* joined in the attack, contributing a glider bomb launched from an He177 to the effort. Both attacks missed their mark. Duly warned, the three destroyers returned to Plymouth on 11 August.

The following week, with *Haida* still undergoing repairs, *Iroquois* and *Ursa*, along with the British cruiser *Mauritius*, encountered the enemy off La Rochelle. The action occurred on the night of 14-15 August, when *Iroquois* detected a lone radar echo south of Les Sables d'Olonne. Starshell revealed an armed merchant vessel. This German merchantman turned away promptly and began making smoke. Just as the Allies were preparing to open fire, a second target came into sight: an Elbing class destroyer. *Iroquois* and her companions quickly abandoned the mer-

chant vessel and opened fire on the warship. In response, the Elbing turned away and fired torpedoes before running for the cover of shore batteries at Les Sables d'Olonne. Forced to abandon the chase, the Allies resumed their patrol just beyond the range of enemy shore guns. With the Germans now alerted to the presence of an Allied patrol, further contacts with enemy vessels seemed unlikely.

This, however, was an incorrect assessment; for, as luck would have it, a second German convoy was located in the early morning hours of 15 August. By 06:15, upon closing within 3,200 yards, the enemy ships were identified as a formation of three German minesweepers. *Iroquois*, *Ursa* and *Mauritius* immediately opened fire and continued to pound the enemy for twenty minutes, by which time two of the German vessels had been driven onto the shoals of the French coast and the third destroyed in an explosion. After missing out on the action in the English Channel earlier that year, it now seemed that *Iroquois* was making up

for lost time by wreaking havoc on the Germans in the Bay of Biscay.

All the while, *Haida* unhappily remained in harbour, although by this time her repairs were nearing completion. On 20 August she was released from the dockyard and on the following day was put to sea for gun trials. Two days later, *Haida* was in all respects ready for duty. She was ordered to sail from Plymouth. Her task was to accompany the cruiser *Bellona* on a three-day patrol off the coast of France between Belle Île and Arcachon.

### *Haida* Rejoins the Patrol

In the weeks since Plymouth Command had first extended its patrols into the Bay of Biscay there had been a steady decline in the level of German naval activity in the region. Having suffered heavy losses throughout the summer of 1944, the Germans had become justifiably reluctant to risk losing their few surviving vessels by sending them beyond the reach of the shore batteries. Instead, they continued to counter with air power. But *Haida*'s patrol of the French coast proved uneventful, and on 25 August she returned safely to Plymouth.

Another Kinetic patrol in the Bay of Biscay had met with greater success than had *Haida*'s latest excursion. While *Haida* and *Bellona* were conducting their sweep between Belle Île and Arcachon, *Iroquois*, *Ursa* and *Mauritius* had become involved in yet another round of skirmishes in Audierne Bay. In their latest engagement, the three Allied ships had been able to close undetected and open fire on a surprised enemy. Within moments, one enemy vessel was destroyed in an explosion while three others were set ablaze and driven onto the rocks along the coast.

Early the next day, at 02:30, *Iroquois* detected a second convoy of four vessels. Closing to within range of the enemy, a starshell was fired, followed immediately by a violent round of gunfire from the Allied ships. The enemy line was thrown into confusion. Two of the German ships were quickly sunk, while the other two collided with each other as they fled for the safety of inshore waters. The impact caused one of the vessels to capsize and sink, while the second was driven full speed onto the rocks and burst into flames. Following this, *Mauritius*, *Iroquois* and *Ursa* turned to seaward and set course for Plymouth.

Unknown to the 10th Destroyer Flotilla as they returned from their patrols, this latest engagement in which *Iroquois* and her companions made such a good showing of themselves marked the conclusion of Operation Kinetic's period of good hunting. German merchant traffic in the area ground to a halt and the *Kriegsmarine* sent no more forces into the Bay of Biscay. From this point onwards, patrols by *Haida* and the 10th DF became a matter of maintaining control over the area and showing the flag to French towns and villages along the coast. Four years

after the defeat of France, the German hold over the country was loosening and soon would collapse entirely.

On 25 August, as *Haida* was making her way up Plymouth Sound following her return from Belle Île and Arcachon, the French 2nd Armoured Division under General Jacques Philippe Leclerc was rolling into Paris. Later that day, as Allied forces moved into the city, the commander of the German garrison, *General-major* Dietrich von Choltitz, surrendered. This was followed shortly by General Charles DeGaulle's entrance into the city and the unrestrained celebrations which ensued. The liberation of Paris was followed by further Allied victories in northern France as British and Canadian troops crossed the River Seine, advancing towards Calais and Brussels, while the Americans captured Châlons-sur-Marne and Reims. In the south of France, the Germans were in retreat as the Americans captured Avignon on 25 August, followed by Toulon and Marseilles three days later. The end of the Third Reich in France was within sight.

*Haida*'s next assignment was to form part of the escort for the French cruiser *Jeanne d'Arc* as she made her way from Algiers to Cherbourg. On board the cruiser were fifty members of the French Provisional Government who were returning to Paris in the wake of the liberation. *Haida* and *Iroquois* met *Jeanne d'Arc* in the Bay of Biscay on 31 August and escorted the cruiser safely to Cherbourg as ordered. Following this, *Haida* was to find herself on regular patrols in the Bay of Biscay, although the character of these patrols differed greatly from those to which the Canadian Tribal was accustomed.

Sweeping south through the Bay of Biscay from Ushant to the Spanish shore in the first week of September, *Haida* was now able to approach the coastline in daylight without fear of German aircraft. In the absence of German resistance, *Haida* was to sail in company with the British destroyer *Kelvin* and investigate the state of affairs at Île d'Yeu, Arcachon and Les Sables d'Olonne. The Allies had military intelligence that the Germans had withdrawn inland and that these towns had come into the hands of the French Forces of the Interior (FFI). Should this prove to be the case, *Haida* and *Kelvin* were to deliver arms and provisions to the FFI and gather intelligence on the local situation.

While en route to these ports, *Haida* and *Kelvin* joined the ring of ships which were blockading Ushant. Arriving off the approaches of the besieged port on 4 September, the crews of *Haida* and *Kelvin* watched as Allied aircraft and German Flak batteries fought throughout the night. At daybreak, the two destroyers departed and continued on their way.

*Haida*'s first port of call on this latest assignment was Île d'Yeu, where she made contact with FFI representatives before proceeding towards Arcachon. There the two destroyers paused to exchange signals with the shore but were met with no response. The coastline seemed all but deserted, despite reports that the FFI had liberated the area. Shortly afterwards, the order was given to continue south towards Les Sables d'Olonne.

As they steamed south along the coast in full daylight, the two destroyers noted the complete absence of German merchant shipping. In their place, the sails of French and Spanish fishing boats could be seen plying inshore waters. As darkness fell, these fishing vessels continued to dot the coastline and could easily be seen by their lights, which were left on throughout the night in order to avoid being mistaken for German vessels.

## Contact with French Forces of the Interior

On the morning of 6 September, *Haida* and *Kelvin* were approaching Les Sables d'Olonne. As the whitewashed buildings of the town came within sight, *Kelvin* was ordered to cover the approach to seaward as *Haida* made her way towards the shore. As the destroyer closed in on the town, the Tricolour of France was raised above a stone tower on the edge of the harbour. Signals were exchanged from ship to shore, and before long a fishing boat was making its way out of the harbour and heading towards the destroyer.

On board were a number of armed FFI men and a young lady who later introduced herself as the group's secretary and interpreter. As the fishing boat maneuvered alongside *Haida*, its occupants began cheering and shouting *"Vivent les Anglais!"* They were met by the equally cheerful crew of *Haida* and five were taken, along with their interpreter, to the captain's cabin for a discussion. There they informed DeWolf that the Germans had withdrawn seven miles inland from Les Sables d'Olonne in order to protect the supply line between German-occupied Gironde and St. Nazaire. It was agreed that *Haida* would send a landing party back with the FFI to investigate the town and to exchange small arms, ammunition and provisions for fresh fruit and vegetables.

Two officers and a petty officer interpreter from *Haida*, along with an officer and petty officer from *Kelvin*, were sent ashore with the French. They were met with great enthusiasm in the harbour by some hundred and fifty FFI guerrillas. From there, the landing party was escorted to the local FFI headquarters and introduced to the mayor of Les Sables d'Olonne. Once again, their arrival was received with spirited cheers, and champagne was produced for the occasion. Here it was agreed that the arms and ammunition would be handed over to the FFI to aid in their fight

THE SHIP WHOSE BLAZING GUNS" 131

against the Germans. The agreeable mayor provided the Allies with further intelligence on German activities in the region, although the discussion was interrupted at one point by a phone call from the local *Wehrmacht* commander. Having just learned that two enemy warships were lying offshore at Les Sables d'Olonne, the German officer wanted to caution the mayor that he was to have no contact with the Allies. Following this telephone call, the mayor, quite non-plussed, returned to the conversation at hand and called for another round of champagne.

The festivities were cut short by an urgent signal from *Haida* that the landing party was to return immediately to the ship. It had been reported that two German vessels were approaching from Gironde and would soon be rounding the headland to the north of Les Sables d'Olonne. *Kelvin* was immediately dispatched to intercept the two vessels. *Haida* hurriedly gathered the landing party before speeding off to join in the fight.

Upon rounding the headland, two German patrol boats, or vedettes, were observed by *Kelvin* as they made their way south along the coast. These fifty-foot vessels were only three miles distant when *Haida* rounded the corner, just as *Kelvin* was firing a warning shot across the bow of the lead vessel. When this warning was ignored by the German boats, a rapid burst of gunfire followed as the British destroyer opened up with its close-range armament. As the two vessels came under a hail of bullets, most of the German crew jumped over the side. A few remained on board in an attempt to fight back using the forward gun, but were killed almost instantly.

With the two enemy vessels silenced, *Kelvin* checked her fire and the two Allied destroyers advanced. The survivors were pulled from the water and taken prisoner while *Haida* and *Kelvin* prepared to take the captured vessels in tow. Prize

crews were dispatched from both ships and, as they boarded the vedettes, found them loaded with loot. It was later learned that the German officers on board the two vessels had been hoping to escape to Spain with all sorts of valuables taken from Brest. Therefore, not surprisingly, when *Haida*'s crew boarded the vessel the men immediately began to gather war trophies such as German uniforms and medals, leather flying suits, silk stockings and perfume. The looting became even more frantic moments later when it was observed that the damaged ship was beginning to take on water and would soon sink.

Following a failed attempt to bring the captured vessel alongside *Haida* and keep it afloat by pumping, the vedette listed to starboard and disappeared beneath the waves, leaving the heavily-laden prize crew floundering in the water. A launch was dispatched and the men were eventually recovered, although a few almost drowned because they were carrying so many souvenirs. In the mad dash to loot the captured vessel for all it was worth, the men also managed to grab several important documents that would later provide valuable intelligence.

As for the boat captured by *Kelvin*, it was towed back to the harbour and handed over to the FFI detachment. Following this, *Haida* and *Kelvin* put to sea and set course for England.

While en route to Plymouth, the two ships made a second brief stop at Île d'Yeu. There they took on seven German prisoners for passage to England. While on the way to Plymouth, *Haida* also had the occasion to assist a formation of British MTBs in the capture and search of a very suspicious German hospital ship off Lorient. On 16 September while searching the ship, it was discovered that many of the occupants were, in fact, high-ranking German garrison officers and their families who had been attempting to escape back to Germany disguised as patients. These, in addition to the prisoners rescued from the waters off Les Sables d'Olonne and those taken from Île d'Yeu, were landed at Plymouth and sent to prisoner of war camps.

This was to be *Haida*'s last week in Plymouth, as word had been received that the destroyer was to return to Halifax for refit. On 19 September, the ship was sent to No. 1 Jetty in the South Yard to take on stores and equipment for the passage across the Atlantic. *Haida* was to depart from Plymouth on the morning of 22 September, make her way to the Azores, and from there to Halifax. While this plan was to be conducted in secrecy, events would prove otherwise.

## Return to Halifax for Refit

On the morning of *Haida*'s departure, Vice-Admiral Leatham came aboard to address the ship's company. Looking over the crew fallen in on the upper deck, the Admiral dispensed with ceremony and asked the men to gather around as he spoke from atop a hatch. His words of praise merit publication here in full:

> I have worked you pretty hard since you joined this Command. Often you have come in from sea, tired and looking forward to having some time off, only to find yourselves under fresh sailing orders, though by all usual rights you had earned your liberty.
>
> It was indeed heartwarming to me to know that not once, though the demands made on you were heavy and onerous, was there the slightest delay, or the slightest slackness in carrying these out. It was no pleasure to me to have to make these demands upon you, but through it all you have supported me magnificently.

> The requirements of war, the demands on this particular Command, made these conditions necessary. We have had a multitude of things to do and a limited number of ships with which to do them. Here we are in the front line. To us is entrusted the Guardianship of the Western Approaches and all that such an important trust involves, including the great convoys and ship movements incidental to the invasion.
>
> We have kept that trust. Our supply convoys, on which the armies in the field are dependent, have passed daily and nightly through the waters of this Command. They offered to an able enemy, based on the French coast within easy striking distance of these movements, a choice and tremendous target totalling close to some six million tons of shipping.
>
> Up to the present time, not a single ton of this vast quantity of shipping has been lost by enemy action in the Plymouth Command. This is a fact of some importance which I feel you will be pleased to know. It will help to make up for the long hours and the ceaseless watch which we have had to maintain.
>
> So much for the defensive side of our operations. On the offensive side, upon which the defence is based, you and the ships with which you have sailed in company have achieved a similarly fine record.
>
> You have engaged in many fierce and spirited actions in enemy waters, actions in which you have emerged the victors on every occasion. You have bot-

tled up enemy shipping and made the movements of his fighting ships an extremely hazardous operation, even in his own waters.

In these encounters you have piled up an enviable score. Your Flotilla figures at the moment stand at thirty-four enemy surface ships, including at least three destroyers and many armed escorts, to say nothing of the transports and other craft, definitely sunk; one enemy submarine sunk, and seventeen enemy surface ships, including destroyers, heavily damaged. Of this, you have the lion's share.

That is only part of what you have done, but it is a part which must give you considerable gratification. It has been achieved with the loss of only one ship, the gallant *Athabaskan*.

These things show how well you have learned your duty ... that duty you have carried out with a courage and coolness that are most commendable. You have displayed a great fighting spirit, coupled with a determination and a persistence which have brought you to victory on every occasion on which you have met and engaged the enemy.

In the future of men like you, I have every confidence. The qualities which each and every one of you has displayed so abundantly must succeed in bringing you to the fore in any walk of life.

Here you have made friends, both ashore and afloat. In this old seaport, reputed to be the worst-blitzed city in Britain, we have, under these wartime conditions, been limited in what we could do for your comfort, but our hearts and our best wishes go with you.

This is an old port....old in history, yet you have shared in making new history here in our times. I would like to think that you will remember us, as we will remember you, and that you will always have a pleasant recollection of this Command.

This is not an official speech. It is just a few words between ourselves that I have wanted to say....to you who have earned so well every praise which can be given to you. Goodbye *Haida*, and good luck!

Following this, three cheers were raised and the Admiral took his leave. The ship prepared to depart. As she made her way down Plymouth Sound, the "secret" departure was given a send-off by crowds of civilians who lined the harbour to say goodbye. One by one, *Haida* was piped by every ship she passed. Among these was *Ashanti*, whose entire crew was gathered on the quarter-deck cheering. Also on hand were the Polish destroyers *Blyskawica* and *Piorun*, and the British cruisers *Mauritius* and *Bellona*, whose signal lamps were blinking away with messages wishing *Haida* well.

It was dusk by the time the Canadian destroyer was passing the Eddystone Light, and as darkness fell, the coast of England faded from sight as *Haida* began her journey home. The great first phase of her work had been completed. She wore the garland of success. All the laurels of victory were hers, proudly won in combat against a dangerous opponent. She was the glamour ship of the RCN, young but already fabled.

*Haida* arrived in Halifax on the fog-shrouded morning of 29 September. She met an enthusiastic welcome from the North Atlantic escort vessels lying at anchor in Bedford Basin. Among the ships on hand was *Huron*, whose entire crew was on deck to welcome *Haida* home. In the background, amidst the sound of hundreds of ships' whistles, the band of HMCS *Stadacona* could be heard playing *Heart of Oak* from the deck of a nearby tugboat. It was, and remains to this day, wrote Sclater, the greatest reception ever received by a fighting ship in Canada.

That night the officers and men of *Haida* heard a CBC broadcast saying they were home. "The crew of the famous HMCS *Haida*, the ship whose blazing guns have written a new and imperishable chapter in our country's history, reached Halifax today," said the announcer:

> The last time I saw this ship was in the historic harbour of Plymouth, England. She was coming in from sea, scarred and blistered with the marks of battle and her battle ensign was flying from her mast. There were holes from enemy fire through her hull…great heaps of empty shell cases lay around her guns and one turret was tilted brokenly over the side…but her crew brought her in as cool and unconcerned as if they had been on a routine patrol. I turned and spoke to an English dockyard matey standing beside me, watching her come in.
>
> 'Quite a ship,' I said, attempting to disguise my pride. He looked at me and in his eyes was a scornful astonishment at my ignorance. 'That's a great ship, mister,' he said; 'that's the *Haida* from Canada. She's been in more fights than any other ship in this harbour, and that's saying something. These boys get free beer in every pub in Plymouth tonight and we're proud to give it to them.'

That was what England thought of them; and now we have them home.

Think well of what they have done. These are men who were mostly untrained for war, lads from the Maritimes and British Columbia, from Quebec and the prairies, from the villages, towns and cities of Ontario. Many of them had never seen the sea until they came to it in time of war.

In the dark and perilous days when the fate of our country and our Commonwealth hung in the balance, *Haida* and her sister ships sailed out to face and fight whatever odds might be against them. Neither the ships nor the men who manned them have come through unscathed. They bear the scars of battle and these men have memories that will never be forgotten.

They did not flinch or fail in the fierce tide of battle. Grim actions took their toll. They saw shipmates fall, wounded and dying beside them, but with steadfast faith in the justice of their cause they honoured those who fell by fighting on.

Now they are home, home from the great series of victories which have brought new honours and added new prestige to our arms, home to the land and people from whence they came.

Take them to your hearts, Canada. This is a great ship which sailed into this old Nova Scotian harbour today, a ship which has earned a great name, a name which will endure forever in our annals of the sea.

# CHAPTER 10

## A NEW TOUR OF DUTY: RETURN TO RUSSIA, LIBERATING NORWAY: 1945

●

SHORTLY AFTER NEW YEAR'S DAY 1945 *Haida* cleared Halifax. She left alone to cross the North Atlantic. Fresh and worrisome in the minds of officers and men was the recent loss of HMCS *Clayoquot*, one of the Bangor class of minesweepers, whose primary duty had been the protection of shipping. Working in the inshore waters around Halifax, this vessel and others were always at the risk of mines and U-boats.

*U806*, commanded by *Kapitänleutnant* Klaus Hornbostel, lingered off the light vessel at Sambro, the Rock of Lamentations, awaiting targets to add to his initial tally, his first victim being the British Liberty ship *Samtucky* of Convoy HHX-327. The Captain (D) at Halifax had ordered *Clayoquot* to investigate, and she sailed on 23 December in company with the frigate *Kirkland Lake* and the Bangor *Transcona*. The next day, the 24th, the

three Canadian vessels were steaming in line-abreast so as to take up a screen around Convoy XB-139, twelve ships bound for Boston, and to sweep through an area where the CNR pre-war liner, converted into the troop ship *Lady Rodney*, and her escorts were to pass en route to St. John's. When the Canadians broke from their position to form the screen, they offered attractive targets. Hornbostel fired a GNAT (German Navy Acoustic Torpedo), a homing weapon. The "fish" struck *Clayoquot*, and in only ten minutes she turned turtle and sank, stern first. Hornbostel then dived to 155 feet and eluded a depth charge attack pressed by the Canadian warships. He got off another GNAT, this time at *Transcona*, but it was destroyed by the latter's anti-acoustic torpedo gear, (a Canadian designed decoy or foxer streamed astern to deflect homing torpedoes targeted for enemy

Haida's crew assembled on deck, 1945. (HMCS *Haida* Naval Museum 991.074.016.001)

propellers) known as CAT. One sailor in the water, knowing vessels were coming to the rescue, issued his own radio news broadcast: "Flash! Canadian minesweeper destroys German torpedo!" Humour was a precious commodity that day. Hornbostel took *U806* to the bottom this time, and there he lay quietly until midnight, when he stole silently and slowly southwards. Twenty hours later he came nearly to the surface and put up his *Schnorkel* to clear the U-boat's air. *U806* was never caught and surrendered to the Allies at Wilhelmshaven in May of the following year. *Clayoquot* lost four officers and four crew; another sixty-seven, including her commanding officer, were rescued and taken to Halifax.

### *Haida*'s New Commander

"We sailed alone," recalled *Haida*'s new commander, Acting Lieutenant-Commander Robert P. Welland, aged twenty-six. He was brother-in-law to the CO of the *Clayoquot*. He was a tough, no-nonsense professional, keenly interested in the well-being of his crew and dedicated to the discipline of his officers and men. He could be a taskmaster and disciplinarian when required. His previous command had been *Assiniboine*, and with him to *Haida* came Lieutenant Gordon Welsh, the navigator, and Lieutenant-Commander William Patterson, the chief engineer. The executive officer was Lieutenant Raymond Phillips. He looked younger than his twenty-two years and had greeted Welland after the latter had been piped aboard.

Welland was impressed with what he saw: "The deck of my new destroyer was heavy steel, riveted, hard, and would stand up to what I would be putting her through. *Haida* was beautiful. She would soon come to life." Welland noted, too, that *Haida* had longer legs than *Assiniboine*, carried 600 tons of fuel, and was primarily a big gun ship, with three mountings of twin 4.7-inch guns that could range out to twelve miles. She bristled with Oerlikon anti-aircraft guns, and down below was 44,000 horsepower that gave her 36 knots at full fuel load. She was "a marvel," he noted. "There were 215 of us on board to make her work." About eighty-five percent of the crew was new.

Welland chose a route via the Azores for good weather so that the ship's company could train hard all the way. It was a rough crossing. *Haida* stopped at the Azores for fuel, food and drink, and then it was on to Plymouth, arriving on the evening of 11 January. *Haida* was taken into dock-yard hands for the installation of new radar equipment, a new two-way radio (then a recent development), new cipher machines that took the work out of decrypting messages, infra red signalling lights that could be used freely in the dark without worry of detection, and new anti-aircraft ammunition with the VT fuse—a tiny radar set in the nose of the shells that caused them to explode as they neared the target. Also placed on board was a new radio receiver and transmitter designed to defeat the glider bomb. "It listened for the glider's radio receiver and activated its transmitter which aped the glider's control signals, causing the glider to go out of control," said Welland. "Now this might work," said *Haida*'s chief radioman. Clever British scientists and engineers were keeping pace with German ingenuity. This greatly increased the chances of survival, noted Welland. As he also noted, there had been a modification to the torpedo control system which would enable *Haida* to fire using radar information instead of depending on visual sightings. Welland had been responsible for this improvement: "They had not even changed my words in the descriptive manual. I was flattered. But not paid for my inventive work."

With this enhanced kit of electronic gear and weapons, and having completed her radar and communications trials, *Haida* sailed north independently on 24 February for lonely Scapa Flow in the Orkneys, there to join the Home Fleet. She came under the supervision of Commodore (D) Home Fleet. In the few months that *Haida* had been in Canada, affairs in European and Mediterranean waters had shifted considerably. With the North Atlantic convoys sailing in relative safety, courtesy of Asdic (or SONAR) equipped ships and increased air cover, the war against the U-boat was being pressed in less customary seas. RAF Coastal Command was carrying the war to the enemy, and the English Channel and Bay of Biscay were being made Allied waters. There was still much to do, and the new duty was to force the Germans out of Norway. The intention was to blockade the country, seal off all its water accesses, and cut off supplies to German forces by sinking their shipping.

## The Offensive in the Norwegian Leads

In Norway, the moderating Atlantic Drift allows more northerly human occupation than otherwise would be possible, and the sea has given Norway its fisheries, merchant marine, and whaling. The sea joins together the fjords and the Norwegian Leads, the channels inside the island fringe linking Stavanger with North Cape. At Narvik, the anvil of the 1940 campaign, a railway allowed Swedish iron ore an outlet, and it was here that ships of the German merchant marine continued to make their regular calls. In German hands the Leads gave continuous shelter to German shipping. Only intervening air power and mines could interfere with the passage of resources destined for Germany or, conversely, supplies destined for the German occupying forces at such places as Narvik and, of particular interest to *Haida*'s story, Trondheim with its near-by air bases.

For the Norwegian campaign of 1945, an unsung and forgotten battle of the war, Scapa was the place for the naval forces to gather, which they did in large number, it being the nearest port from which to mount an assault. "We learned the Germans planned to use their heavy ships to beat us off; battleships with 11-inch guns; fast cruisers with 8-inch guns, and some 6-inch cruisers as well as their very good destroyers, almost as fast as our Tribals." This was what Welland learned in the admiral's cabin in HMS *Rodney*, when he was summoned to a conference of captains. *Huron* and *Iroquois* were part of the force as was a new aircraft carrier HMS *Puncher*. There were also two Polish destroyers, the *Glom* and *Blyskawica*, the latter an old friend from the Plymouth patrol, and the British destroyers *Zealous*, *Zulu* and *Zambezi*. In the past few months British MTBs had penetrated the Leads, destroying ore carriers.

The war had to be taken to the Leads in greater force. In November 1944, as part of Operation Counterblast, heavier units of the Royal Navy had already begun night operations in open waters south of the Leads. HMCS *Algonquin* took part in the action. Two of four merchant ships and all but one of six German escorts were sunk. On another occasion a force encountered a German convoy near Egersund, south of Stavanger, but the race went to the swift. The German destroyers outpaced the British cruisers and found protection under guns mounted ashore. The RAF had fickle weather to contend with, and innumerable hiding places were available to German destroyers. In addition, the enemy countered by sending E-boats and deploying night-fighters, both intended to combat the nighttime operations of Coastal Command against German shipping in Norwegian waters. U-boats were sent to prey on Scapa's approaches. British Intelligence knew of both the German countermeasures and of Dönitz's warning to Hitler in December 1944 that the constant heavy attacks against German forces would soon bring shipping to a halt. Through intelligence gathering and efficient communications the British were able to deploy their forces, the most efficient of these being air attack, which would have fatal consequences to the enemy.

On the eve of *Haida*'s 1945 Norwegian and Russian operations, Operations Intelligence Centre at the Admiralty was passing signals intelligence to headquarters at Rosyth on the Firth of Forth and, on the basis of electronic information, had inaugurated a running plot of all shipping movements. In these circumstances, greater successes would lie ahead for the fighting arms.

Meanwhile, training exercises continued without interruption, and naval forces set forth daily from Scapa to engage in mock combat, all the while readying their weapons and testing their electronic surveillance and communications gear. Friendly fire was a more common occurrence than has been reported. On Friday 9 March *Haida* nearly killed the British submarine HM S/M *Trusty*, commanded by Lieutenant H. Stern. As C-in-C Home Fleet, Admiral Sir Henry Moore stated, "It is fortunate that the chain of circumstances which led to this regrettable accident had no serious consequences."

## Friendly Fire: HM S/M *Trusty*

The weekly exercise known as Serial No. 145 began with two units from Home Fleet, Force A and Force B, out on a night tracking exercise with a

British submarine as part of the group. Although *Haida* received a message that the submarine was not hostile, Welland was for some reason not advised. Data notifying the ship that there was a submarine sanctuary was also disregarded. *Haida* had assumed her customary screening position, altering course as required, and saw in the distance the dim flashes of gunfire that occasionally lit up the night. Thus, when *Haida* chanced upon a submarine, Welland assumed it to be hostile and commenced the attack, driving the *Trusty* down with depth charges—which fortunately did no damage. When *Trusty* rose to the surface Welland identified the submarine as a British T class, with its distinctive bow and large Asdic dome. Everyone yelled "Cease Fire!" Welland called off the attack and quickly brought the ship alongside the sub, which was stopped, blowing tanks, and listing at a precarious down angle. At precisely that moment, a British cruiser opened up with her heavy guns on the destroyer and submarine, with the shells landing short, exploding and throwing up great columns of water. A second salvo followed.

"You stupid bastards!" shouted the chief yeoman, who was flashing signals to the cruiser. *Haida* screened the submarine, which the cruiser had assumed was a U-boat, and escorted *Trusty* to port. Welland tells the remarkable story that, when the conning tower opened, out popped a chap who had been his fellow midshipman from HMS *Glasgow* six years previously. "Dinsy," he yelled, "are you OK?" "Welland, why are you doing this?" came the angry reply. "Nobody told me you were here," Welland yelled back.

The commander of *Trusty* later wryly told the officers of *Haida* that their depth charges had not been very close. To prevent the recurrence of such a disastrous mistake, clearer instructions were issued so that a definite warning signal should be made to, and acknowledged by, all ships about to take part in an exercise. Further, the flag signal NEGATIVE BLUE TACK INTERNATIONAL FLAG E was to be flown during submarine exercises. Admiral Moore stated: "I realize that HMCS *Haida* was in the course of working up at the time of this incident." He went on to inform the officer commanding that he was to take steps to ensure that her communication organization "has been brought to a proper state of efficiency." The court of inquiry blamed the signal officer and the training officer for not logging in the signals and failing to advise the commanding officer. "We consider that the organization and supervision of the Signal Department of HMCS *Haida* is not satisfactory....We are of the opinion that the principal cause of this incident was due to a series of failures in communications, which resulted in the Commanding Officer personally not receiving any information pertaining to the nature of the exercises, other than that it was an air attack exercise. We consider that under these circumstances, he acted correctly." And so the episode was closed.

A few days later, on 13 and 14 March, *Haida* was at sea carrying out gunnery exercises. The location was west of Orkney, and she was in company with and under the orders of the destroyer HMS *Terpsichore* and C-in-C Home Fleet to proceed at best speed to position 58°43' N 04°40'W to hunt a U-boat that had been reported and attacked by HMS *Hastings*. *Haida* quickly reached the position and assumed the chase, dodging some inshore navigational hazards to pursue the U-boat. She dropped a pattern on quite a good echo, and continued her sweep at 12 to 15 knots—good operational speed for her Asdic—all the while streaming her CAT gear. Nothing rose to the surface, and some consideration was given to the fact that perhaps the echo had come from some wreck. The search for the U-boat had been dogged by the necessity of working through about twenty fishing boats. These vessels looked like U-boats on the 293 Radar plan position indicator, and upon investigation *Haida* found that some showed lights and others did not. *Haida* steamed from fishing boat to fishing boat, and those that were stopped in the water were assumed to be fishing craft. Welland was annoyed: "In view of the identification difficulty," he advised Commodore (D) Home Fleet in his after action report, "it is considered that when a U-boat is suspected of being in an area and a hunt is in progress, consideration should be given to ordering all fishermen well clear."

## Escort Duties with the Home Fleet

In the next few weeks *Haida* joined in operations undertaken by the Home Fleet. First came Operation Cupola, a mine-laying strike in the narrow waters off Granesund on the Norwegian coast. In Force One was the escort carrier HMS *Premier*, equipped with eight Avenger aircraft capable of laying mines. Another escort carrier, HMS *Searcher*, carried Wildcats as cover for the Avengers and to provide escort for the carrier *Queen* and the cruiser *Bellona*, well known to *Haida* from 10th DF days. Force One sailed before dawn. An hour before daylight three aircraft were put up to search ahead for German shipping. The carrier decks were ranged with attack aircraft. Eight destroyers, units of 17 DF, accompanied the carriers with HMS *Onslow* as flotilla leader. The aircraft laid their mines in the southern entrance to Askvoll Anchorage. *Haida* was tasked with providing the A/S screen for the strike force, and as such she was safely outside of the mine barrier set up by the Germans. She also acted as aircraft guard during flying operations. Cupola was completed without incident. By the afternoon of 21 March, Force One was back in Scapa.

Force Two sailed three days later and consisted of the escort carriers HMS *Searcher*, *Nairana*,

*Queen* and *Puncher*, the cruisers *Bellona* and *Dido*, and a cluster of destroyers, including *Haida* and *Iroquois*. This time the intention was different: to destroy German shipping along the Norwegian coast by aerial assault. The operation was staged in two parts: Prefix One of 26 March and Prefix Two of 28 March.

Operation Roundel took *Haida* back to far northern waters, to the already familiar Kola Peninsula and Russian naval bases and ports. The route as before lay past deadly North Cape, where in her first action *Haida* had been part of the team that destroyed the dreaded *Scharnhorst*. Eighteen months had passed since *Haida*'s last visit to these seas, and in the interim much had happened. Not only had many of the major surface units of the *Kriegsmarine* been destroyed but Allied radar, communications, and techniques of sub-hunting had improved. Since the loss of the carrier HMS *Glorious* to the *Scharnhorst* and *Gneisenau* in 1940 in Norwegian waters the lesson learned—that air cover was required—had been invariably observed. Now the enemy strength lay in shore-based bombers and fighters, guided by good spotting aircraft, and in the numerous U-boats being gathered by Dönitz at the choke point of the Norwegian Sea leading to the Russian ports. U-boat crews anticipated a happy hunting time. The *Luftwaffe* also kept up its active spotting and attacks on convoys.

*Haida*'s first duty was to escort a party of seven American-built, Russian-manned submarine chasers (Numbers *1482* (SO), *1497*, *1493*, *1486*, *1505*, *1508* and *1511*) for passage from Greenock on the Clyde to Thorshavn in the Faeroe Islands, with an estimated time of arrival of 07:00 on 13 April. There they were to await the arrival and effect a rendezvous with the next Murmansk-bound convoy, JW-66. *Haida* was detached from the Home Fleet for this special duty, and made her way to Greenock. There Welland gave instructions to the commanders of the submarine chasers that they were to follow in line and to keep an eye out for the stern light of the destroyer, which was to be their guide. *Haida* had been fitted with special fueling pumps and hoses, and each of the boats had been brought alongside to demonstrate how refueling at sea was conducted.

According to plan, *Haida* sailed through Greenock boom with the submarine chasers formed astern and proceeded at 12 knots on the standard route through the Minches. Welland and all aboard, including the Russian liaison Lieutenant Nicholai Ivliev, who spoke excellent English, anticipated a normal passage, although they would have to be on the lookout for U-boats and German aircraft. The course was 017 degrees. Early the next day, at 02:30, radar operators in *Haida* observed, when some few miles north of Barra Head, that one of the submarine chasers had detached from the line, headed northeast and then north, and had eventually disappeared altogether from the screen. Welland remembered this as "the night when the sun was stalled below the horizon for a week." Suspicions were immediately raised, and a defection was imagined (although never officially reported). Phillips put it more graphically: "Maybe they don't want to go to Mother Russia."

Welland takes up the tale in his confidential letter of proceedings, dated 5 May, "I endeavoured to recall him, both in English and Russian, I having a Russian Officer and a Russian Signalman on board but received no answer to my calls." The night was clear and dark with the wind at Force 4-5 (11-21 knots) from the northeast. A few hours later the wind had increased, with occasional rain, and the six remaining Russian vessels also broke formation, three heading for South Uist, and the other three remaining in touch, hauled in by Welland's messages. The rest refused, in Russian,

his orders of recall. Because Loch Ewe, the nearest base, was convenient, Welland ordered the compliant three to proceed there and wait. He then went out in pursuit of the remainder, and found the three stragglers. Now the hunt was on for the first defector. Welland took *Haida* close inshore, steaming at 25 knots down the inside coast of South Uist, looking for the missing Russian, No. *1511*. Nothing was seen on this southward search. He ordered 27 knots and a swing to the north, going as high as Cape Wrath along the route, intending to overtake *1511*. Nothing was seen of the submarine chaser. Patrol vessels off the Cape reported no sighting of the vessel. Welland took the destroyer back to Loch Ewe.

By this time the C-in-C Western Approaches and the naval officer in charge of the operation had instituted a formal search. The Admiralty was now annoyed by "the irregular behaviour" of the Russian submarine chaser *1511*, which had caused "grave anxiety to all authorities concerned." Surface craft and aircraft had now carried out extensive searches at a large expenditure of fuel. *Haida* again combed the same shore without success, across the Butt of Lewis and south as far as Ushinish Light, returning to Loch Ewe at 17:00 on 13 April. Air and sea searches likewise met with no success. The officers and men were pondering the disappearance of *1511*. The Admiralty ordered that, if *1511* were not located by 19:00 that day, *Haida* and the remaining six were to sail in execution of previous orders. Before many hours had passed, the naval officer in charge of the Faeroes reported the arrival of submarine chaser *1511* in Thorshavn. Welland gathered up his charges and steamed at 12 knots towards the Faeroes.

Again the weather deteriorated, with winds increasing to Force 7 (28-33 knots). Welland decided to alter course and take shelter in the Orkneys. By 14:00 the wind was Force 8-9 (34-47 knots) from the southeast, and the submarine chasers were practically hove to, but all present and in station. The wind increased to Force 9 (41-47 knots), and the Russian boats behaved dangerously, rolling to an angle of 60 degrees, although they kept the sea right ahead. The Russian senior officer expressed growing concern for their safety. The Admiral in charge of the Home Fleet at Scapa, in constant touch with *Haida* by signal, made plans to bring *Haida* and her charges alongside the famous battleship *Iron Duke* (Jellicoe's flagship at Jutland and now a depot ship). This turned out to be the contingency plan, for at 21:30 on the 14th they all gained the lee of the Orkneys, and received instructions to go into Thurso on the mainland. By 01:00 on the 15th *Haida* was anchored in Thurso and took all boats safely alongside. Two Russians received medical attention, one remaining on board until the eventual arrival in Polyarnoe.

By 11:00 the wind had diminished and Welland ordered all to sea, resuming their station. They arrived at Thorshavn at first light on the 16th without further incident. There, in Skaele Fjord, there was a three-day layover awaiting the arrival of JW-66. Welland took the opportunity to make investigations. This is what he reported on the Russian actions:

> I ascertained that on the night of the 11th and 12th when Number *1511* detached, he did so because he considered it more seamanlike to proceed outside the Hebrides rather than through the Minch. This he did, despite the fact he had been to two conferences and had been given a typewritten copy of the route as far as the Faeroes by myself. This action explains why the searches failed to locate him. He saw my flashing but explained that he knew

what I would say anyway so declined to answer.

Welland also learned that the other three detached and reduced speed because they considered the Minch unduly risky in the darkness. "Until discovering this I had not suspected the reason for their peculiar behaviour," reported Welland with gentlemanly detachment, "The Russian Commanding Officers voiced no fear of the passage through the Minch when I held a pre-sailing conference in Greenock and except for this lapse and even in very bad weather, they kept proper station and were prompt in answering V/S signals."

### Escorting JW-66

At Skaele Fjord in the Faeroes *Haida* and her charges joined with Convoy JW-66. This convoy consisted of twenty-seven merchantmen and sixteen submarine chasers bound for Kola Inlet. The accompanying force was powerful, and comprised two British escort carriers *Vindex* and *Premier*, the cruiser *Bellona*, five British and one Norwegian fleet destroyer, the HNorMS *Stord*, ten corvettes of 7th Escort Group, and the Canadians *Haida*, *Huron* and *Iroquois*. There was also a rescue ship and a tanker. The powerful frigates that the RN kept in 19th Escort Group greeted them as they approached Kola Inlet. The corvettes, sent ahead, were to deploy their forward-throwing Squid mortars and to lob salvoes of depth charges to deter the enemy. A new technological innovation, the sonobuoy, was to be used to listen for U-boats. Dropped from an aircraft, the sonobuoy deployed a suspended hydrophone. Any submarine noises it detected were transmitted to the aircraft by a small radio in the buoy.

The destroyers took up their defence formation according to the orders laid down by C-in-C Home Fleet. The merchantmen in the convoy were split into two columns spaced 500 yards

Depth charge explosion off stern of *Haida*. Fighting her way into Murmansk, 1945. (Courtesy David Ernst)

apart, with the ships keeping 400 yards apart in the line, travelling at 12 knots. The Russian submarine chasers would work the outside perimeter, fighting off aircraft and running down periscope sightings. *Haida* and others laid smoke as they approached Kola, shielding the merchantmen. The destroyers steamed at 18 knots, the best patrol speed at which their Asdic still functioned. Everyone was on the lookout for U-boats.

> At dawn the convoy had formed into two lines [wrote Welland], we were approaching Kola Inlet. Intelligence reports said there were up to ten U-boats waiting for our convoy. Breakfast had been served to all hands; everyone had changed into clean clothing in the event of being wounded. Face masks, ear plugs, and metal helmets were carried by everyone exposed or near the guns. All boilers were coming on line; the electrical supply was split between generators; damage control shores and pumps were placed; sound powered phones were run and tested; emergency steering was made operational; David Ernst, our doctor, had his sick bay ready with morphine. Every man was at fighting position or had a ship-saving duty. We would have only hand-held meals for the next ten hours. We were as ready as could be.

The escort carrier HMS *Vindex* assumed the duties of fighter carrier from 08:00 to 20:00 daily and anti-submarine carrier from 20:00 to 08:00 daily. At 20:00 on 22 April she launched her first anti-submarine patrol aircraft, a Swordfish. This machine was piloted by Lieutenant-Commander S.G. Cooke, the senior spotter and CO of No. 813 Squadron, with his observer Lieutenant (O) G.D. Baring Gould. As the Swordfish left the flight deck the RATOG (rocket assist take-off gear) failed to fire. The Swordfish ditched off the starboard bow of the carrier. *Haida,* as duty rescue destroyer, or duty plane guard, since Welland was the most junior commander, was detailed to rescue the pilot and observer. As Surgeon-Lieutenant Ernst recounted, because Welland was the least senior commander *Haida* got the most interesting jobs.

The sea was extremely cold and the sky was dark. The rescue by *Haida*'s whaler and crew took no longer than twenty minutes, recounted Ernst, and the two aviators were not even wet above their waists, so quick had been the plucking. As a token of his esteem, the pilot gave Ernst one of his jacket buttons, which when opened (with a left-hand thread) revealed a compass beneath the facing. The Royal Navy planned for every navigational contingency. The aviators' watches had been damaged but the machinists on the destroyer were able to repair them and return them to their owners. The two aviators were returned unhurt to *Vindex* at 07:00 next day.

Subsequent to this episode, Commander J.D.L. Williams of *Vindex* came up with an invention to effect recoveries: a marker buoy fitted with light and radar reflectors. One of these was placed on each side of the ship, slung from the aft sponson. When a "let go" buzzer was sounded from the bridge a sentry would release the marker from its gear. Details of this innovation soon appeared in an Admiralty fleet order.

As the convoy approached Kola Inlet the elaborate preparations of the commanders continued. *Haida* and *Iroquois*, working the flanks, continued to cover the convoy with smoke laid at high speed.

Other vessels dropped "scare" depth charges, some three hundred in all. April 25th—the day American and Soviet soldiers met on the Elbe—was the day of greatest anxiety as the convoy came through what was expected to be the U-boat zone. The escort carriers stood off to the northeast providing air cover. "We had to fight our way in," recounted Ernst. *Haida* dropped depth charges every minute in a five-charge pattern, three from the rails and two from the throwers. They towed their CAT gear to attract homing torpedoes. On one occasion *Haida*'s Asdic reported a sub contact. This was *U427*, captained by *Oberleutnant Graf* Karl Gabriel von Gudenus. *Haida* quickly made smoke and no damage was done by the U-boat. After the war a German naval chronicle stated that *Haida* was the specific target of *U427*'s torpedo attack. In addition, the same source said that *U427* had barely survived *Haida*'s depth charge attack.

Two U-boats were sunk, destroyed in the furious approach of JW-66. On the approach to Kola Inlet, relays of Swordfish laid sonobuoys in a series of lines across the swept entrance to the inlet. These buoys were always twelve miles ahead of the convoy. Working in partnership with Avengers the Swordfish provided superb screening and laying of sonobuoys to mark the submarine positions, allowing the destroyers to make their runs and clear out all opposition. The convoy reached Kola unscathed.

By midnight all escorts were riding in safety in Vaenga Bay. Within days *Haida*'s officers and men learned that Naval Intelligence had known that there were fourteen U-boats (of the *Faust* Group) in the vicinity in addition to the one they had sighted.

From the deck of *Haida* a dismal sight met the eye. Everywhere the utilitarian aspect of a war port was obvious. Desolate, snow-covered hills dominated the distance. The five-storey Russian hospital resembled nothing Ernst had ever seen before, with staff walking without shoes or in slippers and always dressed in civilian clothes. The Russians kept close watch on their allies, and liaison officers were required ashore. The drabness of the place could have been expected. Darkness cloaked everything. It was Easter in Kola Inlet. *Haida* refueled, and for four days there was rest. In the Red Navy Club at Polyarnoe crews of escorts, destroyers and corvettes gathered, and it is reported that there was considerable partying and a concert to celebrate the linking of the Russian and British Armies in Germany. The war was nearly over and the scent of victory was in the air.

Meanwhile the return convoy, RA-66, was assembling in readiness for passage to Loch Ewe. Just before RA-66 sailed on the night of 29 April, the trusty frigates of 19 Escort Group and corvettes of 7 Escort Group were sent out to clear the way. They caught and destroyed *U307* and *U286* with concerted depth charge attacks. But they did not get away unscathed. The frigate HMS *Goodall* was torpedoed and went down with considerable loss of life, the last Allied casualty of the Arctic convoys.

The convoy, which consisted of twenty-six merchantmen and the accompanying force that had brought JW-65 to Russia, had to pass through waters patrolled by fourteen U-boats which lay outside, beyond the minefield. Commander Kenneth F. Adams of *Iroquois*, a smart fellow and the senior officer, had determined that there would only be plain language talk between ships, not coded messages, and that this would give the U-boats no additional advantage. Both *Haida* and *Iroquois* escaped torpedoes fired from *U427*, and *Huron* was also subjected to torpedo attack. "Torpedo coming your way," said the chatter, and the helm was put hard over, 30 degrees. The torpedo fired at *Haida* missed by fifteen feet, according to the chief yeoman. *Iroquois* had been able to give the warning. The destroyers now increased speed to 36 knots. All stood to action stations, and the convoy proceeded on course, without further incident. On 8 May the merchant ships of RA-66 arrived safely at the Clyde, despite enemy aircraft, U-boats and snowstorms.

*Haida*, in the interim, had shaped a course for Scapa on the 6th, proceeding with some other members of the escort. *Haida* was in Scapa for VE-Day, where a general celebration was held to celebrate the Allied victory over the Axis in Europe. Churchill's resounding speech—and burp—were subjects of legend to the crew of *Haida*. It was a day to remember. Welland ordered "Splice the mainbrace....and we all had a tot on the Navy....We had been away for so long, we wanted to be home, we had done the job. We were alive and safe. I itched for sailing orders for Canada." Welland's view was shared by the rest.

### The Liberation of Trondheim

"Proceed to Trondheim," the sailing orders ran, for Operation Kingdom, the liberation of Norway. On 16 May *Haida* sailed in company with *Huron* and the British cruiser *Berwick*. The Norwegian ambassador in London had requested that Canadian ships should liberate Trondheim, in recognition of the close association of the Norwegian and Canadian people in Canadian Arctic exploration and development, whaling, sealing and fishing, and because of the joint war effort. (Toronto Island Airport's "Little Norway" was a training base for Royal Norwegian Air Force pilots and crew and the Royal Navy of Norway had Camp Norway at Lunenburg, Nova Scotia.) As the Tribals proceeded, a German M class minesweeper was sighted off the port, and he flashed the message to the Canadians to follow him—through a minefield. *Huron*, the senior ship, took the lead.

Welland ordered all watertight doors shut and all officers and men topside, just in case an errant mine did its dirty work.

"It would have been too ironic to get blown up now," he recalled. "Our men and the German minesweeper crew exchanged waves as we safely entered the harbour. They looked even younger than us; blond haired boys." On 9 April 1940 the heavy cruiser *Hipper* and four destroyers carrying 1,700 troops had passed the Norwegian batteries unscathed and occupied this key port, once the seat of Norwegian kings. The assault troops had forced the surrender of Trondheim after two days' hard fighting. Ever since, Trondheim had been a base for German U-boats and surface raiders including *Tirpitz* and *Scharnhorst*.

Now, five years and one month later, the Allies were asserting their naval superiority. The great cliffs of Trondheim posed the most remarkable backdrop for the human drama then being worked out. In the still, sunny weather of early summer all was jubilation among the Norwegians. On board *Haida* came an old man, the mayor, Ivar Skjoenes, and before long, by Welland's estimate, "the ship soon filled up with visitors, all laughing, shaking hands, kissing." The crew got out goodies for the children and other visitors, and ration boxes were ransacked for food, biscuits and chocolate. "Wide-eyed youngsters and gaunt, sombre-faced adults were welcomed aboard the destroyer and treated to tempting varieties of food." So wrote E.C. Russell, who added: "Everywhere, a festive mood prevailed and grim memories of war faded, if only for a time, from the faces of those who had lived close to its horrors for five long years." A Norwegian liaison officer, Major Ulestad of the Royal Norwegian Air Force who spoke BBC English, told Welland that there were 85,000 German troops still in Trondheim. They were still armed, and since the peace had been proclaimed they had caused no trouble. He told Welland that the mayor wanted shore parties to be landed from the Canadian Tribals to show that the war indeed had been won, and that the time had come for the Germans to go home.

The liberation called for tact and care. Welland and Harold Groos, captain of the *Huron*, decided to put up a show of strength—four hun-

dred officers and men to be put ashore. They were to land unarmed (and were searched before leaving ship) so as to cause no difficulty. The Canadians realized they could not enforce peace and that they were there on sufferance of the German Army. The odds, calculated Welland, were 2,000 to one in the Germans' favour. "I had almost no doubts that this was the right thing to do, the risk was small, our men were our greatest ambassadors." The episode passed without incident. Welland recalls those days as filled with emotion, and surely they were.

The Canadian presence was helped by the show of the cruiser HMS *Berwick*, sporting her eight 8-inch guns. Given the fact that German guns were still watching over and guarding the harbour, when *Berwick* upped anchor and departed for a time there was considerable worry aboard the Tribals. Everyone remained on edge. The Canadian commanders, with the advice of Major Ulestad, proceeded on their tour of eight different harbours. Ships' guns were trained fore and aft, so as to cause no undue worry ashore, and the crews had orders to laze about the decks. A number of German destroyers, minesweepers and U-boats were seen but none gave offence. *Haida* and *Huron* sailed up the long fjord to show that they had taken over, and Welland said that *Haida* wore a White Ensign from the masthead, the *Canadian* blue ensign from the jack staff on the fo'c's'le, and another White Ensign from the quarterdeck. The large maple leaf on the fore funnel had a new coat of paint. "I said there was to be no waving or cheering, even in response. That's the way we did it. The German crews stood idly on their decks, sort of dejected, and not one of them yelled or waved. So I guess we did it right enough. I felt just fine; we had beaten them."

*Haida* went on to take surrender of the nearby *Luftwaffe* base, Vaernes, where air strikes had been launched against convoys and escorts. *Haida* anchored offshore and

Opposite: HMS *Berwick*, a cruiser, with *Haida* at Trondheim, May 1945, as part of Operation Kingdom, the liberation of Norway.
(Courtesy David Ernst)

Above: *Haida* steams from Trondheim, May 1945.
(Courtesy David Ernst)

*Haida, Huron* and
*Iroquois* in Greenock,
Scotland.
(Courtesy Ed Stewart)

a boat was sent in. Waiting on the wharf were two black Mercedes staff cars. A German lieutenant from one car saluted, held the door, and Welland and Ulestad took their seats in the back, the lieutenant getting in beside the driver. The car travelled two miles through countryside reminiscent of northern Ontario until an airfield abruptly came into view. This was infamous in Allied memory as the place from which so many air strikes had been mounted. On the tarmac hundreds of uniformed men were drawn up in ranks. Fifty or more dive-bombing Junker 88s, Dornier 217 bombers, and torpedo-carrying Heinkel 111s, parked in rows, formed the backdrop. They looked smaller than they ever did in the air, noted Welland.

The officer commanding, a colonel, mounted a dias and spoke in German. As interpreted by Major Ulestad, "He is saying he appreciates how well they have fought, they should not be ashamed, and to remember their friends who have died for their country, and the war is now over." The colonel offered his sword to Welland. But Welland graciously declined, in favour of giving it to Ulestad. It was a painful moment for the German officer and difficult all round. Having to surrender his sword, Ulestad told Welland, "hurt him badly."

*Haida* and *Huron* lay in Trondheim Fjord for nearly ten days. Ernst remembers that all the U-boat pens were inaccessible to the Canadians and that the buildings were sealed tight. The surrender and destruction of the German naval units would be undertaken by other authorities. At least eight U-boats were handed over. The Nazi occupation of Norway, in place since distant 1940, was now over. Many Yugoslav prisoners of war were in Trondheim, doubtless as slave workers for this arsenal of German naval and air power. This, with its powerful air base and naval posts, had been the central springboard of Germany's northern maritime missions. Now it, too, had ended its military utility.

The Tribal crews were keen to return home, and the vessels shaped a course first for Scapa, arriving late on 24 May.

"Return to Halifax" was the message awaiting the Canadian Tribals at Scapa, and there was urgency to this order for Canada was still at war with Imperial Japan. They fueled, provisioned, restocked the sickbay, said goodbyes. They called at Greenock, and then sailed for home at their best speed. The course home had been north of Iceland, through Denmark Strait and past Newfoundland. Before long there stood the light on Chebucto Head and the approach to Halifax. "Sirens blew, fire boats streamed hoses, the *Stadacona* band played 'Welcoming Heroes' and peppy naval marches. Our families were on the wharf. Maybe there was a dry eye, just maybe."

*Haida* was taken into the hands of the Dockyard at Halifax, and was readied for tropical work. The intention was to send her to the Pacific, to bolster Canadian and Allied forces. But peace came on 2 September, with Japan's surrender, and all urgency disappeared from the program to modify *Haida*. Her war service was over—although only for a brief while.

*Extra Gangway Adds to Safety.* Able Seaman J.R. Belanger using the gangway, a later addition in Tribal Class Destroyers, to avoid crossing the main deck while heavy seas are running. (Grant Macdonald, courtesy MMGL)

# CHAPTER 11

## COLD WAR WARRIOR: 1945-1951

BY WAR'S END the RCN was operating, manning and maintaining three hundred and eighty-nine warships and fifteen others on loan from the RN. The RCN was also manning two escort carriers for the RN and numerous auxiliary vessels. The total strength in personnel was 95,705. Of these 6,027 were members of the Women's Royal Canadian Naval Service. At the close of hostilities Canada's navy ranked third largest among the Allies. The RCN had deployed four hundred and seventy-one ships during the war. And what of the successes and costs of that war? RCN ships, alone or in company with others, had sunk, damaged or captured forty-two enemy surface ships. They had sunk twenty-seven U-boats and two Italian submarines. The costs were enormous: 2,024 personnel killed by all causes (many buried at sea, with no known grave), three hundred wounded and ninety-five made prisoners of war. Twenty-four RCN vessels were lost. Canadian naval personnel won more than 1,900 decorations and awards, from the Victoria Cross to Mention-in-Despatches. They won forty-seven foreign decorations.

Included in the Royal Canadian Navy as of 1945 were two captured U-boats, *U190* and *U889*. Commissioned into the RCN, they had strange careers. *U889* was allocated to the United States by treaty agreement. *U190*, retained by Canada, was considered unoperational. During the summer of 1945 *U190* toured the St. Lawrence River and Gulf, the very waters U-boats had made a German lake in 1942. For two years she did duty in cat-and-mouse anti-submarine warfare (ASW) exercises, but soon she was valuable only as a target. Thus it was that on 21 October 1947, Trafalgar Day, HMC S/M *U190*, painted red and yellow, was towed to the

*Haida* in Bedford Basin, Halifax, 1948.
(Courtesy Ken Macpherson)

spot where, on 16 April 1945, she had sunk HMCS *Esquimalt* in Halifax Approaches. *Haida*, *Nootka* (senior ship) and the Algerine class *New Liskeard*, along with the naval air arm's Seafires, Fireflies, Ansons and Swordfish put an end to *U190*, first with air-to-sea rockets, then with 4.7-inch guns and Hedgehog mortars. This was termed Operation Scuttled and it ended with the U-boat going down. The RCN's press report noted that "the once deadly sea raider came to a swift and ignominious end." The much vaunted U-boat peril ended with a whimper and comic relief.

In late 1945 the Canadian government authorized a navy of two aircraft carriers, two cruisers, twelve destroyers and 10,000 all ranks—a force half the size of what the Canadian Chiefs of Staff had requested. In 1947 the government further reduced the authorized strength of the RCN to 7,500 all ranks and further slashed the naval budget. By the end of that year *Haida* was one of only four RCN destroyers in commission, with five in reserve. (*Haida* herself had spent most of 1946 in "care and maintenance;" that is, reserve.)

On 3 March 1947 Lieutenant-Commander F.B. Caldwell took command of *Haida*. During refitting and in the working-up exercises the destroyer had a number of mishaps, including a fire in the wheel-house and a burst boiler. As one officer at headquarters observed, this "darling of the fleet" seemed to be in danger of developing a Cinderella complex. Even so, she resumed her obligations at sea, and in 1948, under her new CO, Lieutenant-Commander A.F. Pickard, she exercised with the light fleet carrier *Magnificent*, and on two occasions was dispatched to rescue downed airmen.

## Visiting Arctic Waters

On 2 September, *Haida*, *Magnificent* and *Nootka*, voyaged from Halifax on the first major expedition of the RCN to eastern Canadian Arctic waters. *Magnificent* had replaced the RCN's other carrier, *Warrior*, because she had steam heat and some cold-weather engineering features. At the Magdalene Islands, Sea Furies and Fireflies flew missions in an attack exercise called Operation Grindstone. The force sailed north to Kangirsujuaq ( Wakeham Bay), Ungava. *Haida* and *Nootka* con-

*Haida* in rough seas alongside the aircraft carrier HMCS *Magnificent*, 16 March 1949  (DND PMR 80-353)

tinued on into Hudson Bay, calling at the Hudson's Bay Company's post at Erik Cove, which they found abandoned. Here close-range armament was exercised. Then the Tribals proceeded to Churchill, Manitoba, and made a brief call before setting out on the return to Halifax. The passage back took them to Southampton Island, Hudson Bay, and the Inuit community of Coral Harbour, where a trade in carvings occurred. Then it was on to Killiniq (Port Burwell), where the destroyers refueled from HMCS *Dundalk*, and thence to Halifax.

This northern expedition was designed to test Canadian naval capabilities in Arctic waters, and it was an expression of national commitment to continental defence, especially at high latitudes. At the same time that *Haida* was sailing these seas, the government of Canada, under Louis St. Laurent, expanded the RCN to a manpower ceiling of 9,047. On 4 April 1949, Canada became a signatory to NATO. Under the terms of this agreement, each member nation, with the exception of Iceland, would be required to maintain armed forces pre-committed to the alliance. In the event of war, the role of the RCN would be to protect Canadian and allied shipping across the Atlantic in cooperation with other alliance partners. In 1947, the Canadian Assistant Director of Naval Plans and Intelligence, A.H. Storrs, produced a report suggesting the future role of the RCN as an ASW force. With the containment policy of NATO, *Haida* was slated for ASW duties—in essence, to watch the activities of the growing Soviet Navy and, when necessary, to fight such a war at sea. A refit was required, but not yet.

By 1948 it was essential that HMC ships be given a standard system of type designators and ships' numbers which could be clearly understood. A clear need

*Haida* flying three ensigns to celebrate Newfoundland's entry into Confederation, 1 April 1949. (NAC PA-115054)

existed to have number and type designators that did not conflict with the RN and USN. British practice was to have pendant numbers and type letters allocated to ships, to provide a visual call-sign. American practice was to allocate a serial hull number to each ship of a type built, that number always being unique to that hull. The British scheme lacked continuity; when a ship was lost, and the pendant number was given to another. The American system carried a self-evident signification.

For these reasons the RCN adopted its own system of numbers and type designators for use in the fleet. The ships' numbers were chosen to allow for expansion and still have the minimum similarity between numbers of different classes. They also eliminated confusion with hull numbers in the USN and pendant numbers in the RN. All ships were to have their ship's number painted on their stern and on each side of the ship abreast the bridge. Letters were to be plain block capitals and white in colour. At the same time, in a reversion to pre-war practice, the RCN adopted a system of funnel markings: ships of flotilla commanders were to be marked on the foremost or only funnel with a four-foot-wide black band around the top, and ships of divisional commanders were to carry a two-foot-wide black band three feet from the top of the funnel. Each ship in a flotilla was to paint its flotilla number on each side of the funnel. On 10 January 1949 this new system for allocation and presentation of ships' hull number, type designators, and identification marks was introduced by Ottawa. Accordingly, G63 became DD215.

In October *Haida* took part in a series of exercises off the coast of Labrador. Operation Noramex was a joint exercise with American forces conducted as an amphibious landing exercise in a tundra environment. *Haida*'s role was to form part of the advance fire support unit that would conduct the initial shore bombardment of the landing area. The exercise was designed to provide the landing forces with experience in operating and living in northern conditions. Arriving off Cape Porcupine, Labrador, in late October, *Haida* successfully conducted her part of the mission, bombarding the beach with her 4.7-inch guns prior to the landing forces going ashore. Following that, she returned to Halifax on 27 October and made ready for her next assignment.

## The Rescue of USAF Airmen off Bermuda

On 15 November *Haida*, in company with *Swansea* and *Magnificent*, left Halifax for what was supposed to be a three-week training cruise. This would mark *Haida*'s last training exercise before returning to Halifax and to dockyard hands for an extensive refit, which would see the ship converted to ASW specifications. Two days out of port, on the 17th, *Haida* and others of her group received emergency instructions to proceed to a location approximately four hundred miles northwest of Bermuda. Once they arrived, *Magnificent* launched one of her Fairey Firefly aircraft to search for a downed United States Air Force (USAF) B-29 Superfortress bomber. What transpired would eventually be called by the *New York Times* "the biggest peacetime air-sea rescue search in history."

The bomber had been on a non-stop flight from March Air Force Base, California, to Kindley Field, Bermuda—a distance of some 3500 miles. For the most part, the flight had been uneventful, but on the 16th, as the aircraft was nearing Bermuda, the pilot radioed Kindley Field and asked for a bearing. It seems that the compass was acting up and, with only a couple of hours of fuel left in the tanks, the situation was becoming critical. Two hours later, the pilot reported that he was lost and was preparing to ditch the aircraft. His

**GREETINGS**

WHEREAS, It has been brought to the attention of the nominating committee that

## The Officers and Crew of the Destroyer "Haida"

have been outstanding in *their* field for many years and *rescued the shipwrecked crew of a B-29 Plane whose Co-Pilot was a Texan, and*

WHEREAS, *they* would likely bring further honors to the State of Texas, *they are* hereby made

# HONORARY TEXANS

This entitles *them* to wear cowboy boots, a ten-gallon hat and to generally conduct *themselves* as Texans.     No bronc riding test is necessary at this time in order to conserve horsepower

Date *Nov. 21, 1949*

*Jay B Plangman*
Top Hand—Corral Boss

JAY B. PLANGMAN, 308 W. BROADWAY
FORT WORTH, TEXAS

exact location was unknown, and at the time of his last communication, the aircraft was at a reported height of 900 feet. With no means of positively identifying where the aircraft ditched, the problem of coordinating an air-sea rescue was magnified significantly.

Foremost in the rescuers' minds was the reputation of this particular geographic location—a hazard to shipping, and more recently aircraft, since vessels had plied the waters of the Atlantic. The Bermuda Triangle, a graveyard to many ships over the centuries, revealed few secrets and left fewer traces of the many disasters experienced there. Little effort was needed to recall the events of 1945, in which five US Navy Avenger torpedo bombers were lost in the area, along with a Martin Mariner flying boat sent to search for the missing men and aircraft. However, with over one hundred aircraft, and numerous American, British and Canadian ships searching for the downed airmen, it seemed that the chances for a successful rescue would be high. If the men survived the crash, they were sufficiently well equipped with gear to last

them for ten days. Some of the emergency items included water, food rations, cigarettes, fishing gear, a temporary sail, oars, first aid equipment and flares.

The weather worsened. The winds had risen considerably, making air reconnaissance difficult—if not impossible—and the waves of the Atlantic made all but the most hardened sailor seasick. Suffice it to say, searching for eighteen men in two small canvas dinghies became next to impossible. By late Thursday evening, 17 November, a report was received indicating that red flares had been sighted by an aircraft just before returning to base. The only problem was, the flares had been spotted 240 miles northeast of Bermuda. Meanwhile, *Haida* and company were almost 400 miles northwest of the Islands. The race to the rescue was on. *Swansea*, hampered by high seas, was starting to fall behind and had to turn back towards Halifax. *Haida* and *Magnificent* continued to labour at high speed. Vernon Spurr, a reserve crewman aboard *Haida* at the time of the rescue, remembers: "Only those who have had the

doubtful pleasure of being in an 'old' Tribal class destroyer at full steam in such adverse weather conditions will understand it's a ride that is never forgotten. To look from your ship at an aircraft carrier and see waves continuously breaking over the flight deck is sufficient to humble the bravest and implant a respect for the Atlantic for life."

Later, on Saturday afternoon, a highly modified USAF air-sea rescue B-17 spotted the life rafts from the air. The B-17, piloted by Lieutenant Edward Lynch, was based at Kindley Field, and upon sighting the rafts was able to radio *Haida* and confirm the position of the downed aviators. Then, with great precision, the aircraft dropped its payload—a large semi-collapsible rescue boat it carried in its bomb bay— near the two smaller rafts occupied by the B-29 crew. With the location of the fliers now known, all available ships began converging on the same spot in an attempt to be the first to rescue the men. As much as they were concerned for the lives of the downed airmen, it seems that international reputations were now on the line, with world recognition and the victory laurel going to the rescuers.

Lieutenant-Commander E.T.G. Madgwick, *Haida*'s commanding officer, was determined to be there first. The competition was stiff, however, for quickly approaching the scene was a destroyer, USS *Trout*. Madgwick "opened up the grand old lady to a reported 26 knots, or better, in waves 50 to 60 feet high." Realizing that time was running out, he ordered *Haida*'s 27-foot whaler away. Manned by an experienced crew, the whaler's job was to reach the collapsible boat dropped by the B-17 and recover it. Scramble nets were rigged over *Haida*'s side to help facilitate the transfer of the men aboard. As the whaler pulled alongside *Haida* with the collapsi-

Opposite: Following the rescue, the ship's company of *Haida* were awarded the title of Honorary Texans, while Surgeon-Commander Lee, Lieutenant-Commander Madgwick and Petty Officer Callighan were also awarded the Legion of Merit. (HMCS *Haida* Naval Museum 989.018.010)

Top: Members of *Haida's* crew after the rescue of eighteen airmen from a ditched USAF B-29 off Bermuda in November 1949. L to R: Petty Officer Jim Callighan, Able Seaman Thomas Scratch, Lieutenant Panabaker, Lietuenant-Commander E.T.G. Madgwick, Leading Seaman Gord Munro, Able Seaman "Red" Pugh, Able Seaman Mike Longeuay, Able Seaman Gord Hayes. (HMCS *Haida* Naval Museum 989.018.011)

ble boat in tow, the scramble nets, according to one observer, were deemed unnecessary. The waves were so high, the men simply had to step from the boat onto *Haida*'s deck! A less exuberant account of the rescue suggests that the weakened men were helped aboard by several able seamen, who climbed down the scramble net and assisted the men. By 16:38, all eighteen survivors from the B-29 were safely aboard *Haida*.

A distinctly American version of this particular incident was related in the *New York Times*. According to this report, a second US Navy destroyer in the area, the *Bradbury*, received Lieutenant Lynch's message and radioed *Trout* that the airmen had been discovered. The report then goes on to state that the *"Trout* in turn told the *Haida* to make the rescue." Undoubtedly, there exist as many variations of the rescue as there were participants!

Tired and weak from several days' exposure to the forces of the Atlantic, the grateful crew of the B-29 were quickly made as comfortable as possible. Shortly thereafter, dry clothing donated by the crew was offered to the airmen, and piping hot cups of soup and coffee were quickly consumed. Because of *Haida*'s limited size as a destroyer, however, extensive medical facilities were not available on the ship. Yet the response of the officers and men aboard "was terrific." Bedding was provided, and many of the ship's officers gave up their quarters to the rescued men.

*Haida* made for Bermuda as rapidly as possible so that the men could be transferred to the hospital at St. George's and receive proper medical attention. It should be noted, though, that Surgeon-Commander Eric Lee was transferred from *Magnificent* to *Haida*, where he rendered first aid. Upon *Haida*'s arrival at the harbour on 20 November, the ship was cheered by hundreds of well wishers as she slipped through the narrow

entrance. Amongst the cheering crowd were many members of the world press. *Haida* and her crew, it seems, were heroes!

The honours and accolades soon rolled in. The Minister of Defence, Brooke Claxton, was quick to offer his congratulations to *Haida*'s crew. So did General Hoyt Vandenberg, Chief of Staff of the USAF. United States Defense Secretary Louis Johnson also expressed his thanks to the Canadians: "Permit me to express our profound gratitude to the men of the Canadian Armed Forces whose tireless effort in behalf of their fellow Americans has climaxed one of the most brilliant air-sea rescue operations in peace-time history." The officers and men of *Haida* were also made Honorary Texans since the co-pilot of the B-29 happened to be a Texan, and that's what Texans do! Apparently, no bronc riding test was necessary, says the citation, and the crew were entitled to "wear cowboy boots, a ten-gallon hat and to generally conduct themselves as Texans." Surgeon-Commander Lee, Lieutenant-Commander Madgwick and Petty Officer James Callighan, the coxswain of the whaler, were all awarded the Legion of Merit by a grateful United States Government.

As a result of the crash, and several which had preceded it, all B-29s were temporarily grounded until upgrades could be completed. These done, the bombers were operational again and Strategic Air Command was back in business. As for *Haida*, she completed her originally planned cruise, which culminated in a stopover in San Juan, Puerto Rico. By early December, *Haida* was back in Halifax, in reserve, awaiting her extensive ASW conversion. It would be almost two years before *Haida* plied the waters of the Atlantic again, but interesting days lay ahead for the ship and crew. Indeed, for the first time, her sleek dagger-like hull would grace the waters

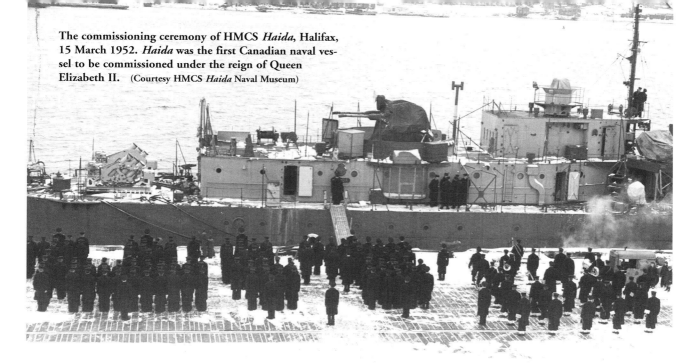

The commissioning ceremony of HMCS *Haida*, Halifax, 15 March 1952. *Haida* was the first Canadian naval vessel to be commissioned under the reign of Queen Elizabeth II. (Courtesy HMCS *Haida* Naval Museum)

of the Pacific Ocean, and she would soon steam towards the Orient with its exotic smells and mysterious ways. *Haida* was about to embark on yet another adventure.

## Conversion to Destroyer-Escort

During the first stages of the Korean War (discussed in the next chapter), *Haida* had been placed in reserve in Halifax while undergoing conversion to destroyer-escort standards—as had her sister Tribals. When she emerged on 15 March 1952, *Haida* not only carried a new array of weapons, she sported a new pennant number, DDE 215. The new designation was representative of *Haida*'s new role and her conversion from the original Tribal class to a vessel more suited to anti-submarine and convoy escort duties.

Some of her new weapons included the ahead-throwing ASW mortar device known as Squid, a new and sophisticated Sperry radar system, enhanced anti-aircraft capabilities in the form of the radar-directed twin 3-inch 50-calibre guns, and a new main armament of 4-inch HA/LA (high angle-low angle) twin guns, which replaced the heavier 4.7-inch gun mounts of Second World War fame. All said and done, *Haida* possessed formi-

dable and versatile weapons systems capable of meeting certain threats of modern naval warfare.

At 09:00 on 15 March 1952, a wintry Halifax day with snow blanketing ship and shore, and *Stadacona*'s band having kept the guests, officers and men entertained and then providing ceremonial music, *Haida* received her colours and commissioning pennant. She was commissioned now for the second time, on this occasion under the Queen. In fact, *Haida* became the first Canadian ship of war to be commissioned under the sovereignty of a queen. She was also the first warship in the Commonwealth to commission under the reign of Queen Elizabeth II.

At the same time, command of *Haida* was passed to Commander Dunn Lantier, RCN, who had previously been aboard *Athabaskan* during the fateful night of her sinking in the English Channel, 29 April 1944. Commander Lantier was one of the officers whom *Haida* had been unable to rescue from the channel, and so he spent the last twelve months of the war as a prisoner of war in Germany. For Dunn Lantier, his new command aboard *Haida* represented a homecoming.

*Return of the Liberty Boat.* Sailors on shore leave return to the ship on the liberty boat, exhausted from their revelries. Clockwise: Able Seaman A.D. Chance, Ordinary Seaman T. Webster, Able Seaman A. Roupee, Ordinary Seaman W.G. North, Able Seaman F. Locker (not shown). (Grant Macdonald, courtesy MMGL)

# CHAPTER 12

## THE KOREAN WAR, TRAIN BUSTING AND OTHER PURSUITS: 1952-1962

On Sunday, 25 June 1950, at 04:00 Korean time, the morning calm of that most beautiful of nations was shattered by the sounds of artillery. North Korean heavy units had moved into position and in a well-timed and coordinated attack commenced firing on the small border town of Ongijin. Several hours later, over one hundred thousand North Korean troops accompanied by armoured units crossed the 38th parallel into South Korea, starting the Korean War. Although the United Nations (UN) response to the crisis was termed a "police action," what transpired over the next three years can only be described as a war—one which required many resources and much versatility from both the equipment and the men serving there.

For decades Korea had been at the mercy of outside powers. Japan established primacy there

in 1905 and proclaimed it a colony five years later. During the Second World War, Allied leaders promised Korea independence. While Syngman Rhee, eventually first president of South Korea, agitated in the United States for independence, Kim Il Sung became a protégé of Stalin. In 1945 Korea was divided between American occupation south of 38° N latitude and Soviet occupation to the north. An intense civil war followed in South Korea (1946-49) culminating in a state under Rhee, supported by American occupation forces. With a continuing US-Soviet deadlock, UN trusteeship for all of Korea was not likely to be effected. By 1948 the US had defined a vague system to contain North Korea, but this failed to prevent the USSR from establishing the Democratic People's Republic of [North] Korea. In fact, the US withdrew its armed forces from South Korea and in

1950 Secretary of State Dean Acheson (and others) even declared Korea to be outside the vital US defence perimeter. Kim Il Sung visited Moscow and promised Stalin that a war begun by a surprise attack would be finished in three days. Stalin suggested that Kim Il Sung first check with Chairman Mao, and in the end both backed him.

Since 1947, the UN and the United States in particular had been attempting to assist the flagging South Korean government in whatever manner it could. The main thrust of their aid was aimed at helping the Koreans, under the mantle of a freely elected democratic government, to achieve national independence. While several United Nations resolutions on the subject of the Korean situation had been passed, the Soviet Union consistently blocked the efforts of the UN's General Assembly to render assistance to the beleaguered nation. Permission to establish contact with the North Korean authorities in order to arrange for a truly national election was never granted to the UN representatives sent to Korea. Thus, the UN's task—and the dream of a united Korea—became all but impossible. Although democratic elections were held in May 1948, they were confined solely to South Korea—hardly an encouraging development. The government of the Republic of Korea (ROK), established as a result of these elections, was tenuous at best. The net result, however, further entrenched the differences between North and South Korea, and border clashes along the 38th parallel soon became regular occurrences.

On the morning of 26 June 1950, after news of the North Korean border thrust became known, the President of the United States, Harry S. Truman, publicly announced that the US would be content to leave the solution to the Korean crisis in the hands of the United Nations. The UN had previously passed a resolution warning North Korea to back down, but this was ignored. By the evening of the 26th, reports were being received in the US that indicated an increasingly serious situation. At that time, Truman, with the assistance of his advisory staff, made the decision to take affirmative action in aid of South Korea. Consequently, the US Seventh Fleet was ordered into action to assist the Southern forces in whatever manner possible and to protect Formosa. The next morning, 27 June, a second UN resolution was passed which augmented the first statement and had the additional benefit of legitimizing the actions taken by Truman in dispatching the US Seventh Fleet. This essentially became a declaration of war, by the United Nations, against North Korea. It should be noted here, that the conspicuous absence of representatives from the Soviet Union was the only reason the Security Council was able to pass these resolutions. As a permanent member of the Security Council, the Soviets possessed the power of veto and could have—and in all likelihood, given their interests in Korea, would have—used this power to negate the UN resolution. The charter of the UN was thus invoked by an ironic twist of fate.

Until this point, Canada, which had neither a seat on the permanent Security Council nor representatives in Korea, had little information on, or input into, the decision making process. In fact, the Secretary of State for External Affairs, Lester B. Pearson, was no better off. He was dependent upon the UN or friendly governments for whatever details could be found. Although questioned in the House of Commons on 26 June, Pearson dealt with the crisis expeditiously yet without much insight. It was not until the 27th, however, after word was received indicating an escalation of the situation, that greater attention was spent on the crisis in Canada. In Ottawa discussions were held on a possible role in the conflict and the appropriate course of action that Canada should follow.

In Parliament, several issues were raised including the current state of Canadian military preparedness. The severity of the crisis was recognized and the decision to support the actions taken by the United States was also made. On 30 June, the Prime Minister, Louis St. Laurent, stated that Canada would not declare war on North Korea or any other country, but as a member of the United Nations would fulfill her obligations, if so called upon, under the UN charter. When asked, Canada responded positively, and for the first time United Nations forces operated "under a unified command to carry out resolutions of the Security Council directed toward the suppression of an act of aggression and the restoration of peace and security."

Several hours after this announcement, Rear Admiral Harry DeWolf, Flag Officer Pacific Coast at Esquimalt, near Victoria, British Columbia, received orders from Naval Headquarters in Ottawa, to sail *Cayuga, Sioux* and *Athabaskan* (second of that name) to Pearl Harbor on 5 July 1950. Of these three, *Athabaskan* was the only Tribal; the other two, despite their names, were wartime-construction fleet destroyers (their distinguishing features being a single funnel and single gun turrets). It was correctly believed that the naval element of the three Canadian armed services was the only service available for immediate deployment—the RCN was the most ready of the three services to go to war. The many preparations needed to bring a ship on line for battle were soon begun.

At the time, Canada possessed one aircraft carrier, *Magnificent*, and two squadrons of carrier-borne Sea Fury fighter-bombers, but the Canadian government refused a British request to commit the *Magnificent* and its aircraft to the Korean theatre, to NATO duties and their responsibilities in the Atlantic. While a formal petition was made by

the air arm of the RCN to Ottawa, it met with little success. Eventually, however, under pressure from the RN, the government acquiesced. The war ended before the squadron could see service in Korean waters.

## The RCN Joins the NATO Task Force

Once official word had been handed down on 30 June, the Pacific Coast squadron began to act quickly. Intended naval exercises were cancelled, as was the customary autumn cruise to Europe for ships based in Halifax. Modifications were made to some of the armament and equipment (such as radar upgrades and additional anti-aircraft weapons). Other repairs were rapidly completed. Ships' crews had to be brought up to full complement—something that had not occurred since the Second World War. Spares and ammunition had to be loaded and the rest of the necessary stores ordered and accounted for. All in all, the dockyard and supply depots at Halifax and Esquimalt were kept busy around the clock.

Other logistical arrangements had to be made. At the time of the Korean War, the RCN lacked any dedicated seagoing fleet support unit, and for all logistical support in distant seas the Canadians would have to depend upon Royal Navy and United States Navy oilers and supply ships to sustain them while at sea. Some personnel changes were also required. Captain J.V. Brock was placed in command of the Pacific Destroyer Division heading towards Korea. He was also to captain *Cayuga* on her first tour. Changes were also made aboard *Sioux*, with Commander P.D. Taylor taking over command of the ship. Commander Robert Welland, *Haida's* previous commanding officer, remained aboard *Athabaskan*. For several days out of Esquimalt, the three ships were accompanied by HMCS *Ontario*—one of two cruisers in the RCN. As *Cayuga, Sioux* and *Athabaskan* sailed out of Esquimalt, past Duntze Head, the traditional

naval salute was taken by none other than Rear Admiral Harry DeWolf.

The nature of the aid Canada could offer was a different matter. With the end of the Second World War, and since the formation of the North Atlantic Treaty Organization in 1949, the RCN had been training and preparing primarily to attack submarines—a task for which the navy had gained some expertise during the previous war. Consequently, equipment changes had been made and tactics had also been modified to reflect the realities of modern warfare. Yet, to a certain extent, the Korean action placed new challenges alongside those of old. Korea became very much a gunnery war—one for which the Tribals were par-

ticularly well suited. But the ranks of the RCN were also filled by many inexperienced young sailors who had never seen action. Thus, the demands placed on the navy and what was required of it in the performance of its duties challenged both man and machine. Shore bombardment and coastal warfare were duties new to the Canadians. The leadership, motivation and skill of the officers and men of the RCN rose to the challenge and Canadians performed with distinction, whatever task they were assigned.

In keeping with official orders to proceed from Esquimalt, the three ships were soon steaming together to Pearl Harbor at a specified 16 knots. It was an uneventful voyage which lasted seven

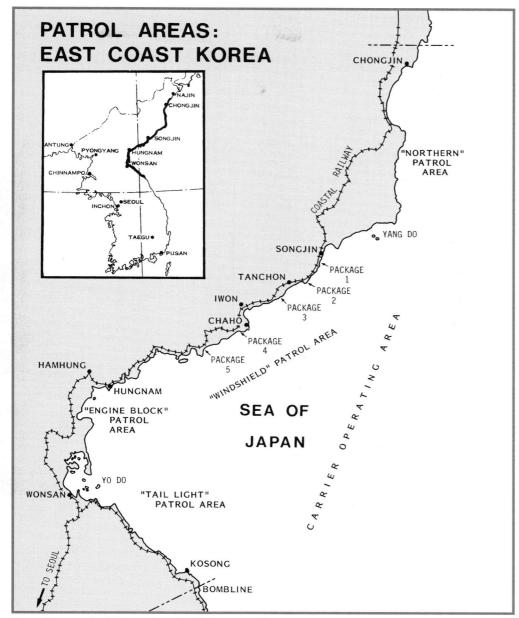

Operations area for 'Ships against shore,' showing packages. (Boutilier, *R.C.N. in Retrospect*)

days. After taking on fuel and supplies at Pearl, the ships then left for Kwajalein. Guam was the next destination. The ships arrived at Sasebo, Japan, on 30 July 1950. Once there, the Canadians found that their main task was to enforce the newly created naval blockade which had been announced by President Truman on 4 July. Opposition from North Korean naval and air forces was minimal, but the abundance of moored and floating mines ensured that alert watch keeping was essential.

Confronting the geographical and hydrographical hazards that Korea presented were another problem which the Canadians shared with the other national navies in the task force. Certainly, both east and west coasts harboured their own special haz-

Opposite: The crew of *Haida's* 3/50 gun in Korea. (HMCS *Haida* Naval Museum)

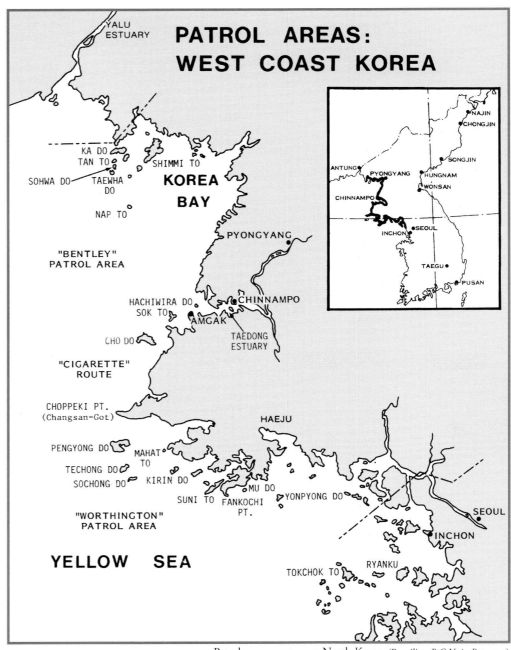

# PATROL AREAS: WEST COAST KOREA

YALU ESTUARY

KA DO
TAN TO
SOHWA DO
TAEWHA DO
SHIMMI TO

**KOREA BAY**

NAP TO

PYONGYANG

"BENTLEY" PATROL AREA

HACHIWIRA DO
SOK TO
AMGAK
CHINNAMPO

CHO DO
TAEDONG ESTUARY

"CIGARETTE" ROUTE

CHOPPEKI PT.
(Changsan-Got)

HAEJU

PENGYONG DO
MAHAT TO
TECHONG DO
SOCHONG DO    KIRIN DO

SUNI TO    MU DO
FANKOCHI PT.
YONPYONG DO

SEOUL

INCHON

"WORTHINGTON" PATROL AREA

**YELLOW SEA**

TOKCHOK TO    RYANKU

NAJIN
CHONGJIN
ANTUNG    SONGJIN
PYONGYANG    HUNGNAM
WONSAN
CHINNAMPO

INCHON    SEOUL

TAEGU

PUSAN

Patrol areas, west coast North Korea. (Boutilier, *R.C.N. in Retrospect*)

ards. The shallow waters which surrounded the myriad small islands of the west coast posed considerable threats to navigation. Strong tides and the seemingly endless mud flats lay close inshore. The east coast was different. Here the coastline was almost completely unbroken by islands and the waters generally ran deep. The land was marked by high mountains interspersed by a series of small plains. And the Korean winter was miserable. To some of the veterans among the crews, the cold and ice seemed reminiscent of the many Arctic voyages made by the RCN during the Second World War.

Opposite: *Haida* on patrol in the icy waters near Chodo, an island off the northwest coast of Korea. (HMCS *Haida* Naval Museum 991.011.001)

Other assigned tasks were handed down to HMC ships while they patrolled on station—each carrying its own potential threat. Some of these duties included carrier screening and plane-guard duty, shore bombardment, fire suppression and, eventually, the grand sport of train busting. Korean duty for the RCN was an odd mixture of extremes. In some cases, it meant days of boring and uneventful patrol, and on others life could get very interesting, very quickly. On more than one occasion, RCN ships (including *Haida*) were straddled by well placed salvoes from enemy shore batteries.

For the most part, life was routine, involving the many little jobs needing attention, such as oiling the ship. This less than exciting task was essential and something the relatively short-endurance Tribals had to complete every two or three days while on patrol. The Canadians soon made a game of this, too, and raised the procedure of oiling at sea to a fine art. Commander Welland, while captain of *Athabaskan* set the top standard, before the competition—judged to be too dangerous—was cancelled. It took only one minute and forty seconds from the time of starting the process until pumping commenced. The *Athabaskan*, with only a few feet separating it from the oiler, completed its fueling. The record was allowed to stand and although the competition was over, no other navy had come close to challenging it.

Operations in Korea also represented an opportunity to work in close cooperation with other navies and a chance to socialize with crews from other countries. Indeed, among various other nations, the Canadians were in contact with the

Royal Navy, the United States Navy and the Royal Australian Navy on a regular basis. Sailors being sailors, comparisons were soon drawn between rates of pay, gear, food and, of course, drink. In most regards except drink, the Americans won hands down. The main American base of operations at Sasebo, for example, was by far the most desirable place to anchor. Steaks, ice cream, first-run movies, not to mention French fries, were tremendous temptations for young Canadian sailors! By comparison, the Commonwealth base at Kure, near Hiroshima, seemed a far less enticing place. British rations of stringy mutton and a serious lack of entertainment seemed to ensure that a dreary time would be had by all. Other differences were noticed. Accommodation aboard American ships seemed spacious when compared to the tight, cramped quarters of the Tribals, and the use of bunk beds, as opposed to the more traditional RN and RCN hammocks, ensured a more comfortable existence for the men.

## The Train Busters Club

Once at sea, friendly competition between the various navies again became a fierce source of pride for the sailors, and train busting was the sport of choice. Originally organized by the US Navy, the Train Busters Club (TBC) was perhaps the most prestigious of all clubs in Korea. Begun in July 1952, it was the brainchild of the commander of Task Force 95, who initiated it after the USN destroyer *Orleck* demolished two trains skirting along the Taeback Mountain range. The rules of the game were simple but rigidly enforced. Admittance into the club was allowed only after the locomotive was confirmed as destroyed. Any additional trains killed were added to the tally, whether the engine was destroyed or not. Membership in the TBC was a particularly difficult task for Canadian ships—something which made it all the more exclusive—because our destroyers were operating with the Commonwealth fleet primarily on the west coast. The trains, it must be understood, operated in the mountainous terrain of the east coast where assignments for Canadian ships were few and far between. It is interesting to note that HMCS *Crusader*, commanded by Lieutenant-Commander John H.G. Bovey, became the undisputed champion of the TBC with four confirmed trains to her credit—three of which were knocked out in a twenty-four-hour period.

## Haida Departs for Korea

These were the circumstances on the eve of *Haida*'s next mission. *Haida*, it will be recalled, re-commissioned on 15 March 1952. After a brief excursion to the United Kingdom as escort for the carrier HMCS *Magnificent*—a voyage which also saw *Haida* revisiting her old wartime haunt of Plymouth— the ship returned to Halifax where she was made ready for service in Korea. *Haida* departed for Korean waters on 27 September. A stopover at Pearl Harbor was planned. While there, an intensive program of "working up" was created for the crew, designed mainly to

Opposite Top: *Haida* on patrol in Korean waters, 1 April 1953.
(Courtesy William Schleihauf)

Opposite Bottom: *Haida*'s stokers in Sasebo, Japan, April 1953.
(HMCS Haida Naval Museum 982.001.010)

increase the efficiency of the men, and was conducted during the middle of October. The ship's company practiced action stations and bombardment drill. Live firing of the main and anti-aircraft guns was also arranged. Lantier's report of proceedings for the month of October 1952 contains telling remarks on briefing for the Korean theatre. He states that: "the CO and four officers were given a full intelligence briefing on the situation in Korea. This briefing is usually given to USN ships proceeding to the operational area and it would appear that this is the first time that it was given to a Canadian ship. It was of very good value and I believe that nothing was omitted."

With loading of ammunition and supplies completed, *Haida* was soon ready. It is interesting to note, too, that this expedition would mark the first occasion in which *Haida* sailed the Pacific Ocean. *Haida* arrived at Yokosuka, Japan, on 6 November, after narrowly avoiding a typhoon. As a precaution, since fuel was running low, Lantier ordered fuel tanks Nos 5 and 6 flooded in an attempt to help stabilize *Haida* should heavy weather be encountered. Although some rough seas were experienced, the precaution, as it turned out, was unnecessary. After a brief stay, *Haida* left Yokosuka on the 10th, arriving at Sasebo Harbor on 12 November. At Sasebo the officers of *Haida* were briefed once again, and the ship re-supplied.

On 19 November, *Haida* sailed in company with the escort carrier USS *Badoeng Strait* in Carrier Task Group 95.1, bound for the west coast of Korea. This patrol was largely uneventful, but on two occasions *Haida* left the carrier escort in order to conduct inshore patrols. On these patrols, *Haida*'s new 4-inch main guns fired rounds of high explosive direct action (HEDA) ammunition at the enemy. This was termed "harassing bombardment." Although no enemy structures were damaged, explosions and flames were observed in the target area. As Lantier reported: "These inshore patrols passed without incident; however, as a newcomer to the area I was very grateful to have a Sperry Radar for night inshore navigation."

Upon returning to Sasebo on 29 November, *Haida* and her crew had just enough time to prepare for yet another patrol—this time as relief for HMS *Constance* off a patrol area named Package 4. These packages consisted of specifically designated patrol areas, numbered 1 to 5, and together made up what was called a Windshield patrol. Typically, the packages ran in an ascending order beginning just south of Songjin and ending northeast of Hungnam. After her rendezvous with *Constance* on 3 December, *Haida* proceeded with her duties, and took over the Windshield patrol. No enemy activity was reported for the day. Later, on the 4th, *Haida* patrolled the northern route in company with USS *Carmick* and returned under a bright moon to complete a solo patrol of Yong Do Island.

On 6 December, *Haida* was to experience a close brush with the enemy. That afternoon, the ship had been assigned fire support duty off Package 1, near Songjin, with USS *Moore*. The area housed several factories and a railroad marshalling yard—the targets of the day—but it was defended by enemy shore batteries. By closing to the optimum range of *Haida*'s 4-inch guns (12,000 yards), the ship risked exposing itself to return fire from positions only 4,000 yards away. The ship pressed on in spite of the danger. As *Haida* moved into position at 14:00, her guns opened up with telling effect but, just as she turned away from the target the enemy's guns opened fire. One shot was observed to fall approximately two hundred yards from the quarterdeck and was quickly followed by others. Commander Lantier then ordered an increase in speed, and the 3-inch 5-calibre gun, capable of firing a hundred rounds

*Haida's* B gun crew in Korea. (HMCS *Haida* Naval Museum 991.011.001)

per minute, quickly responded, silencing the enemy guns. Further activity was reported. After firing her 3/50 guns, spotting aircraft went to observe the results. No enemy activity was reported, leading Lantier to believe that the counter-battery fire had been effective. As they steamed away, however, the Communist battery resumed firing when the two ships were 16,000 yards distant. By this time, *Haida* and *Moore* were steaming at 26 knots and the range was too great for them to return fire.

The following day, 7 December, *Haida* had her first crack at a train while on northern patrol, off Package 4. As exciting as it was to encounter a train, the experience was not very satisfying. As Lantier reported, "a few rounds were fired and due to inexperience and lack of familiarity with the area nil results were obtained." *Haida's* chance to join the Train Busters Club would have to wait. A second opportunity soon arose, on the night of 17-18 December while on patrol off Package 4. A southbound train was spotted at 04:48, speeding towards a tunnel when *Haida's* 4-inch and 3/50 guns opened fire. Although some eighty-four rounds of ammunition were expended between the two guns, the results of the night's work were again disappointing, although some hits were scored.

A navy chaplain is being transferred off *Haida's* quarterdeck by a helicopter from HMS *Glory*, Korea 1953.
(HMCS *Haida* Naval Museum 982.001.009)

Frustration ran high aboard *Haida*, but another crack at this most elusive game was soon to be had. During a routine patrol on the night of 18-19 December, some 3000 yards off Package 2, a northbound train proceeding with all haste was sighted. This time, the response from *Haida*'s gunners was both immediate and effective. With a barrage of starshells and high explosives from the 4-inch and 3/50 guns, the hapless train was soon observed to be afire. Additional rounds were poured into the train, destroying eight or ten box cars. Satisfied that the job had been well taken care of, *Haida* resumed her northern patrol. Later in the day reports from USS *The Sullivans* confirmed that eight box cars were "rather severely bent" but that the engine—the crucial part—had escaped. Wreckage blocked the rail line for some time. Although membership in the TBC was denied— this time—it was still a job well done and the enemy's communications were interrupted. On 20 December, *Haida* took on fuel from a USN oiler and steamed towards Sasebo after having been relieved by the destroyer HMAS *Anzac*. That day, *Haida* received a message from Commander Task Force 95: "Welcome to Train Smasher's club. Good Work."

*Haida* arrived at Sasebo on 22 December where she provisioned and made preparations to leave for the Commonwealth naval base at Kure. The day after arriving at Kure, *Haida* was drydocked for the semi-annual inspection of her Asdic equipment. Through a fortuitous set of circumstances, the crews of all three Canadian ships then in theatre, *Haida*, *Athabaskan* and *Crusader*, were able to spend Christmas together, and all reports indicate that a "very good Christmas was had by all." Repairs complete, *Haida* was moved by tugs to No. 4 Berth. New Year's Day was again spent in the company of fellow Canadians, and many visits were made to the Canadian Army base

as well as to other Commonwealth services stationed near Kure.

On 2 January *Haida* departed for Sasebo, loading additional ammunition, and then proceeding to Onea-Nan where she rendezvoused with the RN carrier *Glory*. While acting as carrier screen, *Haida* was detailed to support ships in the area when the threat of an invasion of some friendly islands near Haeju became known. When nothing materialized, *Haida* returned to screening duties on 10 January. By the 15th *Haida* was back at Sasebo where she stayed for only a brief period of time. Throughout much of the rest of January and early February *Haida* continued with the routine duties that were the hallmark of Canadian destroyers in that war—patrolling, fueling, screening carriers, and occasionally engaging in shore bombardment. At 09:00 on 25 January, while patrolling in the "North Players" area of the "Cigarette Route," *Haida* opened fire with forty rounds of high explosive shells on a North Korean mortar emplacement. Achieving good results, her guns were then turned against a nearby platoon position. On both shoots, the Tribal's guns were directed by the Shore Fire Control Party from Sokto, and "good neutralization" of the Communist positions was reported. This was followed on 3 February by a less successful shoot against North Korean gun emplacements north of Mudo. Although *Haida*'s guns did succeed in silencing the enemy artillery for the duration of the bombardment, Lantier reported it unlikely that the destroyer's guns had done any real damage to the enemy position.

From 9 February until the 17th, *Haida* was back at Sasebo for routine maintenance. After this brief, welcome respite from the rigors of duty the ship was ready for action, this time on the west coast. At Inchon, *Haida* was anchored close to two hospital ships. Lantier noted that, "It is a point of interest that the wounded are flown directly from

Above: The ship's company, *Haida*, Hong Kong, June 1953. Commander Dunn Lantier is seated at the centre, fourth row from the bottom. (HMCS *Haida* Naval Museum 991.011.001)

Inset: Commander Dunn Lantier took command of *Haida* 1 January 1952. He had been aboard *Athabaskan* when she was torpedoed and spent the duration of the war as a German POW. (Courtesy HMCS *Haida* Naval Museum x991.066.001)

Opposite: *Haida* entering Pearl Harbor, Hawaii, January 1954. (NAC PA-115046)

the Korean front lines to the hospital ships at Inchon by helicopter, the helicopter landing on a small deck on the after part of the ship." The 19th saw *Haida* on patrol in the area of Inchon and, later, south through Haeju. Heavy ice was encountered off Chodo on the 22nd —a gift from the cold Siberian winds—and the ship soon left the area for clearer southern waters, joining up with Carrier Task Unit 95.1.1. The remainder of February was filled with the regular tasks of a ship on patrol with little or no enemy activity to report. All appearances seemed to indicate that it would continue to be quiet through early March.

During the middle of March, from the 13th to the 15th, *Haida* was screening the USS *Bataan* off the west coast operational area. After completing this duty, *Haida* again left for southern waters, this time joining Carrier Task Unit 95.2.2. On 18 March, the American destroyer USS *Endicott* reported a submarine contact in the area and proceeded to carry out several ASW attacks. *Haida*, ordered to the same location, could pick up nothing more than a school of fish. After expending all of his ammunition in search of the elusive submarine the captain of the *Endicott* felt that the attack had been successful. When asked if he was sure that his target was a submarine and not something else, he stated that he had "not been to ASW school but that his officers carrying out the attack felt it must have been."

Empty-handed following her attack on the suspected submarine, *Haida* proceeded in company with *Taussig* to the ROK-held island of Yang Do. Here she embarked a South Korean guerrilla for emergency treatment of gunshot wounds suffered in small arms fire the night before during a raid on the mainland. The man was given first aid aboard *Haida* before being transferred by boat to *Endicott* for passage to the medical facilities at Wonson. With that done, *Haida* resumed her patrol duties. By 20 March, *Haida* was again prowling the night off Packages 1 and 2, impatiently searching for trains. *Haida* and her crew were to be disappointed once more. While a southbound train was spotted and fired upon at a range of 2500 yards, no hits were obtained and the train escaped undamaged. All in all, March passed quietly. Commander

Lantier's monthly report concluded with the final statement: "A relatively pleasant but not inspired patrol."

Early April was spent alongside at Sasebo, resting crew and replenishing ship. *Haida* later received orders to escort the carrier USS *Bataan*, which she soon joined on the afternoon of 4 April. Flying operations continued over the next several weeks with *Haida* alternately escorting both *Glory* and *Bataan*. By the 21st, *Haida* had returned to Sasebo after another uneventful patrol. On the 27th, *Haida* was again at sea, screening *Bataan* as she continued flying operations and aerial strikes against inland targets. The beginning of May saw *Haida* taking up station near Wolsari, where enemy activity was expected to coincide with May Day celebrations. Although there was an "air raid warning red" issued during the day, nothing of interest transpired, and the North Korean forces remained quiet. The 2nd and 3rd of May saw

much of the same activity, except fire suppression was conducted against the Wolsari and Amgak gun emplacements.

Much of early May was spent in a similar manner, usually in company with various UN ships and sometimes with *Athabaskan*. On 9 May, *Haida* was relieved by HMS *Cossack* (not the original Tribal, but a wartime-construction sister to HMC Ships *Crescent* and *Crusader*.). *Haida* proceeded to Hong Kong for what Lantier described as "eight very pleasant days of rest and recreation." By 23 May, *Haida* was back at Sasebo for a briefing on the new patrol duties she would be assuming on the east coast. Here at last was another opportunity to try for membership in the coveted Train Busters Club.

## Train Busting—*Haida* Joins the Club

May 26th saw *Haida* arriving in the area of Yangdo to relieve *Anzac* and assume the duties of CTU 95.2.2. That evening, under clear bright skies and calm seas, *Haida* anchored just off Tanch'on—Package 2—and waited. With A and B guns crewed and anticipating action, time seemed to crawl at a snail's pace. As it turned out, however, the crew would not have to wait long. At 23:20, a northbound train came into view. With careful precision, *Haida*'s gun crews lined up the speeding locomotive in their sights and just at the right moment let loose with a devastating barrage of 3- and 4-inch rounds. There would be no question this time. The engine was blown apart and lay in a smoldering heap at the side of the track. For several more hours, the gun crews methodically fired round after round at the wreckage, ensuring that the boxcars—said to number between ten and twelve—were destroyed. In total, 320 rounds of 4-inch high explosive, 11 rounds of 4-inch VT, 108 rounds of starshell and 179 rounds of 3/50 were fired on the train. *Haida*'s formal membership in the TBC was assured. At 02:58, *Haida* was

relieved by USS *Eversole* and proceeded to Yangdo to continue her patrol. The morning brought a message for the jubilant *Haida* from the commander of TF 95, Rear-Admiral C.E. Olsen. It read simply: "Acknowledge receipt of your final dues to Train Buster's Club. Lifetime membership now recorded. Well done."

The 27th and 28th were spent in routine patrol of the Yangdo area, with nothing much to report. On the afternoon of the 29th, *Haida* attempted to oil from the *Mispillian*—a process described by her engineering officer as "unsuccessful." Indeed, it took approximately three hours and three different hoses to complete a job which normally took minutes. Although no specific reason for the problem has been noted, the engineering log does indicate that visibility had been "reduced." Finally, after taking on sufficient fuel, *Haida* pulled away and proceeded to her night patrol station off Package 3. While on station, a northbound train was spotted at about 22:00 and fired upon with the 4-inch guns. The engine, however, managed to escape into a nearby tunnel. Happily for *Haida*, a number of boxcars were destroyed, and the guns crews continued to pound away at these targets until relieved by *Bradford* at 04:00. The ship was soon underway and proceeded with the night's patrol. *Haida* then headed back towards Yangdo. While on passage two things happened. A type M08 mine was spotted and quickly sunk by 40-mm and rifle fire and, for a second time, a message was received from Rear-Admiral Olsen. This message, as recorded in the engineer's log, reads as follows: "Score another goal for *Haida*. Train Busters par Excellence. Well done."

*Haida* had managed to accomplish what few other ships could boast. She had been credited with two train kills while on one patrol—no mean feat indeed. For the rest of May and into early

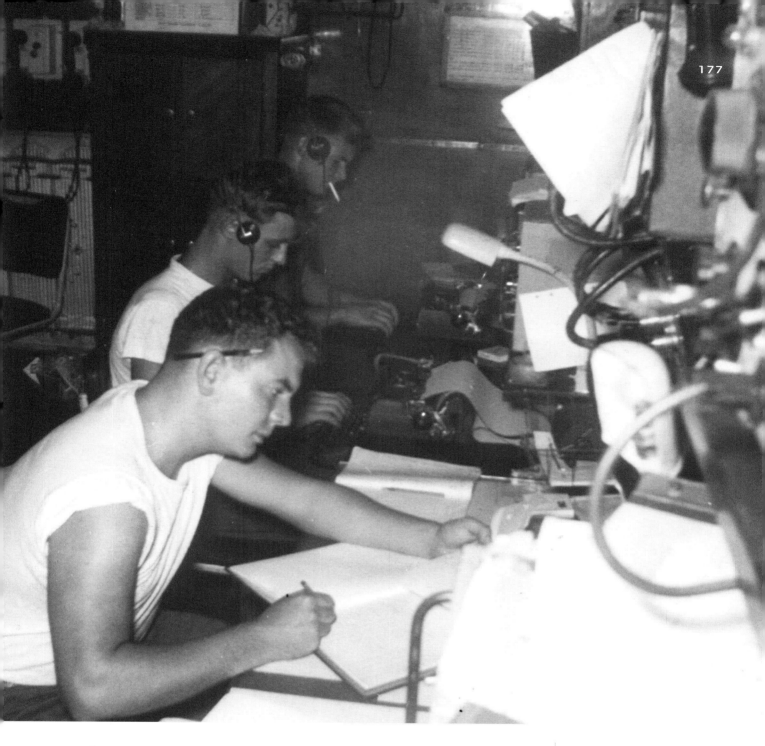

June, *Haida* continued with routine war patrols. She alternately provided gun-fire support, did minesweeper escort duty, bombarded targets of opportunity near the Songjin and Chongjin areas and continued to hunt trains. While stationed off Package 2, on the morning of 2 June, *Haida* spotted and engaged a southbound train. Although the gunners were quick off the mark, and possible hits were more than likely recorded on the target, nothing could be confirmed. After pounding the area for some time, and with a measure of reluctance and a good deal of frustration, *Haida* left for Package 3 where she took on fuel and ammunition. Later that morning, at 11:00, the officers and men of *Haida* "spliced the main brace" and celebrated the

*Haida's* radio room, May 1956.
(HMCS *Haida* Naval Museum 982.001.010)

coronation of Queen Elizabeth II. By 13:00, the ship had resumed station off Yangdo. The evening of the 3rd saw *Haida* off Package 2 for a second night when a northbound train was spotted. The target was quickly fired upon, but due mainly to poor visibility—fog—the train and all of its boxcars managed to slip into a nearby tunnel.

The next few days were spent providing fire-support off Sok-to and Wolsari, and finally, on 8 June, *Haida* waited off Yangdo to be relieved by *Cossack*. Her tour over, and with the turnover conference complete, the ship sailed again to Sasebo. From there, she would leave for Hong Kong—and eventually for Halifax.

## Return Home

The following week was spent in preparation for the voyage home and in saying many good-byes to dear friends on other ships. Visits were exchanged, including one from Rear-Admiral E.G.A. Clifford, RN, the task force commander, and many messages of goodwill were received. As *Haida* was reportedly clearing harbour on 12 June, HM Ships *Tyne*, *Newcastle* and *Morecambe Bay* "cheered ship." *Haida* was the only ship of the Korean theatre to be so honoured. Just out of the harbour, one final message was received from Rear-Admiral Olsen. It read simply: "Your all round performance of duty during your stay in this theatre stands high in the best traditions of the Royal Canadian Navy and is a record of which you and your Ship's Company may be justly proud. Good-bye and GOOD LUCK." Certainly, "Happy *Haida*" had much to smile about.

On the voyage home, *Haida*'s crew re-adjusted to the demands of peacetime sailing and routine without much difficulty, and the tension of war patrols soon faded. The prospect of completing a round-the-world cruise awaited officers and men. The trip home would be an interesting one, rife

with entertainment and the exotic scents and flavors of many foreign ports of call. Some of these included: Singapore, Colombo, Aden, the Suez Canal, Port Said, Malta, Gibraltar and the Azores. With her voyage complete, *Haida* finally arrived at Halifax on 22 July, having circumnavigated the globe.

She had been away from Halifax for almost one year, and had steamed many miles in the service of the UN. Just before entering the harbour, *Haida* was met by Rear-Admiral R.E.S. Bidwell, who boarded the ship and honored her by flying his flag from *Haida* as she entered Halifax Harbour. The welcome given her was astounding. The whistles and cheers emitted from the various ships and crews rang loud in the air. As Commander Lantier later remarked in his log "It was quite a thrill to hear the ships in harbour sounding off to welcome one of Her Majesty's ships home. We really knew that we were home among our own."

"Thus ended," concluded Lantier in his report, "what was considered to be a happy and reasonably successful commission." Afterwards, many of the officers and men were given leave and *Haida* was soon taken in hand for an extended refit. It was also during the month of July that the situation in Korea began to look brighter for the UN. Peace talks, which had begun shortly after the first border incident and had laboured on for most of the war, had finally made headway. The armistice agreement which brought the Korean War to an end was officially signed on 26 July 1953 (or on the 27th, Korean time)—a scant four days after *Haida* arrived home from her first Korean tour of duty.

## The Second Tour

What followed, however, can only be described as an uneasy truce. All too soon, *Haida* was being prepared for a second Korean tour of duty. This time, if the armistice held, her duties would be much more peaceful and would include observation patrols and maintaining the conditions of the armistice.

In October 1953 *Haida* also experienced another change in command, with Captain J.A. Charles, CD, RCN, taking over from Commander Lantier. Preparations for leaving were soon underway, but this time, the crew complement of *Haida* had been reduced to a more "comfortable" level. This was done on the orders of Rear-Admiral Bidwell, who believed that the situation in Korea was quiet enough to warrant smaller crew numbers. He reasoned that should the situation in Korea become more volatile, additional crew could be flown out within a week. With the re-supplying and re-arming of the ship complete, *Haida* departed Halifax on 14 December 1953, and steamed via the Panama Canal for Long Beach, California. From there, *Haida* proceeded to Pearl Harbor, arriving on 7 January 1954. Ship and crew were to spend the next two weeks in intensive workups in order to increase their efficiency after such a long layoff. This was to prove a valuable experience, and Charles commented later in his report that "the efficiency of the ship has improved to a marked degree thanks to the long period at Pearl Harbor."

*Haida* arrived at the Korean Theatre of Operations 5 February 1954, with Captain Charles, as the senior Canadian officer present, assuming the duties of CANCOMDESFE. Within days, the ship and crew were back on patrol, monitoring the peace, and closely interacting with units of the Republic of Korea Navy. For the most part, these patrols were long and tedious, belying their critical nature in ensuring armistice conditions. Reports on proceedings for the next several months are filled with routine entries concerning visits with notables and dignitaries and the occa-

sional comment on the many patrols which were being conducted at the time. One particular entry, however, is noteworthy. Captain Charles, in concluding his report, states that "Kure is much improved as a leave port" and continues by suggesting that "the visit was much enjoyed by all."

From June until September, *Haida* and her crew continued to fill their days observing Korean fishing fleets, and reporting any suspicious craft or activity in their patrol area. It should be noted, too, that many visits were arranged between the ship's company and Japanese notables, and many parties and ceremonies were attended—including outdoor games. Captain Charles felt strongly enough about the situation to record these comments in his report after one particularly successful outing: "It was evident that a tangible contribution to Canadian-Japanese good will was made by the ship's visit, and the observer was in no doubt that Canada enjoys special favor in the sight of most Japanese citizens." After saying many goodbyes and throwing a very successful ship's company party at the China Nights Club in Sasebo, *Haida* prepared to depart for Halifax. It was with some degree of humor, that Captain Charles stated in his report that "some $15,000 worth of personal souvenirs" were aboard and that "there is enough dinnerware on board to serve 1700 persons, 1860 feet of toy railway track with rolling stock to match and approximately 800 fishing rods—to name a few items."

Due to the threat posed by the approach of Typhoon June, *Haida* hastily prepared for departure on 12 September—one day ahead of schedule. As the ship slipped her moorings and proceeded towards the harbour entrance, she was greeted by a rousing three cheers from HMCS *Iroquois*. On the 15th, *Haida* arrived off Sangley Point, near Manila, accompanied by a squall. Although she missed the bulk of Typhoon June's fury, the weath-

Seen here in 1958, *Haida*'s 3/50 gun and Squid mortar at the rear of the ship are readily visible.
(Courtesy Ken Macpherson)

er was nevertheless rough. While in Manila, the ship's company was slated for a three-day stopover filled with entertainment and sporting events. Captain Charles takes up the story. "A terrific sports program had been arranged with beer and food being provided in vast quantities. The remaining events... were enjoyed by everyone of the ship's company." Several receptions were also attended by the officers and men, with many return calls being paid to the ship.

Before leaving Manila, "almost the entire Canadian colony turned out to wave farewell from the jetty and the Philippine Navy band played the ship out of harbour." *Haida* and company had made quite an impression. After a pleasant stay in Manila, *Haida* made for Hong Kong, arriving early in the morning of 21 September. The passage to Hong Kong was uneventful, but while there, two things occurred. Captain Charles, who was leaving the theatre, turned over operational command of CANCOMDESFE to the commanding officer of HMCS *Huron*. After this was accomplished and the new operational commander was briefed, Charles left the ship to take up his appointment as Commandant of Canadian Services College, Royal Roads, near Esquimalt, British Columbia. Following a brief change of command ceremony, the ship's company was placed in the capable hands of Lieutenant-Commander M.W. Mayo, *Haida*'s executive officer. With her new captain in place, *Haida* departed for Colombo, arriving at 09:00 on 2 October after an uneventful voyage. While there, a small reception was held on board *Haida* with approximately forty guests attending. The party was considered a success by all, and after cleaning up, the ship's company relaxed for one more day before weighing anchor. *Haida* left Colombo on 4 October and steamed for Aden. The ship then headed for the Suez Canal, Port Said, and Naples, a major NATO naval base.

*Haida* left Naples for Gibraltar on Trafalgar Day, 21 October 1954, and from there proceeded to Ponta Delgada in the Azores. After taking on fuel and supplies, *Haida* slipped from her berth and steamed towards Halifax—and home. The ship arrived at Halifax on 1 November 1954 amid the cheers of friends and relatives. She had completed her second tour of duty in the Far East. *Haida* had thus circumnavigated the globe for a second time, the only Canadian warship to do so. She had on this occasion celebrated the "crossing of the line" ceremony at the equator, steamed approximately 48,000 miles, and visited thirty-four ports of call in thirteen different countries. As before, the officers and men who could be spared from duty were given leave, and *Haida* was again placed in dry-dock for repairs and refit.

*Haida*'s five-month refit was followed by an intense series of training exercises which saw the ship joining NATO Task Group 301.1 in company with HMC ships, the carrier *Magnificent* and the Tribal class destroyer *Micmac*. Eventually, *Haida* was transferred to the newly-created 1st Canadian Destroyer Squadron in August 1955. At the same time, other events influenced the direction of the RCN which necessitated greater NATO commitments. It was also during this period, from 1956 onwards, that a new series of purpose-built anti-submarine warfare ships, the St. Laurent class of destroyer escorts known as the "Cadillacs," were being introduced into the navy. Armed with 3-inch guns and the new limbo ASW mortars, these ships were intended to kill submarines. Other

innovations soon followed, including the "bear-trap" recovery system which allowed the landing of large ASW helicopters onto the decks of small destroyers—no small feat and a major Canadian invention. Further Canadian innovations were also coming on line, such as Variable Depth Sonar (VDS) which assisted in the detection of submarines lying at differing depths and temperature variations underwater. This towed device was the result of studies conducted by experts in bathythermography, and helped to counteract this problem in submarine detection, recognized during the latter part of the Second World War. Modern warfare was changing, and the technology of hunting submarines—the new "capital ships" of the world's navies—was becoming an increasingly sophisticated business.

*Haida* continued on, training intensively, and participating in cruises and exercises such as New Broom, Seaspray and Maple Royal One. Throughout these years, *Haida* was also an excellent goodwill ambassador, showing the flag at many different ports of call.

By 1960, *Haida* was beginning to show her age. What followed was a frustrating series of repairs and equipment failures. Some minor engine problems occurred, and, on one occasion while entering Halifax Harbour, the steering gear failed. Other problems were discovered. A hull plate on her starboard side needed replacing and several interior frames needed strengthening. She continued to receive her annual inspections and, given her age, seemed capable of continuing. However, time was beginning to run out for the old hunter. Not until March 1962 did real problems begin for *Haida*. While on exercise, cracks began to appear on the port bow plates, and the ship had to depart for Halifax. Placed into refit at the Halifax Dockyard facilities, *Haida* spent the next four months under repair.

With the repairs completed, the ship continued with her duties until several engine bearings failed in December 1962. This necessitated a return to the dockyard at Halifax and *Haida* spent an additional two months under repair. Given the mounting repair costs, the age of the ship—some twenty years—and the fact that the navy was taking delivery of new ships, it was understood that *Haida*'s usefulness was nearing an end. Her career was drawing to a close. The navy decided that she was to go out with a bang and not a whimper. Accordingly a grand tour of the Great Lakes was planned for 1963.

Thus ended the career of the most distinguished Canadian warship in the history of the Royal Canadian Navy. No other ship could boast the victories or wear the laurels of *Haida*. Her Battle Honors were many. The list is impressive: Arctic (1943-1945), English Channel (1944), Normandy (1944), Biscay (1944), and Korea (1952-1953). *Haida* was a fighting ship, and although she appeared destined for the scrap yard, fate had other plans.

# CHAPTER 13

## THE FINAL VOYAGE, THE LAST TRIBAL: 1963 AND AFTER

●

AFTER SPENDING THE BETTER PART OF A YEAR under repair and having seen yet another change of command, *Haida* prepared to embark on a reserve training cruise—what can only be described as a farewell tour of the Great Lakes. Prior to leaving, she spent a brief period of time in Bermuda for clean-up and preparation after her long refit. She then sailed for Halifax to add the final touches before leaving for her last voyage.

During the spring and summer of 1963 *Haida* made a tour of the Great Lakes, a voyage to many cities and towns already known to the crew. She began this voyage in May, calling at Québec City, Trois Rivières, Montréal, Toronto, Cleveland, Sarnia and Hamilton. During June, she made calls at Kingston, Picton, Port Hope, Oshawa, Toronto, Port Dalhousie and Hamilton. In July she visited Toronto, Cobourg, Kingston, Picton and Port Hope. She

closed her long summer by saying goodbye to many of the above mentioned ports and added to her list Rochester, Niagara-on-the-Lake and Grimbsy.

In the course of the summer of 1963 some magic began to appear as publicists and newspapers learned of this final cruise. The crew participated in pirate parties and shore parades for local orphans which soon drew attention to the ship. Reservists, Sea Cadets, war veterans and others were given courtesy tours. After embarking a mobile CBC television studio and crew at Toronto, *Haida* sailed for Montréal. A short film was made about the ship, including some footage showing the firing of her guns for the last time. No one ever expected her to return to Toronto.

### First Steps to Preservation

While the main purpose of this cruise had been one of publicity, the ship caught the atten-

184

Above: *Haida* off
Bermuda in 1963. She
has just been given a
new all-grey coat of
paint and is ready to set
out on her Farewell
Cruise of the Great
Lakes.
(Courtesy William
Schleihauf)

Opposite: The last crew
of HMCS *Haida* – the
reservists from HMCS
*York* who volunteered to
man the Tribal while she
was under tow from
Sorel to Toronto.
(Courtesy William H.
Wilson)

tion of a Toronto-based group that quickly became known as the Preserve *Haida* Organization. No sooner had *Haida* quit her Toronto pier than this group of citizens, small in number but keenly dedicated to the cause, surfaced. Some would call this a BOGSATT—a bunch of guys sitting around a table talking! Spearheading this group was Air Canada pilot Captain Neil Bruce. His brother, Ron, had served aboard HMCS *Iroquois* during the Korean War and it was Ron who had arranged for Neil to be taken on one of the farewell cruises. His associate, Lieutenant Peter Ward, RCNR, military editor of the *Toronto Telegram*, takes up the story: "Neil heard the story of the *Haida*'s past from her officers and fell in love with the ship. He became convinced she could be preserved." Ward was thinking of the same thing. He also had a personal stake in the ship's preservation: his father, Lieutenant Peter Ward, RCNVR, was lost at sea in *Athabaskan*. Also convinced of the need to save *Haida* were Allan Howard of Toronto's Marine Museum of Upper Canada, David Kidd, ex-RCAF, and Norman Simpson, a former naval officer turned lawyer. The officers of *Haida* were also concerned about her future and desperate to maintain her memory as Canada's greatest fighting warship. At their encouragement, Bruce, Howard, Simpson and Ward were brought together early that fall at the Marine Museum. The circle was soon enlarged by Bill Doole, editor and publisher of the *Brampton Times and Conservator*, Joe O'Sullivan, a Goodyear Tire executive, lawyer Jack Graham, Don Smith of Bell Telephone, and Rear-Admiral P.D. Budge, RCN (Ret.).

The need for a tighter, more efficient organization soon surfaced and *Haida*, Inc., became a corporate entity on 30 March 1964, in Toronto. This represented the new and

official legal mechanism for the old Preserve *Haida* Organization, originally established by Neil Bruce. Legal work was donated by Graham and Simpson. *Haida*, Inc. was registered as a non-profit organization. Bruce made many trips to Ottawa and Halifax, lobbying both the government and the navy. He even made a quick trip to Bermuda to consult with Harry DeWolf, *Haida*'s first wartime captain. Meanwhile, Ottawa had shifted the ship from her regular status—out of commission ( 11 October 1963)—to Class C Reserve, that is, mothballed. The ship would be in that category for at least a year before going to the breaker's yard. This gave Bruce and his friends a little breathing room and, as Ward puts it, plenty of time to make their plans.

In fact, this was not the case. There was not sufficient time. At precisely this moment, in the winter of 1963-64, the Department of National Defence began a new phase of its cutbacks. *Haida*, whose military significance had become marginalised by new technology, modern combat conditions and changing fleet requirements for ASW

obligations to NATO, was at the top of the list to be cut. Indeed, she was the oldest of the war-built Tribal class still afloat. *Haida* was declared surplus and handed over to Crown Assets for disposal. One by one Canada's other Tribals had been taken out of service: *Iroquois* in 1962, *Huron* in 1963, *Micmac*, *Cayuga* and *Nootka* in 1964, and *Athabaskan*, the last Tribal in commission, the second of her name, in 1966.

Typical of the last and fragile years of these special warships was their degenerating condition. *Haida* had benefited from a recent refit and was in reasonable condition. But the scrapyard beckoned for them, and the *Athabaskan*, for example, ended her days under the blowtorches and hammers of an Italian breakers yard. Her spirit lives on, for she gave her name, as did *Huron* and *Iroquois*, to a new class of helicopter-carrying destroyers known as the Iroquois, or DDH 280 class.

### *Haida* Retires to Private Hands

When news of Ottawa's axe falling on *Haida* became known to Bruce, Ward and associates,

they hastened their plans. Crown Assets wanted $20,000 for the vessel—presumably her scrap value. She was to be delivered to Sorel, Québec, in her existing state. This put Bruce and company at a disadvantage, for money for ship preservation was unheard of in Canada. *Sackville*, the queen of Canadian corvettes, was still in service as a Canadian naval auxiliary vessel—and at that time her future as a heritage monument to the corvette navy was not even considered.

"Owning a Tribal class destroyer is a luxury we couldn't normally afford," recalled Ward in 1964, "so we approached the Toronto Dominion Bank with our story, and that's where the money came from." Even so, each member of *Haida*, Inc. put up his private residences as collateral against the loan. The $20,000 initially paid for *Haida* was to be repaid in ten yearly installments, with the first due at the end of year one, and no interest charged. The vessel was lying in Sydney, Nova Scotia, and was shifted to Halifax when it was learned she was to be saved. Once the ship's sale had been agreed upon, the navy gave the ship an additional week's grace period, just enough time to load as much equipment and gear at Halifax as would be beneficial for her future as a floating museum of Canadian naval heritage. Items to be included would be naval memorabilia such as ship crests and bells, combat gear and heritage uniforms. The navy also decided that *Haida* should be painted in her Second World War colours and her original pennant number—G63—restored. This, however, would be carried out at a later date. Restoring her to her August 1943 appearance, the date of her commissioning, was out of the question, for over the course of her long career she

Above: HMCS *Haida* in the locks of the St. Lawrence Seaway west of Montreal, just prior to her Farewell Cruise of the Great Lakes, spring 1963.
(Courtesy R. Garant)

Opposite: *Haida* under tow by *Helen M. McAllister*, destined for Pier Six at the foot of York Street, Toronto, 25 August 1964. This was victory day for Haida Inc, saviours of Canada's most famous warship.
Toronto Star Syndicate
(Courtesy William H. Wilson)

had been altered to such a great extent. Her funnel cowls were to be removed and her guns mutilated so that they could never be fired again.

Meanwhile, Bruce and company had to move the ship once she was officially in their possession, so they called for tenders for towing *Haida* from Sorel to Toronto. McAllister Towing of Montreal got the job for slightly more than $6,000, said to be a rock bottom price. Later on, McAllister said that he felt sentimental about *Haida*, and donated $1,000 of his fee back to *Haida*, Inc. The navy had fulfilled its part of the bargain and towed *Haida* to Sorel. McAllister Towing then designated their powerful tug, *Helen M. McAllister*, and one other tug to bring *Haida* to Toronto. It was decided to bring her to Pier Six at the foot of York Street, and then find and develop a permanent shoreside location readily accessible to the public, public transit and automobile parking.

## A Toronto Welcome

The Canadian naval reserve unit in Toronto, HMCS *York*, keenly aided in the transportation and preservation of the ship. *York* volunteered and authorized eighteen officers and men to crew *Haida* as she was towed through the St. Lawrence Seaway to her new home port at Toronto. Ward, who was in the party, recollected that they looked more like a marine camping expedition than a destroyer's crew! Lieutenant-Commander Bill Wilson, *Haida*'s last commanding officer on her last voyage, and, at the time HMCS *York*'s executive officer, played a key role. Lieutenant-Commander J. MacQuarrie, an electrical wizard from *York*, also played a crucial part in the final voyage of *Haida*.

The party boarded the night train bound for Montréal, and one coach looked, Ward remembered, like a wartime draft train heading for

Halifax. The men from *York* found *Haida* at Sorel's Department of Transport jetty, snugged in behind the great navy tug that had brought her from Halifax. They boarded the vessel and made preparations for an early departure. Almost immediately, one particular problem asserted itself: a lack of on board power. However, MacQuarrie and his electrical team were soon hard at work. They scrambled to put together as much gear as was required to switch the ship's current to 110-volt service, all of it run by a four-hundred-pound emergency gasoline generator brought with them on the night train! Once the electrical system was running, the crew took one further precaution. They made sure to load enough beer and Québec rum to satisfy the regulation issue of two bottles per day, and to have a quick tot in the wardroom. McAllister's tugs arrived shortly after, on 22 August, and lines were slipped in mid afternoon. The passage of the ship through the seaway proceeded smoothly enough, but with so small a crew, every hand was needed when the ship approached one of the seemingly interminable number of locks. When this happened, Ward explains, "It didn't matter what you wore on your collar or sleeve, when we came to a lock you tailed on to a line and pulled." As the ship reached Lake Ontario, one of the tugs departed, leaving the *Helen M. McAllister* to complete the journey in company with *Haida*. The entire trip to Toronto

took longer than expected, however—due in part to heavy westerly winds—and three days passed before *Haida* approached Toronto.

Although *Haida* rounded Toronto Island early Tuesday morning, the official arrival at Toronto Harbour was not staged until later that same morning, at ten o'clock on 25 August 1964. It was to be a glorious day for the last crew of *Haida*. The sun shone brightly and bathed the bridge in that wonderful quality of light found only on a beautiful August morning. As the ship passed through the Western Gap, she was greeted by an enthusiastic crowd who waved and cheered as *Haida* came into sight. A fireboat, the *William Lyon Mackenzie,* was also on hand to welcome the proud ship to her new home, and marked her arrival with a fountain of spray from her fire hoses. Reporters and TV crews were present in numbers, not to mention a sizeable contingent of small boats and pleasure craft. *Haida* had successfully completed her last voyage. As Ward said, "there weren't too many eyes completely free of mist."

The next day, the ship was visited by then Minister of Defence Paul Hellyer and three of her previous COs: Vice-Admiral H.G. DeWolf, Rear-Admiral R.P. Welland, who at the time was the deputy chief of operational readiness, and Commodore J. Charles. They were joined by former Toronto Mayor Phil Givens, along with two service bands, for *Haida*'s official handing-over

ceremony. During this event Rear-Admiral Welland presented *Haida* with both the White and Blue Ensigns—an honour not normally bestowed upon an out-of-commission ship. After the ceremonies concluded, a reception was held in *York*'s wardroom where "some pretty salty tales about *Haida*'s past were exchanged among the ship's former captains," remembers Ward.

*Haida*, Inc., meanwhile, faced a growing pile of bills, amounting to $30,000 with no relief in sight until the vessel could be opened to a fee-paying public. These were lonely months for *Haida*'s saviours. The net amount of the towing fee, $5,000, had to be paid. Other costs included a $2,500 bill for insurance to cover the crew members who had brought the vessel to Toronto, insurance for the ship for her last voyage and her first year in Toronto Harbour. On board watchman services were also required around the clock. For this purpose *Haida*, Inc. hired Chief Petty Officer Jack MacDonald, recently retired from the RCN, who took up employment aboard the ship immediately. One of CPO MacDonald's jobs was to get *Haida* into exhibition state at the earliest date possible.

Opposite: *Haida* is being towed into Port Weller Dry Docks by the tug *James E. McGrath*, 1969. (HMCS *Haida* Naval Museum)

Above: H.R.H. Prince Phillip is speaking to Mr. Neil Bruce aboard *Haida*, 1 March 1966. (HMCS Haida Naval Museum x991.072.005.002)

Top: One night in Bermuda, 1959, a sailor from HMCS *Nootka* dropped *Haida's* badge over the side as a prank. Sixteen years later a Royal Navy diver off the cable ship *Sentinel* found the badge on the ocean floor. Pictured here, Vice-Admiral D.S. Boyle, Commander Maritime Command, is presenting the badge to Commander Frank Stockwell of *Haida* May 1975.
(Courtesy Frank Stockwell)

Bottom: Visitors watch from the bridge as the Toronto Symphony Orchestra plays Tchaikovsky's *1812 Overture* accompanied by *Haida's* guns, June 1987.
(Courtesy Lawrence Sibbald)

Other crew members were quickly added to the ship's roster, including Lieutenant-Commander Frank Barlow, who was to be the new commanding officer of *Haida*. Certainly, the challenges which awaited Barlow, MacDonald and crew were many and varied, and, at times, must have seemed overwhelming. The ventilation, for instance, was unable to cope with Toronto's summer heat, while a lack of heat was more than apparent during the winter months. Other problems were beginning to make themselves known. Flooding and leaking were constant concerns for *Haida's* crew, and as Ward later stated, "we almost lost the ship to flooding once or twice!" Indeed, this particular situation was only permanently solved in 1969, when the ship was towed to Port Weller Dry Dock by the *James E. McGrath*. Once there, the hull was inspected, the sea cocks welded shut, and the entire hull given a coat of preservative.

Although more work needed to be done—indeed, there always seemed to be something which required attention—the ship was officially opened to the public on 9 July 1965. Originally, the plan was that in the spring of 1965, when the water level of Lake Ontario would be high, a day would be selected, one with little wind and good visibility, and *Haida* would be shifted from Pier Six, towed outside Toronto Harbour again, pulled to the west end of the Canadian National Exhibition grounds and eased through a gap in the breakwater. As Ward noted, "The ship will then be nursed back to the east end of the grounds, behind the breakwater, and nosed in to shore her bows pointing north, just south of the eastern gates of the CNE." In other words, she was to be berthed on the edge of Coronation Park, a Metropolitan Toronto Park dedicated to the memory of servicemen who fell in the Second World War. The City of Toronto assured *Haida*, Inc. that the ship would make a superb addition to this memorial. It is noteworthy that this military park, which existed for some decades, had among its collection a Lancaster bomber, a Sherman tank, a 90mm anti-aircraft gun and a 25-pdr field gun. However, plans for this project never fully materialized, and had it been pursued, this procedure would have marked Phase Two of *Haida*, Inc.'s original preservation plans.

Still other ideas for a more permanent site for *Haida* began to surface. A critical requirement for *Haida's* safekeeping was that a concrete mole, or breakwater, be built to close her off from the lake. Bruce and his associates of *Haida*, Inc. also reasoned that *Haida* be placed in a permanent drydock, one built for the purpose. Thus it was intended that once the ship was inside the mole, water would be pumped out and the area around the ship filled with concrete. *Haida* would, therefore, be left high and dry and free from the rust which would come to haunt her later. The tag for this was estimated at $250,000. *Haida*, Inc. also proposed a refreshment stand at dockside but all other commercial measures were to be kept at a distance: "Nothing commercial will ever touch the ship herself," wrote Ward in 1964. His words echo down the years.

As a museum the ship continued to attract interest. The ship captured people's imagination and attracted much public attention over the first few years in Toronto. Some corporate sponsors donated either money or material, and a small, but dedicated core of workers and volunteers—many ex-service people—contributed both time and money to the preservation of the ship. Also involved with preserving *Haida*, and able to take advantage of the training opportunities presented by the ship, were the officers and cadets of the Navy League of Canada, the Wrenettes and the Royal Canadian Sea Cadet Corps. During a typical day at summer camp, Wrenettes and Cadets would paint, swab the deck and guide tourists about the ship. In some cases, camp for these young sailors lasted up to five weeks, with most living and sleeping aboard. Later on, in March 1966, *Haida*'s patron, His Royal Highness Prince Phillip, visited the ship for what was supposed to have been a twenty-minute stop. In the end, the Prince enjoyed himself so much that the visit lasted a little over an hour! As Bruce recalled, "... he slid down the companionway to the crowded wardroom where he completely captivated the group." Naval veteran and historian James Lamb of Orillia later said that "If there is a more delightful guest than the Duke, we haven't heard of him."

Although by 1969-70 *Haida*, Inc. began to run in the black, the need for further preservation of the ship, a better location, and the constant financial pressure started taking a toll. With some regret, the decision was made by *Haida*, Inc. to transfer ownership of *Haida* to the government of Ontario. Part of this agreement included a provision for the preservation of the ship in perpetuity, with a new berth to be located by the breakwall of the recently completed Ontario Place Park. *Haida* was officially purchased by the government on 1 September 1970, and the transfer of ownership took place at the end of business, 30 October 1970, with little fanfare. Even though Bruce was reluctant, it was felt that this was the best course of action for the ship. The surrender of the Letters Patent of *Haida*, Inc. was dated 28 December 1971, and the Board of Directors for the former corporation was finally dissolved on 21 February 1972.

Much good had been accomplished for the ship while in the hands of *Haida*, Inc.—not least of which was the saving of this most famous Canadian destroyer. Indeed, over a period of five years *Haida* was painted, had her hull inspected, and had been visited by no less than 315,027 people—a most remarkable achievement.

**The Move to Ontario Place:
In Government Hands**

With ownership now resting in the hands of the government of Ontario, *Haida* was finally ready to be moved to her present location at Ontario Place. On the morning of 17 April 1971, two tugs gently towed *Haida* through a narrow opening in the causeway between Exhibition Park and Ontario Place. Interestingly enough, this man-made causeway was built from the excavations of one of Toronto's subway lines—as were the grounds of Ontario Place itself—and was only intended to be temporary. Once the ship had been securely tied to the breakwall, and after a final inspection, *Haida* was reopened to the public in May of that same year. The second, though modified phase of *Haida*'s original preservation scheme, was now well underway. With a more secure, or at least permanent resting place, her guardians felt that the ship would become more animated—more "alive." To this end, restoration of the ship began in earnest.

Not long after the move to Ontario Place, Frank Stockwell was hired and soon was given the title of Captain. A Sea Cadet officer who had served in both the British Merchant Marine and the Royal Naval Reserve during the Second World War, Stockwell brought a wealth of knowledge and experience to the task. For his dedication to the Sea Cadet programme he was promoted to Lieutenant-Commander, appointed to the Order of Canada as a Member of the Order of Military Merit, and before retirement was granted the rank of Commander. These were hard years for *Haida*, as the management of Ontario Place had little money in their budget for a naval museum and it took all of Stockwell's ingenuity and persuasiveness to keep the ship going. Paint, rope, grease and oil were coaxed out of companies with naval connections and individuals who were interested in maritime affairs. Naval vessels visiting Toronto invariably sailed with a few inches less draft than when they arrived. Volunteers were recruited from Toronto's naval and Sea Cadet community. Copious quantities of body filler, duct tape and "pusser's" grey paint hid the ever growing canker of corrosion. During the last few years of Stockwell's tenure there was a slight turnaround as management, recognizing the potential of the ship, organized the Honourary Company of Noon Day Gunners, and started the process that led to the recognition of the ship as a national historic site. Thanks to Stockwell the ship had survived one of its most difficult periods since facing the threat of war.

In 1986, Stockwell retired.

On 6 September 1986, after an extensive search, Ontario Place found a replacement in the person of Commander Robert A. Willson, RCN (Ret'd). Having served as the navigating officer in *Haida* from 1956 to 1958 Willson had just retired after thirty-five years' service in the RCN. He brought a professional approach to the management of the ship, arranging for the ship as a naval museum to join the Ontario Museum Association, the Canadian Museum Association, the

Organization of Military Museums of Canada, and the international Historic Naval Ships Association (which had its annual meeting in Toronto to celebrate the fiftieth anniversary of the commissioning of the ship, in 1993). An international Tribal Class Destroyers reunion was organized with participants from Canada, the UK, and Australia. A new gift shop was built, and the ship got a bubble harbour to protect it from winter ice and a much needed cathodic protection system. Under Willson's direction, a professional curator was hired, who catalogued the museum collection and established a collections management policy that would serve as a model for other historic naval ships. Meanwhile, the management of Ontario Place faced ever decreasing budgets but the board of directors, led by Clare Copeland and Fred Kasravi, were sympathetic to *Haida*'s needs and helped Willson set up the Friends of HMCS *Haida* to raise money in the private sector.

## Restoration: The Friends of HMCS *Haida*

When Willson retired in 1996 Carla Morse, the curator hired during his tenure, became the manager of the ship. Her professional status within the museum community and her extraordinary ability to network with the other managers at Ontario Place, and the growing body of volunteers from the Friends brought increased awareness of the ship across Canada and internationally. Under Morse's management Parks Canada began to take an active interest in the ship, bringing the resources of the Historic Sites and Monuments Board to bear on the question of the ship's future. *Haida*'s cultural and historical significance was defined in a Commemorative Integrity Statement, and structural surveys were carried out by Parks Canada to begin to define the work that is required to ensure the survival of this, the greatest of Canada's monuments to the Second World War.

Top: Lieutenant-Governor Lincoln Alexander, in anti-flash gear, holds a shell casing after firing *Haida's* noontime gun at Ontario Place, 6 September 1996.
(Courtesy Frank Stockwell)

Bottom: Lieutenant-Governor Lincoln Alexander signs the Log of Noon Gunners in *Haida's* wardroom, with Commander Frank Stockwell.
(Courtesy Frank Stockwell)

## Restoring *Haida's* Guns

Certainly, *Haida* had greater opportunities for public access and exposure while stationed at her new berth, and perhaps this is what attracted a new core of volunteers to the ship—people with valuable and desperately needed skills. While many individuals continued to give their time and help in whatever manner they could, certain names—and the deeds which these people achieved—are worth mentioning. One such individual was Gord Shires.

Having served in the Sea Cadets and undergone training as a gunner, Shires possessed a significant amount of knowledge and experience with naval guns. When approached with the almost impossible job of restoring *Haida's* guns to working order and making them capable of firing a blank round, Shires enthusiastically embraced the challenge. This would be no simple task, for the navy had welded the guns shut to ensure that they could never be fired. There was also some question as to which of *Haida's* guns should first be restored. Of all the different types of weapons with which the ship was equipped—many of them automatic or semi-automatic such as the 3/50 or the Bofors 40-mm anti-aircraft guns—it was decided that the most logical place to start the refurbishing process was with the 4-inch guns. The breeches and moving parts of these weapons were supposed to have been mutilated by the navy and sealed forever. Shires discovered that the breeches and barrels of the mighty 4-inch guns had not, in fact, been ruined after all. Rather, the guns had been spot-welded, or as he stated, they had been slightly done. Here again, it can only be surmised that the navy, realizing that *Haida* was to be a commemorative ship, bent the rules so as to help preserve this great fighting ship—the last of her breed. This, however, does not imply that the guns needed little attention. Indeed, it took Shires approximately four months to get one of B mount's guns working. Most of this work was done at night or over the course of many weekends. Initially, Shires had volunteered his time on *Haida*, but he was soon hired by Ontario Place to complete this and many other duties aboard the ship. Interestingly enough, upon retiring he again volunteered his time, and has been doing so on a regular basis since 1995.

Yet, the job was not finished with smoothing out the barrel, and many scarce parts had to be scrounged to complete the gun and make it ready to fire. After all, finding firing pins, not to mention nuts and bolts for a gun that was no longer in service, was not an easy task. As Shires recalled, "a lot of the knobs and bits came from the east coast or from the navy's gunnery school." His face then broke into a wide grin as he stated, "some of the parts were even filched from *York's* 4-inch mount." Once the gun was restored to a condition in which it could be safely test-fired, a new problem cropped up. Where to obtain ammunition for an obsolete gun? Shire decided to "pack his own!" Using empty brass casings which had been stowed in the forward magazine by the navy before being turned over to *Haida*, Inc., he turned to the dangerous job of reloading. What resulted from his efforts can only be described as the most deadly concoction of powder, cardboard, nylons and canning wax ever to be fired from naval ordnance! Success had been achieved, thanks to hard work and the Department of National Defence, which supplies the blank rounds. *Haida's* big guns now fire every day, at precisely twelve noon. The guns have also been used to salute visiting HMC ships as well as accompanying the Toronto Symphony Orchestra during the playing of the *1812 Overture*.

Still others who were associated with animating the ship must be mentioned. Frank Moore, *Haida's* second "electrical wizard," had been specifically hired by Ontario Place to rewire the ship, and the countless miles of wire and the obvious difficulty of the job which he performed stand as tribute to his skill. One success story is particularly noteworthy. He managed to restore power to the 4-inch twin mounts which can now be trained using the original electrical motors. Certainly, the gun's crew is appreciative of his abilities, for they no longer have to traverse the mounts by hand when firing the noonday gun!

Even though the restoration of the ship was proceeding at a respectable pace, more urgent problems were beginning to manifest. After *Haida* was towed to her berth at Ontario Place and the causeway restored, it was realized that the ship was almost completely encapsulated by a small lagoon. In a warmer climate, this might not have been cause for too much concern, but the harsh Canadian winter soon created a dilemma. Indeed, something had to be done to ensure the integrity of the ship's hull and to help it withstand the pressures of winter ice in a confined space. An innovative solution was eventually found, and the money for the project was raised through the generous contributions of the Ontario Ministry of Energy, Ontario Place and Atlas Copco Inc. In April 1987, Atlas Copco installed a "bubbler" or more specifically, an ice prevention and heat recovery system. The system utilizes compressed air, delivered from lines along the bottom of the lake, to agitate the water lying underneath and beside the hull. This, in turn, causes warm water to mix with the colder surface water, preventing ice from forming around the hull. The excess heat produced by the compressor, which delivers the air to the lines, is then recovered and used to heat the ship's living quarters in the winter—something which was previously done by electricity.

Another innovation, installed in 1989, also helped with the preservation of *Haida*'s hull. This device, designed and built by Cathodic Technology Inc., is a marvel of corrosion engineering. It consists of a series of high silicon cast iron anodes placed under the hull of the ship and on the bottom of the lagoon. These anodes are connected to a computer controlled cathodic protection rectifier. There are also four zinc "reference electrodes" under the hull. They allow for optimal automatic control of the level of cathodic protection being delivered to *Haida*'s hull. This system has assisted tremendously with the preservation of the submerged portion of the ship's hull. However, while the bottom of the hull has been saved from rapid and extensive deterioration, the hull at the waterline, especially where the sun beats against it, is currently in severe jeopardy, and is rapidly decaying. In certain places, the hull could be described as "paper thin." If the ship is going to survive this battle—a battle which very well might be *Haida*'s most important—serious consideration must be given to drydocking the ship and repairing her hull. Whether or not the original plan of *Haida*, Inc. will be pursued, which entailed the draining of the lagoon and the setting of the ship on a concrete pad, is still in question. Other alternatives are being considered, but the final resolution, as with many other museum endeavours, ultimately rests with the cost of the project.

While the plight of the ship attracted much public attention, other important developments occurred which benefited the ship. On 1 January 1989, the Friends of *Haida* was formed at the behest of Clare Copeland and Fred Kasravi. At the time, they were on the Board of Ontario Place Corporation and had the inside track on *Haida*. Kasravi saw the need for an organization capable of raising money to help defer some of the costs of the ship which Ontario Place was finding increasingly difficult to meet. After all, the preservation and running of a museum ship the size of *Haida* is

**HMCS** *Haida* **Naval Museum at Ontario Place.**
(Photo by Barry Gough)

Top: Commander Frank Stockwell greets Lieutenant-Governor the Hon. John Black Aird, arriving aboard to take a royal salute from HMS *Bristol*, 1980.
(Courtesy Frank Stockwell, DND C 84-301)

Bottom: *Haida's* A and B gun mountings. The twin 4-inch HA/LA guns pictured here replaced the ship's original 4.7-inch guns when *Haida* was refitted as a destroyer escort between 1950 and 1952.
(Courtesy Jerry Proc)

neither an easy nor inexpensive task. Costs of maintenance are rising. Copeland, Kasravi, and others have been immensely successful in increasing awareness of the ship and its current battle. Friends of H.M.C.S. *Haida Newsletter* dedicates itself to bits of the ship's history as well as to the activities of the many volunteers associated with *Haida*. Copeland was the first president. Kasravi was president of the organization from 1990 to 1998. John Byrne became president in 1998.

Love for the ship continues to grow, and through the efforts of many other volunteers, *Haida* is being steadily restored. She will never look the same as she did during the Second World War—for the cost would be prohibitive. Even if the money could be found for such a task, the odds of finding the necessary equipment would prove disappointing. For example, obtaining *Haida*'s original armament, the massive 4.7-inch twin guns, would be next to impossible. None of these weapons exist anywhere other than in a museum, and even then there are very few examples to choose from. Yet, *Haida* continues to come alive, bit by bit. Indeed, the ship's large GM diesel generator was recently run for the first time in thirty-five years, thanks mainly to the work and dedication of Margaret Mathers. Mathers had initially served in the navy as a nursing assistant at HMCS *Cornwallis*, the navy's great training facility on the east coast. But years later, Mathers trained as a diesel mechanic at HMCS *Star*, once the navy permitted women to serve in sea trades. Still other individuals, such as Jerry Proc, have made significant contributions. An amateur radiophile, Proc has restored *Haida*'s four radio rooms, written about the ship's radar, sonar and IFF systems and, on special occasions, runs an amateur radio station out of the ship. Proc was also instrumental in establishing a web site for *Haida*. Jim Brewer, Eric Howard, John Brannen, Russ Robinson and

Hayward Sibbald have also made tremendous contributions, in one form or another, to the preservation of the ship. One other person, whose early voluntary interest in *Haida* eventually led to full-time employment, needs to be mentioned. Peter Dixon, still involved with the Sea Cadets, has contributed to *Haida* in countless ways. Currently, Dixon wears a variety of hats, including ship's operational officer and ship historian/archivist.

*Haida* turned yet another milestone as a museum ship on 30 August 1990, coinciding with the 47th anniversary of her commissioning. The ship was honoured with a plaque denoting her importance as a national historic site by the Historic Sites and Monuments Board of Canada. The event, held at Ontario Place in front of *Haida*'s berth, was attended by many dignitaries. These included admirals, representatives from the City of Toronto, Directorate of History and the Department of National Defence, and the Hon. Lincoln M. Alexander, Lieutenant-Governor of the Province of Ontario. The event was a significant recognition of *Haida* as a national museum and as a memorial site.

Meanwhile, concern over the deteriorating condition of the ship's hull prompted further investigation into an appropriate course of action. The hull had been surveyed on several previous occasions, but had last been formally looked at on 8 April 1988. The survey was conducted by Soderholm & Associates Marine Services Inc. for Ontario Place Corporation. Although not considered a formal survey, divers from HMCS *York* inspected the ship's hull on 18 April 1998. The prognosis was not bright, the main problem being along the waterline where cathodic protection stops, and the maintenance of good protective paint coating is impossible. Other problems were noticed as well. Pin holes were visible and water tended to enter the ship through the many rivets along the bottom of the hull. This fact, coupled with the need to increase revenues and continue maintenance and restoration on the ship, prompted a referral to experts in the field of museum consultation. Barry Lord, a world-renowned expert in conservation, was approached. After four months of careful research and professional consideration, the *LORD Report* on *Haida* was produced in February 1996. The report itself is over one hundred pages, and contains no fewer than seventy-seven different recommendations. Some of these include "animating" the ship with various costumed interpreters and allowing greater opportunity for children and young adults to interact with the ship and learn about some of the skills needed by sailors. One suggestion, for example, was to hold demonstration classes in knot tying in which children could participate and learn to tie various nautical knots and other ropework. Another important suggestion was the establishment of a shore-based learning centre. This facility would include a small theatre for viewing films about Canada's naval contribution and about *Haida*. As well it would have archives and a library open to the public, for more serious academic pursuits. Few of these recommendations have been implemented—due mainly to cost—but many of the ideas incorporated into the report have been considered and will eventually find their way into the ship.

*Haida* still lies at Ontario Place, tied peaceably to the breakwall. She is an aging and venerable tribute to a past unknown to children who run her decks, or clamber over the 40-mm anti-aircraft guns, searching the skies for the telltale sign of enemy planes. Her battle ensign no longer flies defiantly from the yardarm as she pulls into Plymouth, announcing yet another victory. Nor do her guns break the morning calm, pounding the shoreline off Korea in quest of another enemy train. No, *Haida* is at peace and yet she fights her most terrible battle of all—the battle for her survival. Fundraising campaigns are underway in order to raise upwards of five million dollars so that the ship can be towed to the drydock facilities, possibly at Port Weller, Ontario, and her hull repaired. This is indeed the challenge of *Haida*'s career. The quest is not without hope, and her one-time site manager Carla Morse confidently stated that the objective will be met. "The ship is an important piece of our heritage. It's very much a living thing, it breathes, and sighs with the wind. As Canadians, we need artifacts such as *Haida* to educate and remind us of our proud past. I'll be doing my best to ensure that *Haida*'s lights keep shining well into the 21st Century. It would be a real disgrace to see her scrapped and that's just something that I'm not willing to even think about at this point."

Many years ago Peter Ward wrote this about his hopes for the ship's future: "The firm intention of the directors of *Haida*, Inc. is to make HMCS *Haida* into a fitting memorial of all sailors who served in the RCN. We hope that by showing the public how seamen lived on board ship, and how they fought their weapons, a greater appreciation of things naval will be passed on to thousands of Canadians. The *Haida* will become a reminder of all the little ships that made our Navy famous. We of *Haida*, Inc., do not consider ourselves the owners of this proud ship; we are merely custodians of her for the people of Canada."

And so, as *Haida* faces an uncertain future, it is with the hope that the vision of the original members of *Haida*, Inc. will be upheld, and that the ship will continue on as a fitting tribute both to those who served, and to a proud Canadian naval tradition.

# CHAPTER 14

## *HAIDA*, REMEMBRANCE, HERITAGE

●

CANADA'S MOST FAMOUS WARSHIP, *Haida,* is a claim on the historical memory of the nation. She is an official national memorial to the Canadian Naval Service and to the sacrifice of the Second World War. She is also designated as a memorial to the Canadian Merchant Marine. *Haida* was a Cold Warrior and took her place in NATO forces. She fought under UN auspices in Korea. Age and technological innovation ended her serviceable life. By citizen initiative she came to make her home in Toronto, a key national city, where she lies as a heritage museum.

In a country where the nation's history is neglected by schools and public, or that such history is warped or faulty, there is just cause for claiming that *Haida* is in need of the preservation and enhancement she deserves. What better memorial to the naval heritage of the Canadian nation and

what better, central location? Saving Canadian naval history—and national history more generally—ranks as the greater aim. *Haida* is an end in herself, and she is the means to an end.

For more than twenty years I have been teaching university courses on naval history. Such courses—on the history of the navies of the world—are conspicuous by their rarity in institutions of higher learning. I know of none such elsewhere in Canada outside of the Royal Military College. In a way, my plight—and my cause—is emblematic of this branch of naval history and national achievement generally. In common parlance, is anyone out there listening? Or, does anyone care? I can say unequivocally that my 18 to 21-year-old students care a great deal. Many shake their heads in disbelief that the nation neglects its own history the way it does. And at another level I am always puzzled by how little the Royal Canadian Navy attends to its own history. In discussion with a serving officer I once made that precise point. His reply was that the Canadian Navy had a website on the Internet. When I went to it to explore its (impoverished) materials, I discovered to my horror and disbelief that most of the photographs of Canadian naval ships had been copied from US naval sources. I should not imagine that the Royal Navy would neglect its own history in such a tawdry fashion and I do know that the US Navy does not. In fact, the US Naval Foundation acts as lobbyist and guardian of such matters. Canada would profit by giving some sensible attention to how other nations attend to their naval heritage. For a country—for a service—that cries out for international recognition, the preservation of national heritage treasures has untold benefits for future generations. We hold *Haida* in trust. She is a claim on our national patrimony.

Often I have thought how *Haida* belongs to others as well. Let's list a few. She took her place, on equal footing with the Royal Navy, in the battle against the *Scharnhorst*, in the struggle for the Narrow Seas of the English Channel and Bay of Biscay, in the liberation of France and Norway, and in the protection of Russian convoys. Then we add to the list her work alongside Polish destroyers in clearing the French coast of German destroyers, torpedo boats and submarines. She fought alongside a Norwegian destroyer in northern operations. To these battle honours are to be added Korea, where she stood in the Commonwealth force in company with British, New Zealand and Australian naval vessels and played escort and support roles for US carriers and cruisers. In NATO she was part of the Standing Naval Force North Atlantic, working with US, Royal, Dutch, Belgian, French and other navies.

In technical terms, *Haida* exhibits the height of naval design of the latter 1930s and early 1940s. She also is emblematic of changing weaponry, from her "sharp end" role as a fleet destroyer to her conversion to a destroyer-escort. Her main armament, torpedoes, and anti-aircraft guns both large and small are prized examples of their kind and age. Her anti-submarine weaponry, especially her Squid mortar, are examples of then state-of-the-art equipment. The radar equipment is testament to the first successful age of night-fighting at sea, and *Haida*'s success was that of those who sat at the screens identifying the position, range and course of the possible enemy. The means of firing shells with technical guidance, as opposed to local or visual control, is equally shown in *Haida*. Her director equipment, the most advanced of its time, enabled her to fire with lethal effect. Her gun crews performed always on the best of technical advice served up by the intricate electro-mechanical network that eliminated guesswork from gunnery. And because the successful prosecution of war at sea means the control of information, the radio kit of *Haida* received and sent messages while operators kept logs and passed along signals. Asdic or SONAR and hydrophone operators provided underwater surveillance upon which the ship equally depended. All of this equipment exists in the ship as of the early 21st century. The friends and volunteers, the paid and unpaid workers, the curators and historical consultants who maintain or keep criteria on *Haida* know that this great material relic, Canada's largest man-made historical artifact, deserves the full attention of the nation that *Haida*'s officers and men worked so hard to protect in war and in peace.

And what of the sailors? "To the men who played a part in the dark pageant there remains only the memory," wrote William Pugsley in 1945, "They went from this province and that town, but they have travelled now and they're coming back Canadians, fond of their country in a way that only those who've been away can really feel." In the crucible of war was forged a nation. "Whether in corvette, minesweeper, or destroyer, no rating will soon forget the first time he clawed his way alone along the open deck at night with a high sea running, or climbed for the first time the swaying rope ladder to the crow's nest." The agony of seasickness, the monotony of endless watches, the fear of storm at sea—these and more—all were conquered by time, teamwork, leadership, fuel and supplies, and a fine man-of-war in which to serve.

> Nor will he forget, [wrote Pugsley], when U-boats attacked the convoy at night, holding on grimly by the depth charges, half drowned by breaking seas, as he waited for the order to fire the pattern; nor his first real storm, listen-

ing anxiously in his reeling hammock as the straining hull thudded warily into another wave and smoking combers thundered triumphantly across the foc'sle no more than inches above his head; nor the mantling millstone of winter ice, today in sunny harbour scintillating with all the magnificence of a ball dress strewn with diamonds, but yesterday in grey rolling seas a clammy shroud that sought to snuff out the lives of all on board, dragging them to the depths, 'without a grave, unknelled, uncoffined, and unknown.'

"Happy *Haida*," they called her. Always, however, there existed a grave foreboding, the price of admiralty, the cost to be paid, for keeping the seas for national and allied purposes, even for those of civilization and humanity.

*Liberty Boats.* Perhaps the most welcome order aboard the ships of Canada's Navy is the call to "fall in for liberty boats" allowing off-duty seamen time ashore to relax from their strenuous duties. Ordinary Seaman D.B. Allan.
(Grant Macdonald, courtesy MMGL)

# APPENDIX 1

## HAIDA'S FIGHTING EQUIPMENT AND GUNNERY

HMCS *Haida* was the last of the British-built Tribal class fleet destroyers, originally called Afridi class destroyers after the lead ship HMS *Afridi*. By the time that *Haida* was commissioned the British had lost twelve of their sixteen Tribals to enemy action. *Haida* benefitted greatly from the experience the RN had with the original ships. The decks were strengthened, adding to the displacement but making the ship more seaworthy. Major changes were made to their armament. Original design specifications for the Tribals called for eight 4.7-inch guns as the main armament and at various times the close-range weapons could be 2-pdr pom-poms in single mounts, quad .5-inch Vickers machine guns and later six single 20-mm Oerlikon guns. *Haida* was fitted with a twin 4-inch HA/LA in place of the 4.7 at X position and the quad pom-pom was located where the British Tribals had their searchlight between the mainmast and X gun. This allowed much improved sky arcs for anti-aircraft defence. In place of the single Oerlikon guns *Haida* was built with six twin power-operated mounts. She had a six depth charge rail at the stern in place of the three-charge rail on the British Tribals.

### Contents, Appendix 1

### ORDNANCE, HMCS *Haida* 1943

Six QF [Quick Firing] 4.7-inch Mk XII guns (3x2) on twin Mk XIX CP [Central Pivot] power mounts, on forecastle (A), fore superstructure (B) & quarterdeck (Y):

| | |
|---|---|
| Max. elevation and depression | +40 to -10 degrees |
| Max. training arc | 320 degrees |
| Training and laying speed | 10 degrees/second in power |
| Rate of fire per minute/gun | 12 rounds (max. power ramming) |
| Projectile weight | 50 lbs average |

| | |
|---|---|
| Cartridge weight | 32 lbs 10 oz full charge 25 lbs 14 oz Starshell [Star] |
| Max. surface range | 16,900 yards |
| Max. vertical height | 15,000 feet |
| Number of rounds per gun | 250 approx. |
| Projectile types | Semi-armour piercing [SAP]    High explosive [HE] Star |
| Fuses | Base percussion [BP] 025 second delay for SAP, Direct Action [DA] for HE Time [T], Time Mechanical [TM] Variable Time [VT] for AA barrage. |

*Note: T is combustion delay, TM is clockwork delay, and VT is a proximity fuse for anti-aircraft actions. T and TM are for HE or Starshell.*

Two QF 4-inch Mk XVI (2xl) guns on a Mk XIX twin High Angle CP power mount on the after superstructure (X):

| | |
|---|---|
| Max. elevation and depression | +80 to -10 degrees |
| Max. training arc | 340 degrees |
| Rate of fire per minute/gun | 12 rounds/minute, manual |
| Total weight of round | 63 lbs average 66 lbs. SAP |
| Weight of projectile | 35 lbs. average |
| Projectile types | SAP, HE and Starshell |
| Fuse types | BP, DA, T, TM and VT |
| Max. Surface Range | 19,400 yards |
| Max. vertical height | 38,000 feet |

**Close-Range Armament *Haida*, 1943**

Four QF 2-pdr Mk VIII guns (1x4) on a Quad. 2-pdr Mk VII (P), mounting on pom-pom platform above and forward of X gun.

| | |
|---|---|
| Max. elevation and depression | +80 to -10 degrees |
| Max. training arc | 710 degrees |
| Max. training and laying speed | 25 degrees/second in power |
| Rate of fire per minute/gun | 115 rounds |
| Ammunition feed | continuous belt |
| Shell weight | 2 lbs |
| Max. surface range | 5,000 yards |
| Max. vertical height | 10,000 feet |
| Number of rounds per gun | 7,200 |
| Shell type | High Explosive |
| Fuse type | Direct Action |

Twelve Oerlikon (6x2) 20-mm Mk IV guns on Mk VC twin power mounts at flag deck (P&S) amidships (P&S) after superstructure (P&S):

| | |
|---|---|
| Max. elevation and depression | +70 to -10 degrees |
| Max. training arc | continuous all round |

| Rate of fire per minute/gun | 480 rounds |
|---|---|
| Magazine capacity | 60 rounds per gun |
| Shell weight | 0.27 lbs (125 grams) |
| Max. surface range | 6,000 yards |
| Max. vertical height | 6,000 feet |
| Number of rounds per gun | 7,200 |
| Shell type | High Explosive Incendiary |
| Fuse type | Direct Action |

*Note: Mk IV Oerlikon guns were manufactured in the United States by General Motors, Pontiac Division.*

## Torpedo Armament *Haida*, 1943

Four 21-inch Mk IX* torpedoes in a quad power mounting amidships forward of the after superstructure on the main deck:

| Total weight of Mk IX* | 3731 lbs |
|---|---|
| Weight of warhead | 750 lbs of high explosive |
| Range and speed | 14,000 yards at 35 knots; 10,000 yards at 40 knots |
| Engine type | Radial diesel |
| Fuse types | Impact exploder or magnetic influence exploder |

## Depth Charge Armament *Haida*, 1943

Forty-six Mk VII depth charges with 2 Mk IV throwers, 1 port and 1 starboard of the after superstructure and a single six-charge rail on the stern:

| DCs normally carried | 22 on deck |
|---|---|
|  | 24 between decks |
| Weight Mk VII | 410 lbs |
| High explosive charge | 396 lbs |
| Sink rate | 10 feet/second |
| Weight Mk VII (Heavy) | 560 lbs |
| High Explosive Charge | 396 lbs |
| Sink rate | 16.5 feet/second |
| Fuse settings for Mk VII* | 50 to 600 feet |
| Fuse type | Hydrostatic |

*Note: Haida was never armed with the Hedgehog ATW. Nor were any of the torpedo tubes fitted to take Mk X depth charges, a special one-ton weapon.*

## Small Arms *Haida*, 1943

One Vickers .303 calibre gas-operated machine gun:

| Magazine capacity | 96 rounds |
|---|---|
| Weight | 21 lbs |
| Rate of fire | 1000 rounds/minute |
| Ammunition feed | 96 round flat circular spring operated magazine |
| Max. effective range | 440 yards |

Two Bren .303 caliber light machine guns (gas operated):

| | |
|---|---|
| Magazine capacity | 30 rounds (28 normally) |
| Weight | 22 lbs |
| Rate of Fire | 500 rounds/minute |
| Effective range | 880 yards |
| Max. range | 3300 yards |

- Thirty-two Lee-Enfield SMLE Rifles No. 1 Mk III.
- Twenty-six Lanchester 9-mm machine carbines (SMGs)
- Four SMLE .22 rim fire rifles
- Twelve revolvers
- Five No.1 Mk II Very Pistols

## *Haida* 1947

The 4.7-inch, 4-inch main guns, the 2-pdr pom-pom, and torpedo armament remained unchanged from 1943. The close-range weapons systems changed as follows.

Four Oerlikon (2x2) guns on Mk VC mounts on the flag decks (port & starboard).

Four 40-mm QF Mk I Bofors guns mounted on the 20-mm Oerlikon Mk VC (4x1) power mounts. This combination, a Canadian initiative, was named the Boffin. Boffins were at the midships and after superstructure positions, port and starboard. Boffin is a combination of Bofors and Oerlikon:

| | |
|---|---|
| Max. Elevation and depression | +70 to -10 degrees |
| Max. training arc | continuous all round |
| Max. surface range | 10,750 yards |
| Max. vertical height | 23,500 feet |
| Rate of fire | 120 rounds/minute |
| Shell type | high explosive |
| Weight of complete round | 4 lbs 14 oz |
| Weight of shell | 2 lbs |
| Fuse type | direct action (graze type) |

*Note: Somewhat later the RN designed a similar mount for the Bofors as the Mk VIII power mount.*
*Note: 2-pdr 40-mm pom-pom rounds and 40-mm Bofors rounds are not interchangeable.*

### Depth Charges

Still with the 1943 depth charge weapons systems, *Haida* carried only ten depth charges on deck, four in the stern rail and three for each thrower. No charges were stored between decks.

## *Haida* 1952
### Main Armament

Four QF 4-inch Mk XVI guns on two Mk XIX twin High Angle/Low Angle CP power mounts (2x2) at A & B. This is the same model and type of gun and mount as X position in 1943.

Two 3-inch 50 calibre Mk VIII Model 2 guns on a twin Mk XXI Model 1 power mount (2x1) in X position:

| | |
|---|---|
| Max. elevation and depression | +85 to -15 degrees |
| Training and laying speed | Training 30 deg/second; Laying 24 deg/second |

| | |
|---|---|
| Rate of fire per minute/gun | 50 rounds |
| Total weight of round, fixed | 24 lbs |
| Weight of shell | 13 lbs |
| Max. surface range | 14,600 yards at 45 degrees elevation |
| Max. vertical height | 29,800 feet at 85 degrees elevation |
| Shell type | high explosive |
| Fuse types | VT and DA |

### Torpedo Armament

Four Mk IX torpedoes in a quad mount as per 1943.

### Anti-Submarine Armament

Two triple Squid ATW (Ahead Throwing Weapons).
Six mortar tubes in two triple mounts on the quarterdeck (3x2):

| | |
|---|---|
| Weight of bomb | 400 lbs |
| Explosive charge | 200 lbs |
| Sink rate | 44 feet/second |
| Effective depth | 60 % kill at 600 feet |
| Fuse Type | Hydrostatic |
| No. of bombs carried | 60 in below-decks magazine |

## SHIP COMPARISON 1944

### German *Z-23* Class (Narvik) (*Z-32*) Also known as Type 36A:

| | |
|---|---|
| Displacement, Standard | 2600 tons |
| Full | 3600 tons |
| Length overall | 416 feet 9 inches |
| Beam | 39 feet 3 inches |
| Draught | 12 feet 8 inches |
| Speed | 36 knots |
| Armament (main) | 5 5.9-inch guns (3x1 and 1x2) |
| Close Range | 6 20-mm (6x1) and 4 37-mm (2x2) |
| Torpedoes | 8 (21 in.) (4x2) |
| Mines | 60 (up to) |
| Complement | 321 |

### Type 39 Class Torpedo Boats (Elbing) (*T-27* & *T-29*)

| | |
|---|---|
| Displacement standard | 1295 tons |
| Full | 1756 tons |
| Length overall | 334 feet 7 inches |
| Beam | 32 feet 10 inches |
| Draught | 10 feet 6 inches |
| Speed | 33.5 knots |

| | |
|---|---|
| Armament (Main) | 4 4.1-inch guns (4x1) |
| (Close Range) | 4 37-mm guns (2x2) |
| | 6 20-mm guns (6x1) |
| Torpedoes | 6 21-inch (3x2) |
| Complement | 198 |

**Tribal Class Destroyer HMCS *Haida* 1944**

| | |
|---|---|
| Displacement Standard | 1960 tons |
| Full | 2745 tons |
| Length overall | 377 feet |
| Beam | 37 feet 6 inches |
| Draught | 13 feet full load |
| Speed | 36 knots (32.5 full load) |
| Armament (Main) | 6 4.7-inch guns (3x2) |
| | 2 4-inch guns (1x2) |
| (Close Range) | 4 2-pdr pom-pom (4x1) |
| | 12 20-mm  Oerlikon (6x2) |
| Torpedoes | 4 21-inch (4x1) |
| Depth Charges | 46 Mk VII |
| Complement | 230 crew plus 18 officers |

## II GUNNERY

By the time of *Haida*'s commissioning, the Destroyer Director Control Tower (DCT), which had been fitted on the first British Tribal class destroyers, had become obsolete. Instead, the entire fire control of the main armament centred on a variant of the Rangefinder Director, known as the Mk III (W). This was similar to the Mk II (W), which on the earlier Tribals had been utilized as a director for AA fire only. The Mk III (W) was almost exactly the same as the Mk II (W), but accommodated an extra crew member—the rate officer—whose duty was to assess the course and speed of a surface target. The other two crew members were the rangetaker and the trainer. The Mk III (W) was located on the bridge.

Information from the Mk III (W) was fed to the Transmitting Station, along with information from radars in the Operations Room and the gun mounting itself. It was in the Transmitting Station that the "firing solution" was generated. This was done by feeding the various bits of information into the Admiralty Fire Control Clock, which was a primitive analog computer, by setting the appropriate dials. *Haida*'s course and speed were also entered, and the Fire Control Clock generated the "firing solution," which was a gun bearing and elevation reading. This was fed to the Director and the gun mountings, and the guns were fired when the control officer in the DCT pushed a button.

In the early 1950s, *Haida*, like the other Canadian Tribals, had their Rangefinder Directors replaced with the Mk 63 Gunfire Control System, which was an American design. This was mounted in the unoccupied DCT position on the bridge. It was an independent self-controlled unit, incorporating its own radar. The aerial was mounted on the elevating gun cradle and full "blind fire" tracking against unseen targets could be carried out.

## References:

Chris Bishop, et. al., *The Complete Encyclopedia of Weapons of World War II* (Etobicoke, ON: Prospero Books, 1998)

Peter A. Dixon, Haida *Docent Manual* (1994).

Bernard Fitzsimons, et. al., *The Illustrated Encyclopedia of 20th Century Weapons and Warfare* (New York: Columbia House, 1971/77/78).

Peter Hodges, *Tribal Class Destroyers* (Surrey: Almark Publishing Co. Ltd., 1971).

H.T. Lenton, *Navies of The Second World War: British Fleet And Escort Destroyers 1* (Garden City, New Jersey: Doubleday and Company Inc., 1970).

H.T. Lenton and J.J. Colledge, *Warships of World War II*, Part Two *Destroyers and Submarines* (London: Ian Allan Ltd., 1962)

NAC RG 24, *Fighting Equipment Reports for HMCS Haida,* 30 August 1943 and 16 June 1947.

Navy Department (U.S.) Bureau of Ordnance: O.P.1566: *3-Inch Loader Mk 2, Models 4, 5 and 6 with Gun Housing Slide* (8 May 1951).

Naval Ordnance Dept., Admiralty, B.R.1632/1953, *Weights and Dimensions of Naval Armament Stores and Gunnery Equipment* (including Naval Aircraft Armament) 12 May 1953.

# APPENDIX 2

## I ASDIC, RADAR, and IFF

### ASDIC

The first device used to locate submarines was known as ASDIC, which comes from Allied Submarine Detection Investigation Committee, and was invented during the First World War by British and French scientists. The more modern term for ASDIC is SONAR, meaning Sound Navigation and Ranging, which came from the Americans during the Second World War, and is now used universally to describe all underwater detection equipment. In the Royal Navy, the term was not formally introduced until 1964.

ASDIC operated by transmitting regular pulses of sound energy that traveled through the water and were reflected by a target. This energy resembled the beam of a searchlight and was projected horizontally. Any resultant echo was received, amplified, and then displayed on a recorder. The time that elapsed between transmission and reception indicated the distance from the ASDIC set to the target. On later Second World War versions, a display mechanism, which had a time base, transformed the echoes into electrical impulses that normally caused a stylus to mark a strip of paper moving on rollers. Together with bearing and depth information, the location of an underwater target could be pinpointed. During the Second World War, the detection range of ASDIC was about 2,000 yards although, under ideal conditions a range of 3,000 yards was possible.

During the Second World War, the ASDIC recorders aboard *Haida* were located in a cabin below the bridge, on the port side and off the plot room. During a normal duty watch, one rating operated the ASDIC set while another stood by. During Action Stations, the ASDIC equipment was manned by three operators.

A Type 144 ASDIC set was fitted-on-build *Haida* in 1943. This was the first attack set based on wartime experience. It was the first attempt at an integrated weapon system with a certain degree of automation, as the set was designed to be used with ahead-thrown weapons, especially the Hedgehog. The main innovations of the set were the electrical, semi-automatic training of the transducer and the new, more sophisticated range recorder, A/S 285.

The Type 144 was designed to cope with U-boats in shallow areas such as the Western Approaches where the depth was not greater than 100 fathoms. This was because the beam from the Type 144 did not go below 10 degrees on the horizontal plane. Two additional sets were created to address the problem of U-boats that dove below this beam. The first was the Q attachment, which was installed as an addition to the Type 144 in *Haida* by the mid 1940s. This was in addition to the ASDIC set, which required separate transmitting and receiving equipment but was suitably interconnected with the main set. The Q oscillator was mounted beneath the main oscillator and trained with it. It projected a beam that was only three degrees wide but could receive echoes at any angle from horizontal to 45 degrees below horizontal. This new arrangement enabled contact to be maintained with deep targets and it also minimized the "dead zone."

The second additional set was the Type 147F, a depth-finding set that was fitted on *Haida* some time after September 1943. It was complementary with the main ASDIC set and the Q attachment. Its sword-shaped oscillator was mounted ahead of the 144 oscillator on the hull, and was retractable. The acoustic beam could be trained up to 65 degrees horizontally and 45 degrees vertically. This new design could accurately track a target to within 20 feet. New style recorders automatically gave the range and direction for steering, while the set itself could automatically set and fire Squid mortars.

Complementary with the Type 147F set aboard *Haida* was the Type 164B. This was a range- and bearing-finding device that was supplemented with depth data from the 147F set and had been designed to be used with the Hedgehog or Squid.

From the mid 1940s onwards, *Haida* was fitted with a Model 761 Echo Sounding Set, which measured depth using a sound impulse. To measure water depth, an underwater sound impulse was sent towards the ocean floor. On reaching the sea bed, the echo returned and was measured and recorded graphically.

When paid off, *Haida* was equipped with AN/SQS-10 azimuth-scanning AM type SONAR. It used a transducer based on the magnetostriction principle, and unlike the roughly 2000-yard limit of the wartime ASDIC sets, this set could operate out to 6,000 yards under ideal conditions when echo ranging.

At the same time, *Haida* was equipped with AN/SQS-501, which was an auxiliary set designed specifically for identifying submarines lying on the ocean floor where the depth of water was not too great. There were three, fixed, quartz transducers mounted in the forward end of the hull. One unit faced port, the second faced starboard, and the third was mounted in the keel facing downwards. They produced a sound beam at right angles to the ship's fore and aft line.

**RADAR**

RADAR, an acronym derived from the fuller term Radio Detection and Ranging, was the name given during the Second World War to an electronic system designed to detect aircraft and/or ships. Credit for the development of the first practical RADAR system is given to the British scientist, Sir Robert Watson-Watt. In RADAR, a transmitter produces radio waves that are radiated from an antenna which "illuminates" the airspace with those waves. A target, such as an aircraft or ship, that enters this space scatters a small portion of this radio energy back to the antenna. This weak signal is amplified and displayed on a cathode ray tube (CRT). Because radio waves travel at a constant speed (186,000 mi/sec), the range can be determined by measuring the time taken for a radio wave to travel from the transmitter to the target and back to the receiver. Practically speaking, this translates to 328 yards per microsecond.

The following were the RADAR fits aboard the *Haida* at various points in her career:

**1944** Foremast top: 291 combined;

After boathouse: 271 combined with 241 IFF pitchfork antenna;

Mainmast: HF/DF birdcage antenna.

**1948** Foremast top: HF/DF birdcage;

Foremast midpoint: 293 cheesecake;

Mainmast: 291 combined.

**1953** Foremast top: 293 WC type (Warning Combined).

Descending order: IFF dipole; Sperry HDWS RADAR (Mk II);

Mainmast stump: 291 combined.

**1954** Foremast top: 293 WC type (Warning Combined);
Descending order: IFF dipole; AN/SPS6C; Sperry HDWS;
Mainmast: 291 combined (rarely used).

**1956** SHF/DF antenna added to foremast top for AN/UPD501 RADAR DF set.

A Type 271 air/surface warning set was installed in *Haida* during her January 1944 refit in Plymouth. The RADAR compartment was located astern between the searchlight and the pom-pom guns. An integral, perspex, hat-box antenna was mounted directly above the 271 office. Its finer and narrower beam permitted escorts to detect trimmed-down U-boats at long distances, consistently and accurately. As well, a battleship was detectable at 13 miles. Since the 271 set operated at the 10 cm wavelength, the antenna could be made small enough to be housed in its own perspex bubble and mounted on top of the operator's cabin.

The Type 285 set was a secondary-battery gunnery RADAR, which on *Haida* was fitted-on-build in 1943. The gunnery office was located at the base of the foremast, while the aerial was mounted atop the director control tower on the bridge. Bearing accuracy was 3 to 4 degrees typical, with an accuracy of 100 yards on the 15,000 yard scale. At maximum range, it could detect a cruiser at seven miles. However, the 285 was fundamentally flawed due to its inability to follow aerial targets in elevation and was replaced with the Model 275. As the director was manually controlled, it was difficult to follow fast-moving aircraft.

Both the Type 291 and the Type 293 RADAR sets were installed on *Haida* at the same time. The 291 office was located on the flag deck below the bridge, while the antenna, fed by pyrotenax cable, was located at the top of the foremast. The

291 was a small ship/air search RADAR set. The antenna was similar in concept to that of a 281 type, but the dipoles were supported by an X-shaped structure. This antenna had a beam width of 40 degrees and was of the lazy H construction. It had the capability of detecting a bomber at fifteen miles.

The 293 was an S-band target indicator (sometimes referred to as "Warning Combined" type) which used the same transmitter as the 277 type and was equipped with the new, azimuth-stabilized, "cheese" antenna. It acquired that name because it resembled a block of cheese cut in half. Stabilization was essential. Otherwise, the roll of the ship would tilt the beam, and air targets might be displayed at wildly wrong bearings. The beam was wide in the vertical plane so that the ship's roll would have little effect. Typical detection range was fifteen miles for an aircraft at 10,000 feet. Type 293M, which used an 8-foot antenna, was introduced into service in 1945. Type 293P was similar to a previous model but it was modified for easier maintenance. A post-war RADAR program introduced the 293Q set with a redesigned 12-foot antenna. *Haida* was fitted with the 293 type until the late 1950s.

When *Haida* was paid off, she was equipped with two AN/SPA-4A Range-Azimuth Indicators. One was located in the RADAR hut and the other unit was on the bridge. The SPA4 was designed to be used with any naval search RADAR system having a pulse frequency between 140 and 3000 pps. It employed a remote PPI type indicator using a 10-inch, flat CRT. Azimuth was determined by means of a mechanical cursor coupled to an electronic cursor, and jointly they were accurate to within one degree. An electronic range strobe was accurate to within one percent of the maximum range being viewed.

The *Haida* was fitted with the AN/SPG-34 (X-band) fire control RADAR for AA guns. The antenna was a 40-inch-diameter dish that could produce a 2.4 degree beam.

Prior to her second tour of duty in Korea, *Haida* was fitted with the AN/SPS6-C shipborne, long-range, air search RADAR, and continued to be so equipped until she was paid off. This set was designed to supply target bearing and range data to its 5-inch A-scope indicator. As well, it was equipped with automatic frequency control and anti-jamming features.

In the early 1950s, *Haida* was fitted with Sperry HDWS (High Definition Warning Surface) Marine RADAR (Mk 2). This was a medium range, surface search RADAR. While its primary use was to locate other ships, helicopters, navigation aids and shorelines, it was also very effective in detecting submarine periscopes.

## IFF

The IFF acronym is derived from the term *Identification, Friend or Foe*. IFF is used to determine the identity of RADAR contacts. An IFF system consists of a searching RADAR (or interrogator) that emits interrogating pulses, and a transponder in the RADAR contact (i.e. an aircraft or ship) that responds with the correct reply when it detects an interrogating pulse. IFF was initially developed for installation in RAF aircraft.

The Mk III IFF was the standard Allied IFF system used in the Second World War. The IFF challenge and response signals were each to occupy a separate, specialized band, and they operated in conjunction with the main RADAR sets so that the transmitted pulses were synchronized. As well, to ensure that the returning signals gave an accurate indication of target bearing, not just target range, the IFF interrogator was located on the RADAR antenna, rotating with it to give directional indications. The same device also received the response, which was known as an interrogator-responsor system. The system had no problem with sea returns, and as the transmitters required much less power for a given range, the fitting of IFF presented few space problems. Initially, the interrogator aerials consisted of directional "Yagi" arrays mounted on a horizontal U-bar. But in 1944, the most commonly used aerial system consisted of four, broad-band cage dipoles in a rectangular configuration and capable of power rotation.

*Haida* was equipped with Type 242 IFF series interrogation equipment in the 1940s, which was located on a platform abaft the fore top. In conjunction with Type 291 and Type 275 RADAR sets, they provided A band interrogation using the standard Mk III IFF system. When the interrogator pulse was fired by the transmitter, a secondary trace, displaced from the main trace, was displayed as an A scope presentation. Interrogator signals received by the responsor unit were displayed on this secondary trace as inverted signals, along with the normal RADAR echoes. Correspondence of the interrogator pulse and the RADAR echo identified the target. The associated shipborne transponder was the Type 253 or alternatively the Mk III IFF when fitted on an aircraft.

Type 242M interrogator equipment, utilized in conjunction with Type 277 and Type 293 RADAR sets, was also used aboard *Haida*. Type 242M is similar to Type 242, except for a few minor modifications, such as being selectable between low and high power outputs, a variable output frequency and the incorporation of a pre-amplifier. When the Type 242M operated in conjunction with the 276/277/293 RADAR types, it consisted of four broadband vertical dipoles with power rotation.

*Haida* was fitted with the Type 253P transponder during the mid 1940s, which was located on a short strut on the foremast. This was a shipborne transponder, compatible with the Mark III IFF system and operated in response to triggering pulses from any interrogator or RADAR set in the same frequency band. When triggered, it responded with various coded signals as required. To limit mutual interference, the antenna for 253P was located at least 12 feet or more from the nearest interrogator on a ship. Normally the power output was 10 watts, although a low power setting of 0.75 watts was also available as an anti-direction finding measure.

**References:**

Peter Hodges, *Tribal Class Destroyers* (Surrey: Almark Publishing Co. Ltd., 1971).

Willem Hackmann, *Seek & Strike: Sonar, Anti-Submarine Warfare and the Royal Navy, 1914-1954* (London: Her Majesty's Stationery Office, 1984).

Derek Howse, *Radar at Sea: The Royal Navy in World War 2* (Annapolis: Naval Institute Press, 1993).

Jerry Proc, *ASDIC, RADAR, and IFF Systems Aboard HMCS Haida* (19 June 2000, http://webhome.idirect.com/~jproc/sari/sarintro.html).

## II RADIO

By 1941, low powered, medium, and high frequency radios were widely fitted for voice communications within task groups and convoys. VHF voice radio was slowly being adopted, thanks to developments in the RAF. During the period 1943 to 1945, the most important advance in wireless communications was the tactical use of voice radio. This rapid increase of voice radio reduced the amount of communication passed by flag or light signals.

High frequency direction finding (HF/DF), also known by the sobriquet Huff Duff, was a relatively new development at the start of the war. By the end of 1942, HF/DF was an essential part of the equipment that vessels had to carry. It served essentially two purposes. The first was to act as a navigational aid by taking cross bearings on a series of shore-based Huff Duff stations. The second was to intercept German radio transmissions and from these establish the position of U-boats, etc. On *Haida*, the Huff Duff cabin was mounted aft, and the ship had to carry three additional Wireless Telegraphy (W/T) operators from the Huff Duff branch.

Of interest was the function known as Headache, which applied to the shipborne sections of Y Intelligence who were charged with the interception and reading of German low-grade radiotelephone traffic. Headache operators came from a special branch of the RN and were fluent in German. On *Haida*, the action station for the Headache operator was a small office just below and aft of the bridge, with communication with the bridge transmitted through a voice pipe. *Haida*'s Headache receiver was the Hallicrafters S27, whose frequency coverage was 27 Mcs to 143 Mcs, and was removed in 1949.

During the Second World War, confidential documents and reference materials were filed in a black box in the coding and decoding area of the main wireless office by the POTEL (petty officer telegraphist). The POTEL reported to the signal officer and was briefed regarding the level of secrecy prior to each operation. Telegraphists were given information only on a need-to-know basis—information such as the names of ships, radio call signs, and frequencies.

*Haida*'s Radio Equipment (1944 or 1945)

| Qty | Functional Designation | Original Equipment | Description |
| --- | --- | --- | --- |
| 1 | Loran | DAS | Loran A position-finding receiver |
| 1 | MF/DF | FM12 | MF/DF receiver; 42 to 1060 kc |
| 1 | HF/DF | FH4 | HF/DF receiver; 1 to 24 Mc |
| 1 | HF/DF | B28 | HF/DF Receiver; 60 to 420 kc; 0.5 to 30 Mc |
| 1 | W/T Tx | TV5 | Transmitter; CW/MCW/RT |
| 1 | W/T Tx | TBL12 | Transmitter; 175 to 600 kc; 2 to 18 Mc |
| 1 | W/T Tx | 4T | Transmitter; 100 to 17,000 kc; freq multiplication unit |
| 1 | W/T Tx | 60FR | Transmitter; 100 to 17,000 kc; CW/MCW/RT |
| 1 | W/T Tx | 60EM | Transmitter; 100 to 17,000 kc; CW/MCW/RT |
| 2 | W/T Tx/Rx | 53 | Battery Rx/Tx; 3 to 6 Mc |
| 1 | W/T Tx/Rx | TBS | Transmitter/Receiver; 60 to 80 Mc; 50 watts |
| 1 | W/T Tx/Rx | 86M | Transmitter/Receiver; 100 to 156 Mc; 9 watts |
| 1 | W/T Rx | B29 | Receiver; 15 to 550 kc |
| 7 | W/T Rx | B28 | Receiver; 60 to 420 kc; 0.5 to 30 Mc |
| 2 | W/T Rx | B19 | Receiver; 40 to 13,500 kc |

## Radio Rooms

Radio Room One (formerly the Main Wireless Office) was fitted-on-build in 1943, and was subsequently modified in 1950, 1957, and 1962. It was located on the upper deck, off the port passageway, aft of the bell room. Among the equipment located here in 1943 were the FM12 MF/DF receiver, the 7 B28 receivers, the Admiralty-pattern wavemeter, the TBL12 transmitter, the 4T transmitter, and the TV5 transmitter. As well, the coding and decoding area was located in this office. It was always the main receiving and transmitting office for the ship for any long distance communications. Modernization of this room provided *Haida* with reception and transmission capabilities in the high frequency (HF), very high frequency (VHF), and ultra high frequency (UHF) radio bands. Also located here was a CM11, the Navy's workhorse transmitter/receiver in the two decades following the Second World War.

This office contained the four operating positions, each being equipped with a Marconi CSR5 receiver and a typewriter. Operators copied the Morse code broadcast sent to all ships by Halifax Radio at speeds up to 25 words per minute and the messages were logged on Royal Telegraphic typewriters. From 1943 to 1946, *Haida*'s radio call sign was CGDK, and for voice traffic, Idiot. From 1946 to 1963, it was CGJD and King Cobra.

In its modernized configuration, Radio Room One had sound powered telephone connections with Radio Room Four, the OPS room, and the bridge. A normal crew complement would be five radio operators and a clerk. The staff could consist of the following: a Petty Officer 1st Class Radioman (P1RM), a Petty Officer 2nd Class Dayman (P2), a Leading Seaman Radioman (LSRM), an Able Seaman Radioman (ABRM), and an Ordinary Seaman (Watchkeepers 3 OS).

The Message Centre, part of Radio Room One, was installed in February 1957, modified in 1962, and had a crew complement of one. This was the main focal point for the processing, distribution, and filing of all messages that were sent to or from the ship by radio, flashing lights, flags, and (in harbour) messenger. It had telephone connections with Radio Rooms Two and Three.

The Coding Office was also part of Radio Room One, and was installed in 1950. It was manned as required, and its purpose was to code and decode messages using a KL7 off-line crypto machine. There were two such units in the coding office, with one usually set up with the previous day's "keys" in case there were any late-arriving messages. The crypto office was always locked unless someone was working there.

Tribals also had a second wireless office on build. In this room was the emergency transmitter, the codebook safe, a gyro repeater and DF unit, and two receivers (the first used with a speaker and the second used with headphones). Originally, this fifty-square-foot office was located on the port side, aft. During the September/December 1944 refit, it was moved to a position inside the "new" mast. The room was fitted with only one chair, so it can be assumed that there was only one operator per watch. In 1950, Radio Room Two was modernized and the crew complement grew by one operator. It had telephone connections with the Message Centre and Radio Room Three. It was the main transmitting room for high frequency radioteletype and CW transmissions, all under remote control from Radio Room One. This was also a backup in case Radio Room One was ever put out of action, and it also provided additional radio circuits when Radio Room One was overloaded. As well, the Marconi PV500 transmitter was located here.

Radio Room Three was installed in 1950, and was located on the port side, on the flag deck, below the lattice mast. It was purely an equipment room and provided four additional UHF voice circuits. The station was normally unmanned and remotely controlled unless frequencies had to be changed and equipment tuned up. However, it

could be locally controlled under emergency conditions. It had telephone connections to Radio Room Two and the Message Centre.

Radio Room Four was installed prior to 1956 and was located on the starboard side below the lattice mast. Its crew complement was two, both of whom (and anyone else in this room) had to be cleared for top security. This was an electronic warfare room. It was capable of providing direction-finding services in the MF radio bands, plus the interception of RADAR transmissions in the SHF bands. Whenever NATO ships were on exercises, they would be shadowed by Russian intelligence gathering ships. When the Russians radioed home their coded reports, these signals were intercepted by Radio Room Four using a Hammarlund SP600 general coverage receiver. Simultaneously, the transmissions were recorded on a reel-to-reel recorder and sent to Ottawa for analysis. Depending on the type of ship, the room was also known as the Electronic Warfare Room (EW), Electronic Warfare Control Room (EWCR), EW Shack, or EW Hut.

When *Haida* was paid off in 1963, she had the radio capabilities that are shown below. Due to the fast-paced developments in technology, some of these modes or functions are obsolete in today's navy:

### UHF AM Voice (200 to 400 MHz):

NATO requirements of the day stipulated that ships participating in exercises must have seven UHF voice channels or circuits. Each circuit consists of a URR35 receiver, a URT502 (TED3) AM transmitter and a Channel Amplifier Unit. Three circuits were fitted in Radio Room One and four circuits in Radio Room Three. AM voice was replaced with FM voice in this band.

### VHF:

Radio Room One housed a four-channel, 45-watt Model TDQ transmitter and its companion receiver, the RCK. These gave *Haida* the ability to guard the 121.5 MHz VHF aeronautical distress channel and to communicate with aircraft. In today's world that functionality is replaced with a small hand-held radio. Properly "crystallized," this vintage equipment could still be used to communicate with aircraft.

### RADIOTELETYPE (RATT):

*Haida*'s radioteletype system was completely modernized in 1962 and was consistent with the rest of the fleet. Encrypted broadcast was turned into plain text by the KWR-37 on-line crypto receiver. Model 28 teletypes, the TD14 transmitter/distributor, and the Model 14 reperforator were used to originate or receive radioteletype messages. Signals were received with the RAK (LF) or CSR5 (HF) receivers and modulated/demodulated by the AN/SGC1A terminal unit or the FSC107 frequency shift converter. The RATT transmitter, namely the Marconi PV500, was located in Radio Room Two and was remotely controlled from Radio Room One. The RATT system has only lim-

ited capability today because the only source of signals originates on the amateur radio bands, and they are few and far between.

### HIGH FREQUENCY (HF):

There were four operating positions in Radio Room One which were used to receive the CW broadcast at 25 wpm. The Communicators also had control over three HF transmitting circuits using the Marconi CM11 transmitter/receiver. One circuit was fitted in Radio Room One. The other two were in Radio Room Two, under remote control.

### DIRECTION FINDING:

The Marconi FM12 MF/DF direction finder was moved to Radio Room Four in 1962. From here, *Haida* had the ability to detect radar emissions from various sources on the super high frequency (SHF) radar bands using the UPD501 receiver. Because *Haida*'s fitting was an early version of the system, it only had X band capability. This system is now obsolete.

**References:**

Jerry Proc, *Radio Systems Aboard HMCS Haida*, 3rd ed. (18 July 2000, http://webhome.idirect.com/~jproc/rrp/toc.html).

William Schleihauf, "The Last of Her Tribe: HMCS *Haida*," *Warship International*, No. 4, 1996, pp. 344-77.

# APPENDIX 3

## COMMANDING OFFICERS, HMCS *HAIDA*, 1943–1963

30 August 1943–18 December 1944
 Commander H.G. DeWolf, CBE, DSO, DSC, RCN

19 December 1944–2 September 1945
 Lieutenant-Commander R.P. Welland, DSC, RCN

3 March 1947–11 December 1947
 Lieutenant-Commander F.B. Caldwell, RCN

12 December 1947–15 May 1949
 Lieutenant-Commander A.F. Pickard, OBE, RCN

16 May 1949–12 January 1950
 Lieutenant-Commander E.T.G. Madgwick, RCN

13 January 1950–31 December 1951
 Commander R.A. Webber, DSC, RCN

1 January 1952–28 October 1953
 Commander Dunn Lantier, RCN

29 October 1953–15 December 1954
 Captain J.A. Charles, CD, RCN

16 December 1954–10 July 1956
 Commander Victor Browne, CD, RCN

11 July 1956–6 April 1958
 Commander H.R. Beck, CD, RCN

7 April 1958–2 September 1960
 Commander John Husher, CD, RCN

3 September 1960–2 August 1961
 Commander G.S. Clark, CD, RCN

3 August 1961–19 July 1962
 Commander D.C. Rutherford, CD, RCN

20 July 1962–22 September 1963
 Commander W.H. Atkinson, DSC, CD, RCN

23 September 1963–11 October 1963
 Lieutenant-Commander D.K. Gamblin, CD, RCN

# APPENDIX 4

## TRIBAL CLASS DESTROYERS MASTER LIST

| | |
|---|---|
| Displacement: | 1,870 tons, except RAN and RCN vessels 1,927 tons (approx. 3,000 tons loaded) |
| Dimensions: | 355½ (pp) 377½ (oa) x 36½ x 9 ft. |
| Machinery: | Two-shaft geared turbines, S.H.P. 44,000–36 knots |
| Armament: | RN vessels eight 4.7-inch (4x2), four 2-pdr A.A. (1x4) 8.5-inch AA (2x4 guns; four 21-inch (1x4), TT, RAN and RCN vessels, six 4.7-inch (3x2), two 4-inch AA (1x2), four 2-pdr AA (1x4), eight .5-inch AA (2x4) except *eight 4-inch AA (4x2), four 40-mm AA (1x2 & 2x1), four 20-mm AA (2x2) guns, four 21-inch (1x4) TT. |
| Complement: | 190 (219 in *Afridi, Cossack, Somali* and *Tartar*) except RAN vessels, 250; and RCN vessels, 240/250. |

| Service | No. | Name | Builder | Built | Fate |
|---|---|---|---|---|---|
| Royal Navy | F07 | *Afridi* | V-A (Tyne) V-A (Barrow) | 8.6.37 | Lost 3.5.40 |
| | F03 | *Cossack* | V-A (Tyne) V-A (Barrow) | 8.6.37 | Lost 27.10.41 |
| | F20 | *Gurkha* | Fairfield | 7.7.37 | Lost 9.4.40 |
| | F24 | *Maori* | Fairfield | 2.9.37 | Lost 12.2.42 |
| | F31 | *Mohawk* | Thornycroft | 5.10.37 | Lost 16.4.41 |
| | F36 | *Nubian* | Thornycroft | 12.12.37 | Scrapped Briton Ferry, S. Wales 25.6.49 |
| | F18 | *Zulu* | Stephen | 23.9.37 | Lost 14.9.42 |
| | F51 | *Ashanti* | Denny | 5.11.37 | Scrapped Troon, Scotland 12.4.49 |
| | F67 | *Bedouin* | Denny | 21.12.37 | Lost 15.6.42 |
| | F75 | *Eskimo* | V-A (Tyne) Parsons | 3.9.37 | Scrapped Troon, Scotland 27.6.49 |
| | F59 | *Mashona* | V-A (Tyne) Parsons | 3.9.37 | Lost 28.5.41 |
| | F26 | *Matabele* | Scotts | 6.10.37 | Lost 17.1.42 |
| | F21 | *Punjabi* | Scotts | 18.12.37 | Lost 1.5.42 |

|  |  |  |  |  |  |
|---|---|---|---|---|---|
|  | F82 | *Sikh* | Stephen | 17.12.37 | Lost 1.5.42 |
|  | F33 | *Somali* | Swan Hunter: Wallsend | 24.8.37 | Lost 24.9.42 |
|  | F43 | *Tartar* | Swan Hunter: Wallsend | 21.10.37 | Scrapped Newport, Wales 22.2.48 |
| Royal Australian Navy | I30 | *Arunta* | Cockatoo | 30.11.40 | Scrapped |
|  | I91 | *Bataan* (ex-*Kurnai*) | Cockatoo | 15.1.44 | Scrapped |
|  | I44 | *Warramunga* | Cockatoo | 6.2.42 | Scrapped |
| Royal Canadian Navy | G07 | *Athabaskan I* (ex-*Iroquois*) | V-A (Tyne) Parsons | 18.11.41 | Lost 29.4.44 |
|  | G63 | *Haida* | V-A (Tyne) Parsons | 25.8.42 | Disposed-Navy Memorial-1964 |
|  | G24 | *Huron* | V-A (Tyne) Parsons | 25.6.42 | Scrapped |
|  | G89 | *Iroquois* (ex-*Athabaskan*) | V-A (Tyne) Parsons | 23.9.41 | Scrapped |
|  | R04 | *Cayuga* | Halifax | 28.7.45 | Scrapped |
|  | R10 | *Micmac* | Halifax | 18.9.43 | Scrapped |
|  | R96 | *Nootka* | Halifax | 16.4.44 | Scrapped |
|  | R79 | *Athabaskan II* | Halifax | 4.5.46 | Scrapped |

Note: V-A denotes Vickers-Armstrong

## TRIBAL CLASS DESTROYERS: *HAIDA'S* SISTERS

### HMS *Afridi*

After her acceptance trials, *Afridi* sailed from Portland, England, on 27 May 1938 to join the Mediterranean Fleet at Malta. When war broke out, she was ordered to Alexandria in preparation for convoy duty. However, Italy's neutrality meant that convoy escorts were not required in the Mediterranean, and *Afridi* was ordered to return to England with the rest of the 4th Destroyer Flotilla. From April 1940 onwards, she participated in numerous actions off the Norwegian coast. On 2 May 1940 at 08:00, while escorting a convoy off the Norwegian coast, she and the other ships around her were attacked by German Ju87 and Ju88 bombers. The French destroyer *Bison* was hit and her forward magazine exploded. *Afridi* joined *Grenade* (France) in rescuing survivors and in fighting off two more air attacks. Another Ju87 dive bombing attack developed at 14:00. Since *Afridi* was the common target for two aircraft coming in from each side, evasive maneuvers were not possible. One bomb hit her No. 1 Boiler Room, starting a severe fire at the after end of the messdecks. Another bomb hit the port side just forward of the bridge. *Imperial* came alongside and *Griffin* stood by to carry out rescue work. At 14:45, *Afridi* went down bow-first. She took with her forty-nine officers and men, thirteen soldiers, and over thirty *Bison* survivors. It was the second anniversary of her commissioning.

### HMAS *Arunta*

The newly completed *Arunta* arrived in Port Moresby on 24 August 1942. Her duty was to protect merchantmen from Japanese submarines. On 24 August, she carried out four depth-charge attacks on the 700-ton Japanese submarine *RO-33*. In the first month of 1943, she carried out a hazardous mission to the Japanese-held island of Timor, where she picked up a guerilla force that had failed to push back the Japanese invaders. After returning to Sydney at the end of the month, she underwent a much-needed refit. After returning to escort duties in March, she joined Task Force 74 in May 1943. As part of this force, *Arunta* covered US landings at Saidor, New Guinea, between 8 January and 7 February 1944. On New Year's Day 1945, *Arunta*, accompanied by her sister ship *Warramunga*, left Manus bound for the Philippines as part of the Lingayen Gulf assault force. Kamikaze attacks developed as they passed through the Sulu Sea. At 04:50 on 5 January, two kamikazes attacked *Arunta*. One kamikaze, a Zero, aimed straight at the bridge. *Arunta* turned hard to starboard and the Zero skimmed the port side of the bridge and hit the sea alongside the gear room. The explosion sent shrapnel through the *Arunta* and severed her steering cables. She continued to steer in circles until the end of the attacks, when she lay dead in the water for five hours while the damage was repaired. Two men were killed and five wounded. After further operations in the Philippines, *Arunta* participated in attacks on Japanese positions in New Guinea and Borneo. After the war, she continued in the Royal Australian Navy. She underwent modernization as an anti-submarine destroyer from 1950 to 1953 and, hence, missed the Korean War. She was laid up in 1957 and sank while being towed to Taiwan in 1969.

## HMS *Ashanti*

*Ashanti* was the only Tribal class destroyer to actually visit the tribe for which she was named, arriving in Ghana on 27 February 1939. At the outbreak of war, she was attached to the 6th Destroyer Flotilla, and spent the last months of 1939 on anti-submarine patrols and the occasional stint on escort duty. She participated, as part of the Home Fleet, in the Norwegian campaign, surviving a near miss from a German bomber while exploring a fjord. During the summer months she continued anti-submarine patrols and escort duty. In October 1941, *Ashanti* and five other destroyers were ordered to perform a high-speed run through the channel leading to the Tyne in preparation for the transit of the new battleship *King George V* from the Vickers-Armstrong yard to Scapa Flow. In a drizzle, HMS *Fame* ran straight onto the beach at the Whitburn Rifle Range, and *Ashanti*, too, ran aground. She suffered serious damage, and it was not until August 1941 that she was recommissioned. After participating in a raid on the Loften Islands in December 1941, she spent January and February 1942 escorting Murmansk convoys. In August, she and other Tribals escorted a large convoy to Malta before returning to Arctic waters. She was part of Force H for the Torch landings in November 1942, after which she spent several months on North African patrols and in drydock for repairs. Beginning in 1944, *Ashanti* participated in patrols in the English Channel in preparation for D-Day, and worked closely with the Canadian Tribals, especially *Haida*. On 16 September 1944 she arrived at Palmer's Jarrow Yard for a major refit. However, once the refit was completed, it was discovered that she still needed more work. This time she was passed over and put into reserve. In 1948 she was used in damage control tests, and was broken up in 1949.

## HMCS *Athabaskan*

The first two Canadian Tribal class destroyers were laid down as *Iroquois* and *Athabaskan* but *Iroquois* was delayed by bombing while on the stocks. *Athabaskan* was therefore renamed *Iroquois* and launched as the lead ship, while the original *Iroquois* was launched as *Athabaskan*. After her commissioning on 3 February 1943 at Newcastle-on-Tyne, she was assigned to the British Home Fleet but *Athabaskan* was plagued with mishaps during her short service life. The ship left on 29 March 1943 to patrol the Iceland-Faeroes Passage, there to search for blockade runners. Weather induced stress caused hull damage, which took five weeks to repair at South Shields. In June 1943, *Athabaskan* took part in Operation Gearbox III, the relief of the garrison at Spitzbergen. On 18 June, she collided with the boom defence vessel *Bargate* at Scapa Flow, resulting in a month of repairs at Devonport. In July and August 1943, she was based in Plymouth, carrying out anti-submarine patrols in the Bay of Biscay, and on 27 August was hit by a glider bomb off the Spanish coast. She managed to reach Devonport where she remained under repair until 10 November. Returning to Scapa Flow in December, she escorted convoy JW-55A to Russia and in February 1944 she rejoined Plymouth command and was assigned to the newly formed 10th Destroyer Flotilla. On 26 April, she assisted in the destruction of the German torpedo boat *T29* in the Channel off Ushant. Three days later on 29 April, was sunk by a torpedo from *T24*, an Elbing class destroyer, north of the Île de Batz. Her commanding officer, John Stubbs, and one hundred and twenty-eight men were lost, eighty-three taken prisoner and forty-four rescued by *Haida*.

## HMCS *Athabaskan II*

The last of her class to be completed was commissioned at Halifax on 20 January 1948. After the main part of her crew arrived from British Columbia, sea trials were completed and the *Athabaskan* sailed to her appointed station on the West Coast on 15 May 1948. There, she spent the first part of her service career with *Cayuga* and other RCN ships, showing the flag along the Pacific shores of Canada and the US. On 15 September 1949, *Athabaskan* began a comprehensive refit. In the process, two triple-barrelled Squid mortars were fitted in place of Y mounting. The Asdic Control Room and the Operations Room were enlarged, and electronic gear was installed to link the Squid directly to the submarine detection instruments. The two depth-charge throwers were removed but the depth-charge chute was retained. Her complement was now at two hundred seventy-eight men, and it was intended that *Athabaskan* should concentrate on training personnel in the use of equipment, while the other ships on the west coast got on with their more complex exercises. She sailed from Esquimalt on 5 July 1950 for the first of three tours of duty in Korean waters, finally returning on 11 December 1953. For *Athabaskan* and *Cayuga*, the years between 1955 and 1959 meant pilotage and amphibious exercises in the narrow inlets of British Columbia, air defence, gunnery and anti-submarine exercises off California and Pearl Harbor, goodwill visits, reviews, regattas, refits and sea trials. When this training was completed in January 1959, she left for Halifax to become part of a homogeneous Tribal class squadron. In October 1962, she was in European waters once again, only this time it was to hold a memorial service over the resting place of her namesake, the first *Athabaskan*. After five years of training cruises and NATO exercises she was placed in reserve at Halifax and on 21 April 1966, paid off for disposal. In July 1969 *Athabaskan* was towed to La Spezia, Italy, to be broken up.

## HMAS *Bataan*

*Bataan* was the only Tribal class destroyer *not* to be named after a people or nation in the British Empire. She received her name as a gesture to the US, who had named one of their cruisers USS *Canberra*. She was commissioned on 25 May 1945. Her first task was to join Task Force 74 in Subic Bay, Philippines. She was preparing for the final assault on Japan when the war ended. She was part of the naval task force that was present in Tokyo at the official Japanese surrender on 2 September 1945. Afterwards she participated in rescues of POWs and internees. When the Korean War began, the Australian government placed *Bataan* at the disposal of the UN, and by 5 July 1950 she was operating in the Yellow Sea. For most of the time, she was employed in routine escort and anti-submarine duties. She underwent a refit in 1951, but was back in Korean waters by early 1952. During one operation, a 76-mm shell hit the captain's cabin. Fortunately there were no casualties. In May of 1952, she provided bombardment support for landings by ROK forces. By July, she joined *Warramunga* and HMCS *Nootka* and *Iroquois* in providing carrier screens in the Yellow Sea. In 1954, she was laid up in reserve in preparation for conversion to an anti-submarine escort. However, the conversion was cancelled in 1957, and by the end of 1958 she was sold for scrap.

## HMS *Bedouin*

On 7 April 1940, *Bedouin* left Scapa Flow destined for Norway as part of the Home Fleet destroyer force, and fought in the Second Battle of Narvik. She spent the summer of 1940 standing by to prevent a possible German invasion of the UK. She underwent a refit in October 1940, and when completed she rejoined the 6th Destroyer Flotilla at Scapa Flow. The flotilla spent the winter of 1940/41 escorting capital ships and participated in a commando raid on Norway in March 1941. Following another refit, she rejoined the Home Fleet in September 1941, and participated in the Loften Islands raid in December 1941. After a refit in May 1942, she was assigned to the Mediterranean, where she was to escort an eastbound convoy from Gibraltar to Malta. On 15 June, the convoy was met by units of the Italian Navy off the Algerian coast. In the ensuing battle, *Bedouin*'s superstructure was severely damaged. The ship was burning and stopped in the water. Dense smoke screens laid by the British prevented the Italians from any further assaults. In all, she had been hit twelve times by 6-inch shells, although not all of them had exploded. Splinters from one shell perforated the gear casing and started a fire in the Gear Room. The main and steering engines were dead and there was no electricity. HMS *Partridge* took the Tribal in tow and she was ordered to rejoin the convoy. However, two Italian cruisers soon appeared, and *Bedouin* slipped the towline and laid smoke. At the same time, she was attacked by an Italian torpedo bomber. While the aircraft was shot down, her torpedo hit *Bedouin*'s engine room, blasting a hole clear through the ship. She quickly rolled over to port and sank with twenty-eight men. Two hundred and thirteen survivors, plus the torpedo bomber pilot, were rescued by an Italian hospital ship.

## HMCS *Cayuga*

Although *Cayuga* was built on the east coast of Canada, she was intended for service on the Pacific coast. A skeleton crew carried out her acceptance trials, followed by commissioning at Halifax on 20 October 1947. After being fitted with fire control equipment, a full crew complement arrived from British Columbia, and she set sail for Esquimalt on 4 February 1948. This was to include a lengthy call in Bermuda. Along the way, many steam leaks and other defects developed, the most serious being the complete breakdown of the port, low-pressure turbine. Most of the passage to Esquimalt was on one engine at a maximum speed of 8 knots. On her arrival, she assisted with the Fraser Valley floods, then accompanied *Athabaskan* in a series of exercises. Following this, she was preparing for a tour of European waters, which was cancelled when hostilities broke out in Korea. *Cayuga* left Esquimalt on 5 July 1950, as Senior Officer's ship of the first three Canadian destroyers to serve in Korean waters. She carried out three tours of duty there, the last in 1954 after the armistice. In 1952, between the second and third tours, she was rebuilt as a destroyer escort. On 5 March 1953 as she was docking an order was misinterpreted, and *Cayuga*'s engines went half ahead instead of half astern and drove her bows twenty-five feet into the jetty. She was only slightly damaged, but a few days later the engines failed altogether when berthing and a collision was barely avoided. It is recorded that "henceforth the ship's return from sea invariably drew an interested audience." The above incidents sent her to drydock in order to repair the low pressure turbines. Four years after her return from Korea in mid-December 1954, *Cayuga* carried out training on the west coast, transferring to the east coast in January 1959 for five more years in the same capacity. During her service life, *Cayuga* had three fires aboard. On the morning of 9 September, while at anchor in Nanoose Harbour, BC, a fire broke out in No. 1 Boiler Room. Two men received burns and were landed at the Nanaimo General Hospital for immediate attention. They were subsequently moved to Royal Canadian Naval Hospital, Esquimalt. A Board of Inquiry was convened on arrival in Esquimalt. On 16 September, she sailed with no limitations from fire damage noted. During the evening of 14 March 1961, there was a fire in the Ops Room. The other was a fire in the No. 1 Boiler Room on 2 July 1959, while the ship was on passage from Montreal to Halifax after the St. Lawrence Seaway opening ceremonies. This was dealt with quickly and the record clearly states that no one was burned or injured. Paid off at Halifax on 27 February 1964, she was broken up at Faslane, Scotland, the following year.

## HMS *Cossack*

*Cossack* spent the last year before the Second World War in the Mediterranean, visiting Istanbul with *Afridi,* and conducted exercises with other Tribal class destroyers as the leader of the 8th Division. Once war began, she was engaged in convoy duties until a collision on the night of 7/8 November 1939, which killed four men, caused her to be sent back to England for repairs. When she was ready in January 1940, Captain Philip Vian assumed command as his ship, *Afridi*, was in for repairs. *Cossack* was now leader of the 4th Destroyer Flotilla. In February, she led the raid on the German supply ship *Altmark*, which was carrying British sailors captured from the *Atlantis*. She was located in Norwegian territorial waters, but *Cossack* seized *Altmark* after fruitless negotiations with Norwegian authorities. This action elevated *Cossack* to fame. After this incident Vian returned to *Afridi*, and *Cossack* fought in the Second Battle of Narvik, where she sustained damage. Her repairs were completed on 15 June, Vian reassumed command, and she became the

leader of 4th Destroyer Flotilla from then on. She prepared for a possible German invasion, and engaged a German convoy bound for Norway in October. She participated in the hunt for the *Bismarck*, and subsequently was sent to Plymouth to battle German destroyers and E-boats. On 14 July, she arrived in Gibraltar to take part in Operation Substance, which was the reinforcement of Malta's garrison. In October 1941, she left Gibraltar escorting a slow, UK-bound convoy. On the night of the 23rd, she was hit by a torpedo from *U563* which struck forward of the bridge and killed Captain Berthon and one hundred and fifty-eight of his officers and men. Ammunition had exploded, and No. 1 Boiler Room was flooded. The survivors abandoned ship, but the fire extinguished itself and the ship remained afloat. The survivors returned to the ship and managed to get the engines to run astern. However, it was too far to Gibraltar, and in worsening weather the crew abandoned *Cossack* once again. She sank the next day.

## HMS *Eskimo*

At the outbreak of war, *Eskimo* was in refit due to problems with her turbines. Soon thereafter, she returned to Scapa Flow and shot down one German aircraft when the *Luftwaffe* attacked on 17 October 1939. That winter consisted of convoy and escort duty. During the Second Battle of Narvik, she sustained torpedo damage to her bow, and after receiving temporary repairs in Norway, she sailed for the Vickers-Armstrong yard at Newcastle-on-Tyne for a rebuild. When she was ready again in September, she rejoined the 6th Destroyer Flotilla, and spent the next few months escorting capital ships of the Home Fleet. In March 1942, she helped screen convoys PQ8 and PQ 12, and participated in an abortive sweep in search of the *Tirpitz*. She took part in the Pedestal convoy to Malta, and under Captain Eaton, *Eskimo* became the leader of the Force H destroyer screen for the Torch landings. She participated in Operation Retribution, the effort to sink Axis vessels passing through the Sicilian Narrows, and during Operation Husky, she was struck by a German dive bomber, which necessitated her return to England for repairs. In May 1944, she was assigned to the 10th Destroyer Flotilla at Plymouth, and participated in anti-shipping sweeps and escorting minelayers. With HMCS *Haida*, she sank *U971* on 24 June 1944. In the winter of 1944, *Eskimo* was sent to join the Australian Tribals in the Far East. After participating in operations south of Burma, she was sent to Durban, South Africa, for a refit—just as the Japanese surrendered. Her final days were spent as a headquarters and accommodation ship for minesweepers and salvage craft in the Thames and Medway Estuaries. She was sold for scrap on 27 June 1949.

### HMS *Gurkha* (originally spelled *Ghurka*)

*Gurkha*'s first assignment was to the 1st Subdivision of the 1st Destroyer Flotilla at Malta in December 1938. After escorting French troop convoys, she was transferred to the Atlantic and escorted convoys in the North Sea, followed by escort duty with the Home Fleet. On 21 February 1940, she and the French destroyer *Le Fantasque* depth-charged and sank the 753-ton submarine *U53*. While escorting a convoy on 9 March, her propellor gashed a hole in HMS *Kelly*'s bow when the two ships momentarily connected. *Gurkha* participated in the very first moves of the Norwegian campaign, sailing with a force of cruisers and destroyers from Rosyth, Scotland, on 7/8 April 1940. At 14:00 on 9 April, the force was attacked by Ju88 and He111 bombers. One bomb struck *Gurkha* aft and blew a 40-foot hole in her starboard side. The stern caught fire and the aft magazine had to be flooded. Soon the stern was awash and she had a 45-degree list to starboard.

The usable guns were fired to attract anyone's attention, and HMS *Aurora* came within 200 yards and lowered her boats. She managed to pick up a hundred and ninety survivors. At 19:00 *Gurkha* rolled over and sank. She was the first Tribal to be sunk and the first British destroyer to be sunk by an aerial attack.

### HMCS *Huron*

Commissioned on 19 July 1943, at Newcastle-on-Tyne, *Huron* was assigned, as was *Haida*, to the 3rd Destroyer Flotilla of the British Home Fleet. As part of Operation Holder, she sailed in October 1943 to Murmansk with technical personnel and special naval stores. For the rest of the year, *Huron* escorted convoys to and from North Russia. In February 1944, after one more trip to Murmansk, she joined the 10th Flotilla at Plymouth for pre-invasion duties, spending the next seven months in the Channel and the Bay of Biscay. On 25/26 April 1944, *Huron*—along with *Haida*, *Athabaskan*, and *Ashanti*—was involved in a scrap with German Elbing class destroyers in the English Channel. After the action, she and *Ashanti* collided, damaging *Huron*'s port hull and the main bulkhead between No. 1 and No. 2 Boiler Rooms. The port cutter and its davits were smashed, the guard rails and stanchions bent inwards, and the torpedo-davit damaged. *Huron* managed to return safely to Plymouth and repairs were completed on 7 May, just in time for D-Day operations. *Huron* arrived in Nova Scotia for a refit on 13 August 1944. It was completed and her sea trials were over by 20 November. She called at the Azores and then arrived at Cardiff for new radar and target indication equipment. Sea trials of this gear were completed on 20 January 1945, but *Huron* still had to finish her work-ups at Scapa Flow. During February and March she was assigned to escort duties in the Western Approaches. In April, *Huron*, *Haida* and *Iroquois* escorted their last convoy to Russia. After sharing in the liberation of Norway, all three returned to Halifax in preparation for service in the Pacific. Their refits were suspended in August and *Huron* was placed in reserve. She was paid off on 9 March 1946. *Huron* was recommissioned at Halifax for training purposes in 1950, but sailed on 22 January 1951 on the first of two tours of duty in Korean waters. The second was carried out in 1953/54. On that January day, it was so cold in Halifax that *Huron*'s siren and the band instruments froze up and had to be thawed before any sound would come out. Like so many other destroyers, *Huron*'s first Korean mission was to screen carriers on the west coast. On her return from Korea, she reverted to her peacetime role until she was finally paid off on 30 April 1963 at Halifax. *Huron* was broken up at La Spezia, Italy, in 1965.

### HMCS *Iroquois*

*Iroquois* was the first of the Tribals to commission and was assigned to the 3rd Flotilla, Home Fleet. *Iroquois* returned from her first patrol off the Faeroes with broken plating, twisted frames and a bent keel. The ship was dispatched to her builder, Vickers-Armstrong, in order to have this damage repaired and by 30 January 1943, she was considered operational. She was assigned to northern waters in the Western Approaches and the constant onslaught of the weather strained the crew. By mid year, she was eastward bound in order to join the Home Fleet and operate from Plymouth. One of the ship's notable achievements occurred in July 1943. Three troopships being escorted by *Iroquois* to Freetown were attacked by German aircraft three hundred miles off Vigo, Spain. Two ships were sunk but *Iroquois* rescued six hundred and twenty-eight survivors from the *Duchess of York*. In February 1944, she arrived in Halifax for a refit, then joined the 10th Destroyer Flotilla in Plymouth in preparation for the Normandy inva-

sion. After D-Day, she carried out patrols in the English Channel and the Bay of Biscay, and provided escort service for capital ships and troopships in United Kingdom waters. Throughout the winter of 1944/45, she remained on escort duty with capital ships and troopships in British coastal waters. On 16 March 1945, *Iroquois* left Plymouth to rejoin the Home Fleet at Scapa Flow and for the rest of the month joined *Haida* in screening carrier strikes on Norwegian targets and escorting convoys bound for Russia. When the war ended, *Iroquois* celebrated V-E day at Scapa Flow with *Haida* and *Huron* and then shared in the liberation of Norway. From Copenhagen, *Iroquois* escorted the German cruisers *Prinz Eugen* and *Nürnberg* to Kiel for their formal surrender. Following that, *Iroquois* returned to Halifax in order to prepare for the Pacific, but with war's end imminent, her refit for the tropics was suspended and she went into reserve on 22 February 1946. Toward the end of 1947, a refit was begun, and was completed by June 1949. The ship's conversion to an escort destroyer was started in June 1950 and completed by October 1951. The work consisted of the installation of two triple-barreled squid mortars, 4-inch forward guns and a 3/50 aft gun. These alterations raised her displacement to 2200 tons and she received her new pennant, DDE 217. After work-ups were completed at Norfolk, Virginia, *Iroquois* returned to Halifax for a pre-Korea refit on 15 March 1952. When the loading of ammunition and stores was completed, *Iroquois* left Halifax on 21 April and arrived in Sasebo, Japan (via the Panama Canal) on 12 June. This was the first of two tours of duty for the ship. While in Korea, her main duties were to provide screening for aircraft carriers, attack coastal defence batteries and destroy trains. *Iroquois* was the only Canadian destroyer to sustain casualties in Korea. During an exchange of fire with a shore-based North Korean artillery battery near Songjin, she sustained damage to B mounting on 2 October

1952. The resultant explosion killed three of her crew, severely injured two and left eight others lightly wounded from splinters. By 26 November 1952, her tour of duty was completed and she arrived back in Halifax on 8 January 1953. In June of that year, *Iroquois* returned to Sasebo, together with *Huron*. This time the primary mission was coastal patrol on Korea's west coast. When the Korean conflict ended on 27 July 1953, *Iroquois* remained to assist with evacuations. On New Year's Day 1954, she began her homeward voyage via the Mediterranean and she arrived in Halifax on 10 February. After a short refit and a visit to Newfoundland, *Iroquois* was dispatched to Korea again on 1 July for patrol duties and she returned home together with *Huron* on 19 March 1955. In her last years, she visited ports in the United States and Europe, escorted the Royal Yacht *Britannia* and participated in various NATO exercises. On 24 October 1962, *Iroquois* was paid off at Halifax and went into operational reserve. After being towed to Sydney, Nova Scotia, she was scheduled for disposal, and in 1966 was scrapped at Bilbao, Spain.

### HMS *Maori*

*Maori* was the last Tribal to go to war in the Mediterranean, spending the first month escorting convoys. In October 1939 she returned to England and performed convoy duty as well as patrols in the North Sea. After a refit in March 1940, she began the Norwegian campaign by screening the capital ships of the Home Fleet. She then escorted French troops to Namsos, Norway. Subsequently, during the evacuation of Namsos, *Maori* suffered two near-misses, with five men dying from splinters that struck the ship. After the Norwegian campaign, she participated in a search for German vessels near Iceland. An effort was made to seize four Italian-built warships that were being bought by Sweden, but was abandoned once it was realized that the four ships were essentially worthless.

After a refit in January 1941 and patrols in the Channel, *Maori* was sent to the eastern Mediterranean to join the 14th Destroyer Flotilla. She participated in the action that resulted in the sinking of the Italian cruisers *Alberico da Barbiano* and *Alberto di Guissano*. At the end of 1941, as Force K was weakened due to human torpedo attacks on HMS *Queen Elizabeth* and *Valiant*, HMS *Maori*, *Sikh*, and *Zulu* were ordered to a base at Malta as the 22nd Destroyer Flotilla, to assist in escorting convoys. Early in 1942 the *Luftwaffe* began a major air offensive against Malta. At 02:00 on 12 February 1942, *Maori* was attacked from the air, and a bomb found its way into her engine and gear room. She exploded and sank at her moorings. Since most personnel slept ashore while at Malta, only one man was killed. The wreck, still partially visible, was struck several more times during bombing raids. Finally, on 5 July 1945, she was scuttled in deep water far from the harbour.

### HMS *Mashona*

The first wartime operation for *Mashona* was the rescue of the crippled British submarine *Spearfish* in German waters in September 1939. After being one of the first destroyers on the scene after the German invasion of Norway, *Mashona* and three of her sister ships participated in the evacuation from Trondheim. Afterwards, she helped screen HMS *Ark Royal*, escorted troop convoys bound for Narvik, and then helped cover the withdrawal in June. She was drydocked in late June after receiving damage to her bottom plating due to severe weather. In the last months of 1940, she was engaged in convoy duty in the Western Approaches. She was damaged in January 1941 when she collided with *Sikh* while attempting to exit Scapa Flow. After repairs had been completed on 3 March, she resumed patrols in the North Atlantic. As part of the Home Fleet, she joined in the search for the *Bismarck*. During the pursuit,

*Mashona* ran low on fuel and was ordered back to base. On 27 May, she was located and bombed by German aircraft. One bomb struck her port side, abreast of the fore funnel. It penetrated No. 1 Boiler Room and blew a huge hole in the ship. *Mashona* listed farther and farther to port with every wave, and orders were given to abandon ship. *Tartar* picked up survivors; forty-six men were lost.

## HMS *Matabele*

*Matabele* arrived at Plymouth, England, on 26 January 1939, and after sea trials was assigned to the 2nd Tribal Destroyer Flotilla. She participated in the rescue of the British submarine *Spearfish* in September 1939. In April 1940, *Matabele* joined the Home Fleet destroyer screen in the North Sea as part of the Norwegian campaign. She ferried troops ashore at Namsos and screened transports at sea. In Norway, she ran ashore on the Fasken Shoal, necessitating several months of repairs. In the first months of 1941, she underwent a further refit at Barrow-in-Furness, and then needed more repairs when she ran aground when leaving Barrow. She finally rejoined the Home Fleet in August 1941, and shortly thereafter was assigned to escort convoys to Russia. On 8 January 1942, *Matabele* and *Somali* were ordered to join the escort for convoy PQ8. On 17 January, just off Kola Inlet *Matabele* was torpedoed, and she sank in two minutes. Many of the men who managed to abandon ship froze to death in the Arctic waters.

## HMCS *Micmac*

*Micmac* was the first Tribal built in Canada, but she was completed too late to see service in the Second World War. She was commissioned at Halifax on 18 September 1945, and by October she was in service. Alone of her class, she never fired a shot in anger, but spent her entire career as a training ship. It was suggested that *Micmac* spend part of 1946 visiting ports on the Pacific coast, but

since she was the only destroyer in commission on the east coast, it was decided to keep her there. Over her lifetime, the pattern of events were repeated over and over—training programs, exercises, visits, dockings and an occasional special assignment. On 16 July 1947, she collided in fog with the 10,000-ton freighter SS *Yarmouth County* off Halifax, suffering very extensive damage to her bows. While under repair, she was partially converted to a destroyer escort. The A and B mounts were removed. A triple-barrelled Squid mortar was mounted at A position and quadruple 40-mm guns at B position. *Micmac*'s keel had been damaged at the time of collision so the ship could not support heavy mountings in A and B positions. This was the reason she was never deployed to the Korean theatre. The keel damage was repaired when *Micmac* received the full DDE modernization. There were two twin 4-inch mountings aft and a further four single Bofors. All the work was completed in November 1949 and *Micmac* found her way into Caribbean waters. After completing duties there, she was paid off 30 November 1951 and made her way into the dockyard to complete her conversion to a destroyer escort. Just like the other Tribals, 4-inch guns were installed in the A and B positions, and two triple-barrelled Squid mountings were installed aft. A 3/50, two-barrelled gun was fitted on the aft superstructure and *Micmac* received a new, lightweight lattice foremast. She was recommissioned in Halifax on 14 August 1953. A mid-year refit in 1956 saw the installation of funnel caps. *Micmac* experienced a number of difficulties during exercises in the Caribbean in 1957. Her port condenser gave trouble at Puerto Rico, and later, due to a buoy being moved, she struck her port propeller on a coral pinnacle near Bermuda. Dockyard examination showed that one blade had a 5-foot 9-inch dent. Severe vibration set in at any speed except 14.5 knots, and *Micmac* was sent to Quonset Point,

Rhode Island, for repairs. The autumn of 1963 saw *Micmac*'s last cruise—a visit to European waters. At the end of that year, after many strenuous years of training, NATO exercises and "showing the flag," more and more mechanical defects were occurring, so she was declared surplus on 13 December 1963. On 31 March 1964, *Micmac* was paid off at Halifax and broken up at Faslane, Scotland, in 1964.

### HMS *Mohawk*

After completion, *Mohawk* arrived at Malta on 13 October 1938, and spent the last months of peace on patrol in the Mediterranean. Shortly after the outbreak of war, she was ordered to the Atlantic. While providing an escort for a North Sea convoy on 16 October 1939, she was attacked by a Ju88 bomber. Two bombs exploded on the surface just beside *Mohawk*, showering her with splinters. Fifteen men including Commander Jolly and many experienced executive officers were killed. Jolly lived long enough to command his ship until it reached port, for which he was posthumously awarded the George Cross. Early in 1940, she participated in convoy escorts and fleet sweeps in the North Sea and the Atlantic. In June, she was ordered to the Mediterranean as part of the 14th Destroyer Flotilla. *Mohawk* participated in a battle between the British and Italian Fleets on 8 July. For the remaining months of 1940, *Mohawk* was engaged in escorting convoys to Malta and screening the capital ships of the Mediterranean Fleet, encountering Italian forces on several occasions. On 10/11 April 1941, she and HM Ships *Jervis*, *Janus*, and *Nubian* arrived at Malta to act as a night strike force. On 15 April, the 14th Destroyer Flotilla engaged a Tripoli bound convoy in a night action. Just as *Mohawk* was about to fire, a torpedo struck her just abreast of Y mounting on the starboard side. The crew of Y gun were killed, and *Mohawk* was awash as X mounting. Meanwhile, A

and B guns continued firing and set the lead merchantman on fire. However, a second torpedo struck *Mohawk*, hitting portside between No. 2 and No. 3 Boiler Rooms. *Mohawk* immediately began to sink. Forty-one men were lost, and the survivors were picked up by *Nubian*.

### HMCS *Nootka*

Commissioned on 7 August 1946 at Halifax, *Nootka* served as a training ship on the east coast and in the Caribbean until her conversion to a destroyer escort in 1949 and 1950. A minor calamity occurred on 1 April 1949 when *Nootka* was refueling at sea. The quick release coupling on the hose accidentally released itself and a fountain of high pressure oil sprayed all over the ship—including the chief stoker and the engineering officer—from the 293 radar antenna to the waterline. There was so much of it to clean up that *Nootka* used up all of her cotton waste and had to get more from HMCS *Magnificent*. After completing more exercises, she was paid off on 15 August 1949. During her conversion to an escort destroyer, *Nootka*'s 4.7-inch guns were replaced with 4-inch mountings by February of 1950. It was decided that she should be further altered. The Y mounting was removed altogether and two triple-barrelled Mk IV Squids were installed. After some trials, she returned to port for additional alterations to fit two Boffin gun mounts. These were single 40-mm Bofors on a twin 20-mm Oerlikon powered mounting. Earmarked for Korean duty, she transited the Panama Canal in December 1950 for the first of two tours. Returning to Halifax via the Mediterranean at the end of 1952, she underwent further conversion and modernization in 1953 and 1954 before resuming her original training duties. March 1961 saw *Haida*, *Huron*, and *Nootka* battling through an icy gale to help search for a Nova Scotia fisherman who had encountered difficulties in the

Atlantic. *Nootka*'s evaporator pump, turbo-generator and sonar gear gave trouble in spite of regular and extensive refits. In 1963, with *Haida*, she toured the Great Lakes in the course of a summer's cruising. *Nootka*'s last series of exercises found her in Bermuda. While docking at the jetty, the wind pushed her hard up against the jetty and she sustained some damage. A temporary concrete patch allowed her to return home. She was decommissioned at Halifax on 6 February 1964 and broken up at Faslane, Scotland, the following year.

### HMS *Nubian*

*Nubian* was the last to join her flotilla, arriving at Malta on 2 February 1939. When war began, she was employed on convoy escort and contraband control in the eastern Mediterranean. At the end of 1939, she reported to Scapa Flow and then to her base at Rosyth, from which she escorted Norwegian convoys and participated in the Norwegian campaign. On 14 May 1940, she arrived at Alexandria to join the 14th Destroyer Flotilla. She was to remain in the Mediterranean throughout 1943, winning battle honours for Calabria (1940), Mediterranean (1940), Libya (1940), Malta Convoys (1941), Matapan (1941), Mediterranean (1941), Greece (1941), Crete (1941), Mediterranean (1943), Sicily (1943), and Salerno (1943). During 1944 she served in the Arctic. In January 1945 *Nubian* left the UK en route to the Indian Ocean via Alexandria. She helped the British Army drive the Japanese out of their coastal fortifications in Burma. After the war, *Nubian* served as a Reserve Fleet accommodation ship alongside Whale Island, Portsmouth. She was scrapped at Briton Ferry, S Wales, on 25 June 1949.

### HMS *Punjabi*

At the outbreak of war, *Punjabi* began to patrol the North Atlantic with the rest of the 6th Destroyer Flotilla. During the Second Battle of Narvik on 13 April 1940, she was damaged by six shells, but was back in action an hour later. She sailed with the Home Fleet on 22 May 1941 in pursuit of the *Bismarck*. However, two days of high speed searching depleted the destroyers' fuel, and they all had to return to Hvalfjord, Iceland, on 24/25 May to refuel. As part of Force K, *Punjabi* sailed to Spitzbergen to investigate its feasibility as a naval base. However, it was determined that it could not be used throughout the year. After the German invasion of Russia, *Punjabi*'s operations focused on escorting convoys to Russia. After a refit at Palmer's Jarrow Yard in January 1942, she returned to the Home Fleet. While on duty with convoy PQ15 on 1 May 1942, visibility suddenly diminished, and the 35,000-ton battleship HMS *King George V* crashed into *Punjabi*'s port side just abaft the engine room. *Punjabi*'s stern sank almost immediately. Fortunately, *Punjabi*'s forepart sank quite slowly, allowing a hundred and sixty-nine survivors to be saved by HM Ships *Martin* and *Marne*.

### HMS *Sikh*

Once her trials were completed, *Sikh* sailed for the Mediterranean, arriving at Malta on 2 December 1938. At the outbreak of war, she was in the Red Sea, but quickly returned to the Mediterranean to escort convoys. She returned to the UK on 26 December 1939, and after a quick refit, she joined the 4th Destroyer Flotilla in early 1940. During the Norwegian campaign, she dodged aerial attacks off Namsos and helped cover the evacuations from central Norway and Andalsnes. The rest of 1940 was taken up with routine screening, patrols, and escort duties in the North Sea and the Western Approaches. On 21 May 1941, *Sikh*, along with three other Tribals, left the Clyde to escort a troop convoy through the Western Approaches. Detached to screen the capital ships of the Home Fleet in their pursuit of the *Bismarck*,

*Sikh* witnessed the destruction of the *Bismarck* at dawn on the 27th. Subsequently, she joined Force H at Gibraltar, and participated in the action that saw the sinking of the Italian cruisers *Alberico da Barbiano* and *Alberto di Guissano*, as well as the First Battle of Sirte. It was then decided that *Sikh* should return to Malta to form part of the 22nd Destroyer Flotilla. On 12/13 September 1942, while *Sikh* and *Zulu* were supporting an assault off the coast of Africa, they came under fire from 88-mm shore batteries. One shell exploded in *Sikh*'s gear room, while another blew up the ready-use ammunition locker for A gun and started a fierce fire. Soon thereafter, a third shell disabled her direction finder, while at the same time she was losing speed. As *Zulu* attempted to tow her, two more shells struck *Sikh*, starting more fires. As daybreak came, two more shells struck her, including one that severed the tow line. *Zulu* abandoned efforts to tow her, while the crew aboard *Sikh* continued to respond to German fire. Finally, once the ammunition was gone, the ship was abandoned, and all the survivors became prisoners.

### HMS *Somali*

On 3 September 1939, *Somali*, as part of the 6th Destroyer Flotilla, was screening British and French battlecruisers south of Iceland, and two hours after war was declared they captured the 2377-ton *Hannab Bööge* of Hamburg, Germany, the first prize taken in the war at sea. In April 1940, she was with *Afridi* and other Tribals when *Gurkha* was lost. While coming to the aid of a sinking ship off Norway on 14 May 1940, she was struck by a German bomb. After repairs, she again became leader of the 6th Destoyer Flotilla, and spent much of the winter of 1940/41 screening Home Fleet sweeps. She participated in the hunt for the *Bismarck* in May 1941. Subsequently she was part of the escort for HMS *Prince of Wales* during the Prime Minister's journey to Newfoundland in

August 1941, although the destroyer escort was forced to turn back. Around Christmas 1941, *Somali* participated in the raid on the Norwegian Lofoten Islands. From April 1942 onwards *Somali* was assigned to convoy duty on the Murmansk run. She was escorting convoy PQ18 in September 1942 when a pack of U-boats attacked the convoy. At 19:20 *Somali* was struck by a torpedo that blew her torpedo tubes over the side and cut all the port-side main stringers. The ship was held together only by the upper deck and starboard side as far as the keel. The port engine fell through the bottom of the ship and the engine and gear rooms filled with water. Most of the crew transferred to other ships while *Ashanti* attempted to tow *Somali*. After 420 miles the towline snapped, and in a snow squall *Somali* folded in half and sank.

### HMS *Tartar*

When war began, *Tartar* was assigned to fleet screening. During the Norwegian campaign, she helped escort forty merchantmen from Norway to the UK in the first days of the invasion, escorted troop convoys, and screened HMS *Ark Royal*. The rest of 1940 and early 1941 was spent either being refit, on escort duty, or screening capital ships. On 4 March 1941 she participated in a raid on the Lofoten Islands, and later hunted German weather reporting trawlers in the North Atlantic. In one case, *Tartar* was able to board a trawler before she could destroy her confidential code books, which was a valuable catch for British Intelligence. She also helped escort HMS *Prince of Wales* back to England from Newfoundland after the Atlantic Charter meeting. After a major refit in the fall, *Tartar* returned to screening capital ships of the Home Fleet, as well as providing cover for the early Murmansk convoys. She participated in the Pedestal convoy to Malta in August 1942, as well as the Torch landings. She was assigned to a striking force designed to attack enemy convoys, and on 28/29 April 1943, she and HMS *Caforey* engaged a number of E-boats that were running supplies to Tunisia. Admiral Cunningham witnessed the Allied landings at Rezzio, Italy, from the bridge of *Tartar*, and afterwards *Tartar* escorted an assault convoy to Salerno. On 21 January 1944, she completed a major refit, and for most of 1944 she was the leader of the 10th Destroyer Flotilla as they patrolled the Channel. During one patrol, they were attacked by four German vessels, and *Tartar* was hit three times. Although four men were killed and all communications were knocked out, she was able to return to port. She spent the last months of the war in the Indian Ocean. After returning home in November 1945, she served as an accommodation ship at Devonport before being scrapped on 22 February 1948.

## HMAS *Warramunga*

*Warramunga*'s career almost reads like a history of the war in the Southwest Pacific. Like HMAS *Arunta*, she saw her first action in Australian waters soon after completing work-ups in 1942. During March and April 1943 she was assigned to convoy escort duty between Queensland Territory and New Guinea, but in May, *Warramunga* joined Task Force 74 in the Coral Sea. There, she participated in almost all of the Southwest Pacific landings. The ship continued with general destroyer duties around the Philippines during the first part of 1945 and was present at the official Japanese surrender in Tokyo Bay on 2 September 1945. Peacetime exercises, cruises and refits were interrupted by the Korean War. On 6 August 1950, *Warramunga* left Sydney, Australia to join HMAS *Bataan* in Korea, where the two ships spent most of their time screening carriers off the Korean west coast in the company of RCN Tribals. After completing her first tour of duty, she sailed for Australia on 5 August 1951 and after a refit she returned to start a second tour of duty. In

November 1952 *Warramunga* was converted to an anti-submarine destroyer. The refit was completed on 5 October 1954 and for the next five years, *Warramunga* exercised and cruised with other ships of the Royal Australian Navy. By 1960, she had been placed in reserve and was scheduled for disposal in 1962. She was sold to a Japanese firm for break-up, and in January 1963, she began her last voyage from Sydney—under tow.

## HMS *Zulu*

After completing sea trials, *Zulu* sailed for the Mediterranean and arrived at Malta on 18 November 1938. There she joined *HMS Afridi* and the 1st Tribal Destroyer Flotilla. When war broke out, *Zulu* and her sister ships began convoy escort duties and contraband control. *Zulu* was given a part to play in Plan R4—the projected landing in Norway that would forestall German reaction to Operation Wilder. As it happened, Germany invaded Norway first and the Home Fleet put to sea. In early 1941, *Zulu* was mainly employed in escorting convoys in and out of the Western Approaches. She was escorting such a convoy on 26 May, when she was ordered to join the C-in-C, resulting in the 4th Destroyer Flotilla sharing in the destruction of the *Bismarck*. After the excitement of the chase, the 4th Destroyer Flotilla returned to the Home Fleet and escort duties in the Western Approaches. For the better part of 1942, *Zulu* was attached to Force H at Gibraltar, striking against Axis supply convoys. *Zulu*'s final operation was the attack on Tobruk, Libya, on 13/14 September 1942. As a result of shelling from coastal batteries, *Zulu* was hit but she could still make 30 knots. Her crew had been at full watch since dusk on the 13th, and daylight on the 14th brought no rest. In spite of surviving multiple bomb attacks during the day, *Zulu* was mortally wounded at 16:00. A bomb from an enemy aircraft pierced her side and exploded in the engine room, flooding it along with Boiler Room Three and the gear room. She stopped dead in the water and settled two feet deeper. HMS *Croome* came alongside to take off any remaining personnel except for a towing party. *Zulu* was taken in tow by HMS *Hursley*. By 19:00, and only a hundred miles from Alexandria, Egypt, she was sinking fast. The towing party was rescued after a strafing pass by an enemy aircraft. Suddenly, *Zulu* rolled to starboard and sank. In both attacks, twelve men had been killed, twenty-seven went missing and one was wounded.

**References:**

Martin Brice, *The Tribals: Biography of a Destroyer Class* (London: Ian Allen, 1971).

Jerry Proc, *Canadian Navy Tribal Class Destroyer Association* (http://webhome.idirect.com/~jproc/cta/).

Simon L. Taylor, "A Short History of Tribal Class Destroyers," in *The One Ten Bulletin* (Trenton, Ontario: Royal Canadian Legion Branch 110), Oct. 1996, pp. 4-7, and Nov. 1996, pp. 7-10.

*Tribal Reference Section* (http://www3.sympatico.ca/hrc/haida/27trib.htm).

## RESULTS OBTAINED BY 10TH DESTROYER FLOTILLA IN ENGLISH CHANNEL AND BAY OF BISCAY, 15 APRIL–15 SEPTEMBER 1944

(NAVAL SERVICE)

FROM:     Captain (D) Halifax

DATE:     23 October, 1945                    File:D.9-3-0

TO:        The Commanding Officer

           H.M.C.S. *Haida*

### TENTH DESTROYER FLOTILLA

The enclosed copy of Captain (D) Tenth Destroyer Flotilla's report dated 15 September, 1944 giving a list of results obtained by the Tenth Destroyer Flotilla in the Channel and Bay of Biscay is forwarded for information and inclusion in Ship's Book.

encl.

(J.C. Hibbard)
ACTING CAPTAIN, RCN
CAPTAIN (D) HALIFAX

H.M.S. *Tartar* 15th September, 1944

**SECRET**

Sir,

I have the honour to submit for your information a revised list of results obtained by the 10th Destroyer Flotilla in the Channel and Bay of Biscay, during the five months' period from 15 April to 15 September, 1944.

All actions were at night with the exception of the sinking of U.971, and the A.M.C. on August 12th.

| Date | Ships Engaged | Enemy Losses | |
| --- | --- | --- | --- |
| | | **Sunk** | **Damaged** |
| 25-26 April | *Haida, Huron, Ashanti, Athabaskan* & *Black Prince* (S.O.) | 1 Elbing | 1 Elbing |

| 28-29 April | *Haida* & *Athabaskan* (*Athabaskan* sunk) | 1 Elbing | — |
|---|---|---|---|
| 8-9 June | *Tartar* (D.10) & all ships of 10th D.F. | 2 Narviks<br>1 Elbing | 1 Narvik |
| 13-14 June | *Piorun* & *Ashanti* | 2 M Class Minesweepers | 2 M Class Minesweepers |
| 24 June | *Haida* & *Eskimo* | Submarine U.971 | — |
| 17-28 June | *Huron* & *Eskimo* | 2 Trawlers | 1 Trawler |
| 5 July | *Tartar* (D.10) & *Ashanti* | — | 4 Armed L.C.T.'s (Retired over shoal water to Lannion River) |
| 9 July | *Tartar* (D.10) & *Huron* | Not known | 4 Trawlers (Retired into St-Malo) |
| 15 July | *Tartar* (D.10), *Haida*, & *Blyskawica* | 2 Merchant Ships<br>1 Trawler | 1 B.P.T. |
| 5-6 Aug. | *Bellona* (S.), *Tartar* (D.10), *Haida* *Iroquois* & *Ashanti* | 4 Merchant Ships<br>2 Minesweepers<br>1 Trawler | 2 Minesweepers |
| 12 Aug. | *Piorun* with *Diadem* (S.) & *Onslow* | 1 Armed Merchant Cruiser | |
| 15 Aug | *Iroquois* with *Mauritius* (S.O.) & *Ursa* | 2 Minesweepers<br>1 Flak Ship<br>2 Medium M.V.'s<br>1 Small M.V.<br>1 Small Tanker | 1 Narvik |
| 23 Aug. | *Iroquois* with *Mauritius* (S.O.) & *Ursa* | 5 Armed Trawlers,<br>1 Sperrbrecker<br>1 Coaster<br>1 Flak Ship | — |

making a total of thirty-five surface ships and one submarine sunk and fourteen damaged.

I have the honour to be,
Sir,
Your obedient Servant,

THE COMMODORE (D) HOME FLEET
(Copy to:- THE COMMANDER-IN-CHIEF,
  FLOTILLA HOME FLEET.)

CAPTAIN (D),
TENTH DESTROYER

**Additional details supplied by Peter Dixon:**

Enemy vessels sunk or damaged by 10th DF 25 April–6 September 1944 are as follows, with date of operation:

*T-29* sunk 25-26 April; *T-27* damaged same night.

*T-27* sunk 28-29 April; *T-24* damaged same night.

*Z-32*, *ZH1* sunk 8-9 June; *T-24* damaged same night.

*M83* sunk 13-14 June; *M343, 412, 422, 432, 442, 452* damaged same night.

*U971* sunk 24 June.

2 trawlers sunk 28 June, one damaged.

Not known sunk 5 July; 4 trawlers damaged.

*M605* and *M4601* sunk 9 July.

UJ 1420 [*Eylan*] and UJ 1421 [*Deltra II*] sunk 15 July; battle practice target damaged same night.

*M263, M486, V414,* and SG 3C sunk 5-6 August.

Sperrbrecker 157 sunk 12 August; *M275, M385* damaged same night.

Trawlers *V702, 717, 720, 729* and *730* sunk 23 August.

Trawler *Vedette* sunk 6 September.

# BIBLIOGRAPHY

## PRIMARY SOURCES

**Directorate of History & Heritage, National Defence Headquarters (DH &H), Ottawa, Canada:**

DHist File 4000 (A-Z) German Channel Action Evaluation

DHist File 4000 (A-Z) Canadian Tribal Channel Actions

DHist File 4000 (A-Z) History of HMCS *Huron*

DHist File 4000 (A-Z) The RCN's Part in the Invasion of France

DHist File 8000 (A-Z) Tribal Class Destroyers built in UK

DHist "Interview with Commander DeWolf, April 23, 1944, Plymouth,"

DHist "Interview with Vice-Admiral DeWolf, June, 1982, Ottawa."

**National Archives of Canada (NAC), Ottawa:**

RG24, Accession 1983-84/167 Collisions, Groundings, Mishaps – Warships – HMCS *Haida* – DDE-215 (1945-1963)

RG24, Accession 1983-84/167 General Information – HMCS *Haida* DDE-215 (1944-1964)

RG24, Accession 1983-84/167 General Information – HMCS *Haida* DDE-215 (1964-1965)

RG24, Accession 1983-84/167 Movements – HMCS *Haida* – Tribal Class Destroyer (1943-1949)

RG24, Accession 1983-84/167 Movements – HMCS *Haida* – Tribal Class Destroyer (1949-1954)

RG24, Vol. 6790 Damage by enemy or other action – HMCS *Athabaskan* (1943-1944)

RG24, Vol. 6890 Sinkings – Warships – HMCS *Athabaskan* (1944-1945)

RG24, Vol. 11525 [Flag Officer Atlantic Coast] – Reports of proceedings – HMCS *Haida* (1947-1950)

RG24, Vol. 11525 [Flag Officer Atlantic Coast] – Reports of proceedings – HMCS *Haida* (1952-1959)

RG24, Vol. 11730 Tribal Class Destroyers – HMCS *Athabaskan*, general (1944)

RG24, Vol. 11730 Tribal Class Destroyers – HMCS *Athabaskan*, loss of, personnel (1944)

RG24, Vol. 11730 Tribal Class Destroyers – HMCS *Haida*, general (1944-1945)

RG24, Vol. 11730 Tribal Class Destroyers – HMCS *Haida*, reports, general (1944-1945)

RG24, Vol. 11730 Tribal Class Destroyers – HMCS *Haida*, reports of action (1945)

RG24, Vol. 11730 Tribal Class Destroyers – HMCS *Haida*, nominal lists (1944-1945)

RG24, Vol. 11730 Tribal Class Destroyers – HMCS *Huron*, general (1944-1945)

RG24, Vol. 11730 Tribal Class Destroyers – HMCS *Huron*, reports of action (1944)

RG24, Vol. 11731 Tribal Class Destroyers – HMCS *Iroquois*, general (1944-1945)

RG24, Vol. 11731 Tribal Class Destroyers – HMCS *Iroquois*, reports, general (1944-1945)

RG24, Vol. 11731 Tribal Class Destroyers – HMCS *Iroquois*, reports of action (1944-1945)

RG24, Vol. 11747 HMCS *Haida* – Commissioning, working up, operational.

RG24, Vol. 11747 HMCS *Haida* – Equipment, repairs, As and As.

RG24, Vol. 11939 Sinkings – HMCS *Athabaskan* (1944)

**Public Records Office (PRO), Kew, London, United Kingdom:**

Adm.1/1571 In-letters and enclosures re: destruction of U.971, 24 June 1944.

Adm.199/263 Vice-Admiral R. Leatham, "Report of Action on the Night of April 28th/29th," 1 June 1944.

Adm.199/263 Captain St. J. Crodyn, "Minutes on Action of 29 April 1944."

Adm.199/531 LtCdr J. Cartwright, "Report by Senior Officer, 52nd MTB Flotilla...Operation Hostile 26," 25 May 1944.

Adm.234/366 BS No.39, "Operation Neptune: Landings in Normandy, June 1944" (1947)

Adm.234/369 BS No.22, "Arctic Convoys 1941-45" (1954)

**Primary Sources, Publications**

Canada. Department of National Defence. *Particulars of Canadian War Vessels*. Ottawa: 1944.

Canada. Department of National Defence. *Navy List*. Various issues.

Great Britain. Admiralty Historical Section. "Cruiser and Destroyer Actions in the English Channel, 1943-44," *Battle Summary No. 31*. London: 1945.

Great Britain. Admiralty Historical Section. "Operation Neptune: The Landings in Normandy," *Battle Summary No. 31*. London: 1945.

Jackson, Norman. *Engineer Officers Note Book and Ship's Diary, 1952-53*. Transcribed by Frank Moore, 23 February 1991.

**Memoirs**

Churchill, Winston S. *The Second World War*. 6 vols.; Boston: Houghton Mifflin, 1948-1953.

Dönitz, Karl. *Memoirs: Ten Years and Twenty Days*. Translated by R.H. Stevens. London: Weidenfeld and Nicholson, 1959.

Hill, Roger. *Destroyer Captain*. London: William Kimber, 1975.

Jones, Basil. "A Matter of Length and Breadth," *The Naval Review* 38, No. 2 (May 1950): pp. 136-42.

_____*And So to Battle: A Sailor's Story*. Battle, East Sussex: Battle Martlets, Tollgates, by the author, 1979.

_____*The Tenth Destroyer Flotilla in the English Channel*. Extracts from *And So to Battle*. n.d.

Welland, Robert P. Memoirs. Unpublished, 1999.

**Other**

"An Afternoon with Vice-Admiral H.G. DeWolf," *Maritime Warfare Bulletin*, Commemorative Edition (1985), pp. 7-25.

Interviews with Carla Morse, July, August 1998.

Interviews with David Ernst, 1999.

Interviews with Neil Bruce, July 1998.

Interviews with Michael Whitby (by telephone), Sept. 20, 1999.

Interviews with Peter Ward (by telephone), July 1998.

Interviews with Gord Shires, July 1998.

*New York Times*. 17-23 November 1948 [B-29 crew rescue].

*Vancouver Daily Province*, 1 May 1944 [loss of *Athabaskan*].

# S E C O N D A R Y   S O U R C E S

Barnett, Correlli. *Engage the Enemy More Closely: The Royal Navy in the Second World War*. New York: W.W. Norton & Company, 1991.

Bartlett, Norman, ed. *With the Australians in Korea*. Canberra: Australian War Memorial, 1954.

Beesley, Patrick. *Very Special Intelligence: The Story of the Admiralty's Operational Intelligence Centre, 1939-1945*. London: Hamish Hamilton, 1977.

Bekker, Cajus. *Hitler's Naval War*. Translated by Frank Ziegler. Garden City: Doubleday, 1974.

Bishop, Chris, et al. *The Complete Encyclopedia of Weapons of World War II*. Etobicoke, Ontario: Prospero Books, 1998.

Blair, Clay. *Hitler's U-boat War: The Hunted, 1942-1945*. New York: Random House, 1998.

Boutilier, James, ed. *R.C.N. in Retrospect*. Vancouver: University of British Columbia Press, 1982.

Brice, Martin. *The Tribals: Biography of a Destroyer Class*. London: Ian Allan, 1971.

Bruce, J. Neil. "Haida," *Sentinel* 8, No.6 (June 1972): pp. 21-25.

Burrow, Len, and Emile Beaudoin. *Unlucky Lady: The Life and Death of HMCS Athabaskan, 1940-44*. Toronto: McClelland and Stewart, 1987.

Burt, R.A. *British Destroyers in World War Two*. London: Arms and Armour Press, 1985.

Busch, Fritz-Otto. *The Sinking of the Scharnhorst: A Factual Account From the German Viewpoint*. Translated by Eleanor Brockett and Anton Ehrenzweig. London: Futura Publications, 1956, 1974.

Busch, Rainer, and Hans-Joachim Röll. *Der U-Boot Krieg, 1939-1945*. Hamburg: E.S. Rittler & Sohn, 1999.

Butcher, Alan. *I Remember Haida: A Brief History of Canada's Most Famous Warship*. Hantsport: Lancelot Press, 1985.

Campbell, Sir Ian, and Donald MacIntyre. *The Kola Run: A Record of Arctic Convoys 1941-1945*. London: Frederick Muller, 1958.

Cave Brown, Anthony. *Bodyguard of Lies*. Toronto: Fitzhenry & Whiteside, 1975.

Cloutier, Edmond. *Canada and the Korean Crisis*. Ottawa: King's Printer, 1950.

Cooper, Bryan. *The E-Boat Threat*. London: MacDonald & Jones, 1976.

Connel, G.G. *Fighting Destroyer*. London: William Kimber, 1976.

Cresswell, John. *Sea Warfare 1939-45*. Berkeley: University of California Press, 1963.

Cruickshank, Charles. *Deception in World War II*. Toronto: Oxford University Press, 1979.

Dickens, Peter. "Narrow Waters in War," *Journal of the Royal Service Institute* 114, (March 1969): pp. 42-45.

Dixon, Peter A. *HMCS Haida Docent Manual*. Toronto: HMCS *Haida* Museum, 1994.

_____ "I Will Never Forget the Sound of Those Engines Going Away: A Re-examination into the Sinking of HMCS *Athabaskan*, 29 April, 1944," *Canadian Military History* 5, No. 1 (Spring 1996): pp. 16-25.

Douglas, W.A.B. "Conflict and Innovation in the Royal Canadian Navy 1939-1945." In Gerald Jordan, ed. *Naval Warfare in the Twentieth Century, 1900-1945: Essays in Honour of Arthur Marder*. New York: Crane Russack, 1977.

Douglas, W.A.B., ed. *The RCN in Transition, 1910-1985*. Vancouver: University of British Columbia Press, 1988.

Edwards, Kenneth. *Operation Neptune*. London: Collins, 1946.

Fitzsimmons, Bernard, et al. *The Illustrated Encyclopedia of 20th Century Weapons and Warfare*. New York: Columbia House, 1971, 1977, 1978.

Franks, Norman L.R. *Search, Find and Kill: Coastal Command's U-Boat Successes*. London: Grub Street, 1995.

Friedman, Norman. *Naval Radar*. Annapolis: Naval Institute Press, 1981.

Friends of HMCS *Haida* Newsletter, 8, No.3 (Fall 1997).

Friends of HMCS *Haida* Newsletter, 9, No.1 (Spring 1998).

Friends of HMCS *Haida* Newsletter, 9, No.2 (Summer 1998).

Friends of HMCS *Haida* Newsletter, 9, No. 3 (Fall 1998).

Friends of HMCS *Haida*, Newsletter, 10, No.1 (Spring 1999).

*Fuehrer Conferences on Naval Affairs, 1939-1945*. Foreword by Jak P. Mallman Showell. Annapolis: Naval Institute Press, 1990.

Gardner, W.J.R. *Decoding History: The Battle of the Atlantic and Ultra*. Annapolis: Naval Institute Press, 1999.

German, Tony. *The Sea Is At Our Gates: The History of the Canadian Navy*. Toronto: McClelland and Stewart, 1990.

Goodman, S.V. *H.M.C.S. Haida: 10th Destroyer Flotilla – Force 26 and the Plymouth Connection, 1944-1945*. Plymouth: Port Admiral's Department, 1986.

"HMCS *Haida* Commissions: Well-Known Destroyer Resumes Career," *The Crowsnest* 4, No.7 (May 1952), p. 6.

"Howdy, Tex!" *The Crowsnest* 4, No.12 (December 1949), pp. 33-34.

Harbron, John D. *The Longest Battle: The RCN in the Atlantic, 1939-1945*. St. Catharines: Vanwell Publishing Limited, 1993.

_____ "The R.C.N. at Peace, 1945-55: The Uncertain Heritage," *Queen's Quarterly* (Fall 1966), pp. 311-34.

Hargreaves, Reginald. *The Narrow Seas: A History of the English Channel*. London: Sidgwick and Jackson, 1959.

Hinsley, F.H. *British Intelligence in the Second World War: Its Influence on Strategy and Operations*. 3 vols.; London: Her Majesty's Stationery Office, 1979-88.

Hodges, Peter. *Tribal Class Destroyers, Royal Navy and Commonwealth*. London: Almark Publishing, 1971.

Hodges, Peter, and Norman Freidman. *Destroyer Weapons of World War 2*. Greenwich: Conway Maritime Press, 1979.

Hoyt, Edwin P. *The Invasion Before Normandy: The Secret Battle of Slapton Sands*. Leicester: Ulverscroft, 1987.

Humble, Richard. *Fraser of North Cape: The Life of Admiral of the Fleet, Lord R. Fraser, 1888-1981*. London: Routledge and Kegan Paul, 1983.

"In Hudson's Wake," *Crowsnest Magazine* 1, No. 1 (November 1948).

James, Sir William. *The British Navies in the Second World War*. London: Longman, Green & Co., 1946.

Kemp, Paul. *U-Boats Destroyed: German Submarine Losses in the World Wars*. London: Arms and Armour Press, 1999.

Kosiarz, Edmund. *Poles on the Seas, 1939-45*. Translated by Jan Aleksandrowicz. Warsaw: Interpress Publishers, 1969.

Lawrence, Hal. *Victory at Sea: Tales of His Majesty's Coastal Forces*. Toronto: Macmillan of Canada, 1989.

Lenton, H.T. *German Warships of the Second World War*. New York: Arco, 1976.

_____ *Navies of the Second World War: British Fleet and Escort Destroyers*. Garden City: Doubleday and Company, 1970.

Lenton, H.T., and J.J. Colledge. *Warship Losses of World War II: British and Dominion Fleets*. London: Ian Allan, 1964.

_____ *Warships of World War II, Part Two, Destroyers and Submarines*. London: Ian Allan, 1962.

Lewis, Nigel. *Channel Firing: The Tragedy of Operation Tiger*. London: Viking, 1989.

MacIntyre, Donald. *The Naval War Against Hitler*. London: B.T. Batsford, 1971.

Macpherson, Ken, and John Burgess. *The Ships of Canada's Naval Forces, 1910-1985*. 2nd revised ed. St. Catharines: Vanwell Publishing, 1993.

Manning, T.D. *The British Destroyer*. London: Putnam, 1961.

March, Edgar J. *British Destroyers, A History of Development, 1892-1953, Drawn by Admiralty Permission from Official Records & Returns, Ships' Covers & Building Plans*. London: Seeley Service, 1966.

Martienssen, Anthony. *Hitler and His Admirals*. London: Secker and Warburg, 1948.

Matthaes, R.E. *Canadian Tribal Class Destroyers Across the Drawing Board to the War Zone: A Case Study of the H.M.C.S. Haida to Justify and Identify the Merit of the Tribal Class Destroyer Purchase*. B.A. Hon. thesis. Waterloo: Wilfrid Laurier University, Department of History, 1989.

McAndrew, William, Donald E. Graves and Michael Whitby. *Normandy 1944: The Canadian Summer*. Montreal: Art Global, 1994.

McKee, Fraser and Robert Darlington. *The Canadian Naval Chronicle, 1939-1945: The Successes and Losses of the Canadian Navy in World War II*. revised ed. St. Catharines: Vanwell Publishing, 1998.

Meyers, Edward C. *Thunder in the Morning Calm: The Royal Canadian Navy in Korea 1950-1955*. St. Catharines: Vanwell Publishing Limited, 1992.

Milner, Marc. *Canada's Navy: The First Century*. Toronto: University of Toronto Press, 1999.

_____*U-Boat Hunters: The Royal Canadian Navy and the Offensive against Germany's Submarines*. Toronto: University of Toronto Press, 1999.

Morse, Carla. "HMCS *Haida* Photo Essay," *Canadian Military History* 5, No.1 (Spring 1996), pp. 85-89.

Niestlé, Axel, *German U-Boat Losses During World War II*. Annapolis: Naval Institute Press, 1998.

Ostertag, Reinhard. "Torpedo Boats in Battle with Destroyers," *Truppenpraxis* 12 (1980): pp. 3-6.

Poolman, Kenneth. *Escort Carrier: HMS Vindex at War*. London: Leo Cooper in association with Martin Secker & Warburg, 1983.

Proc, Jerry. *Asdic, Radar and IFF Systems Aboard HMCS Haida*. Toronto: privately printed, 1995.

Pugsley, William H. *Sailor Remember*. Toronto: Collins, 1948.

_____*Saints, Devils and Ordinary Seamen: Life on the Royal Canadian Navy's Lower Deck*. Toronto: Collins, 1945.

Robertson, Terence. *Walker RN*. London: Evans Brothers, 1956.

Rohwer, Jürgen, and G. Hummelchen. *Chronology of the War at Sea, 1939-1945*. Translated by Derek Masters. Edited by A.J. Watts. London: Ian Allan, 1972-1974.

Roskill, Stephen. *The War at Sea*. 3 vols.; London: Her Majesty's Stationery Office, 1954-1961.

Ruge, Friedrich. *Sea Warfare 1939-45: A German Viewpoint*. London: Cassel and Co., 1957.

Russell, E.C. *H.M.C.S. Haida: A Brief History*. Ottawa: Naval Historical Section, Naval Headquarters; [1959] new cd., n.d.

Salmon, Patrick, ed. *Britain and Norway in the Second World War*. London: Her Majesty's Stationery Office, 1995.

Schofield, Brian Betham. *The Arctic Convoys*. London: MacDonald and Jane's, 1977.

_____*Operation Neptune*. Vol. 10 of *Sea Battles Close-Up*. London: Ian Allan, 1974.

_____*The Russian Convoys*. London: Pan Books, 1984.

Schull, Joseph. *Far Distant Ships, An Official Account of Canadian Naval Operations in World War II*. Toronto: Stoddart, 1987. First published 1950 by Ottawa: King's Printer by authority of the Minister of National Defence.

Sclater, William. *Haida*. Toronto: Oxford University Press, 1946.

Schleihauf, William. "The Last of her Tribe: HMCS Haida," *Warship International*, 4 (1996), pp. 344-77.

Scott, Peter. *The Battle of the Narrow Seas: A History of the Light Coastal Forces in the Channel and North Sea, 1939-1945*. London: Country Life, 1945.

Smith, Peter C. *Hold the Narrow Sea: Naval Warfare in the English Channel, 1939-1945*. Annapolis: Naval Institute Press, 1984.

Stacey, C.P. *Arms, Men and Governments: The War Policies of Canada 1939-1945*. Ottawa: Department of National Defence, 1970.

Stern, Robert C. *Type VII U-boats*. London: Brockhampton Press, 1991.

Thorgrimsson, Thor and E.C. Russell. *Canadian Naval Operations in Korean Waters 1950-1955*. Ottawa: Queen's Printer, 1965.

Tucker, Gilbert N. *The Naval Service of Canada; Its Official History*. 2 vols.; Ottawa: King's Printer, 1952.

Venier, Mark Richard. *Ready, the Brave! A Chronicle in the Wake of HMCS Huron, Volume I: 1943-46*. Woodstock: The HMCS Huron Association, 1989.

Ward, Peter. "Haida, Inc.," *The Crowsnest* 16, No.9 (September 1964), pp. 5-9.

_____"*Haida*'s Last Cruise," *The Yorker*. HMCS *York*, Toronto (October 1964), pp. 1-4.

_____"So... No-one Told You Who Brought *Haida* Up? Well...We Did!" *The Yorker.* HMCS *York*, Toronto (October 1964).

Watkins, John. "Destroyer Action, Île de Batz, 9 June 1944," *The Mariner's Mirror* 78, No. 3 (August 1992), pp. 307-325.

Watts, A.J. *Loss of the Scharnhorst.* London: Ian Allan, 1970, 1972.

Whitby, Michael J. "'Fooling' Around the French Coast. RCN Tribal-Class Destroyers in Action—April 1944," *Canadian Defence Quarterly* 19, No. 3 (Winter 1989), pp. 54-61.

_____"Instruments of Security: The Royal Canadian Navy's Procurement of the Tribal Class Destroyers, 1938-1943," *The Northern Mariner*, 2, No.3 (July 1992), pp. 1-15.

_____"Masters of the Channel Night: the 10th Destroyer Flotilla's Victory Off Île de Batz, 9 June 1944," *Canadian Military History* 2, No. 1 (Spring, 1993), pp. 5-21.

_____*The "Other" Navy At War: The RCN's Tribal Class Destroyers 1939-1944.* M.A. thesis. Ottawa: Carleton University, Department of History, 1984.

Whitley, M.J. *Destroyer! German Destroyers in World War II.* London: Arms and Armour Press, 1985.

Wilson, J.L. "*Haida* and Her Spirit," *Canadian Forces Sentinel* 10, No.1 (January 1974), pp. 17-19.

Wood, Herbert F. *Strange Battleground: The Operations in Korea.* Ottawa: Queen's Printer, 1966.

Woodman, Richard. *The Arctic Convoys 1941-1945.* London: John Murray, 1994.

Zerter, Wilhelm. "My Experiences During the Last Days of April 1944," *Haida Newsletter* (January 1983): pp. 5-6.

Zimmerman, David. *The Great Naval Battle of Ottawa.* Toronto: University of Toronto Press, 1989.

# REFERENCE SOURCES BY CHAPTER

## Chapter 1: The Tribals and the War at Sea

This chapter rests on National Archives of Canada (NAC), RG24, Vol. 11747 "HMCS HAIDA—Equipment, repairs, As and As;" and comments on Harry DeWolf: William H. Pugsley, *Saints, Devils and Ordinary Seamen* (Toronto: Collins, 1945), pp. 200-225. The standard source for the study of Canadian Tribals in the Second World War is Michael J. Whitby, *The "Other" Navy at War: The RCN's Tribal Class Destroyers, 1939-1944* (MA thesis, Department of History, Carleton University, 1988). Also of value: R.E. Matthaes, *Canadian Tribal Class Destroyers Across the Drawing Board to the War Zone* (BA Hon. thesis, Wilfrid Laurier University, 1989).

On destroyers generally, and Tribals in particular, the following have been used: Edgar J. March, *British Destroyers, A History of Development, 1892-1953* (London: Seeley Service, 1936), ch. 39; H.T. Lenton, *British Fleet & Escort Destroyers 2* (Garden City: Doubleday, 1970); H.T. Lenton and J.J. Colledge, *Warship Losses of World War II* (London: Ian Allan, 1964), esp. p.127; T.D. Manning, *The British Destroyer* (London: Putnam, 1961), pp. 99-101; and Peter Hodges, *Tribal Class Destroyers* (London: Almark, 1971), esp. ch. 1. Fighting equipment particulars came from Peter Hodges and Norman Friedman, *Destroyer Weapons of World War 2* (London: Conway Maritime Press, 1979), ch.2, which contains excellent line drawings and descriptive material.

## Chapter 2: *Haida* On the Murmansk Run: October–December 1943

Primary documents pertaining to HMCS *Haida*'s actions and activities from October to December 1943 are available from the NAC. Of particular interest are the monthly Reports of Proceedings (ROPs), which provide details on *Haida*'s operations at sea, movements, actions in defence of the convoys, and even the health and behaviour of the crew. Details of Andrew Gillespie's appendectomy were provided by these reports. Also available from the NAC are Reports of Proceedings for *Haida*'s sister Tribals which took part in the Arctic convoys during this period. For *Haida* and *Huron*'s ROPs, see NAC RG24, Vol. 11730, and for *Iroquois* Vol. 11731. Details of *Haida*'s work-ups prior to being deployed on operations are in RG24, Vol. 11747 "HMCS *Haida*—Commissioning, working up, operational." For memoirs and recollections of *Haida* crew members during this period, see Alan Butcher, *I Remember Haida: A Brief History of Canada's Most Famous Warship* (Hantsport: Lancelot Press, 1985), pp. 15-40.

Also used extensively in this chapter were a large number of secondary sources dealing with the Arctic convoys. For an overview of the war in Arctic waters, see Jürgen Rohwer and G. Hummelchen, *Chronology of the War at Sea, 1939-1945* (London: Allan, 1972-1974), esp. pp. 244, 250. Two accounts of the Russian convoys are by B.B. Schofield: *The Russian Convoys* (London: Pan Books, 1964, 1984), pp. 148-88, deals with the events leading up to the sinking of *Scharnhorst*, while *The Arctic Convoys* (London: MacDonald and Jane's) provides a detailed description of each convoy to Murmansk. A more general work is Sir Ian Campbell and Donald MacIntyre, *The Kola Run: A Record of Arctic Convoys 1941-1945* (London: Frederick Muller, 1958). On the tragedy of PQ-17, see Correlli Barnett, *Engage the Enemy More Closely* (New York: W.W. Norton & Company, 1991), pp. 710-22; and for the details of negotiations between the British and Soviets regarding the resumption of the convoys, see Winston S. Churchill, *The Second World War: Closing the Ring* (Boston: Houghton Mifflin Company, 1951), pp. 256-99. For the situation in Arctic waters as seen by the German High Command, Karl Dönitz, *Memoirs* (London: Weidenfeld and Nicholson, 1959), pp. 371-87, and Cajus Bekker, *Hitler's Naval War* (Garden City: Doubleday, 1974), pp. 339-61, are instructive. On the Battle of North Cape, see Richard Humble, *Fraser of North Cape* (London: Routledge and Kegan Paul, 1983), pp. 187- 224; Fritz-Otto Busch, *The Sinking of the Scharnhorst: A Factual Account From the German Viewpoint* (London: Futura Publications, 1956, 1974); and A.J. Watts, *Loss of the Scharnhorst* (London: Ian Allan, 1970, 1972). For the British intelligence on *Scharnhorst*'s movements, see Vol. III, Part 1,

F.H. Hinsley, *British Intelligence in the Second World War* (London: H.M.S.O., 1984), pp. 537-41; and Patrick Beesley, *Very Special Intelligence* (London: Hamish Hamilton, 1977), pp. 204-218.

For *Haida*'s activities from her arrival in Scapa Flow to the Arctic convoys, and in the Battle of North Cape, see William Sclater, *Haida* (Toronto: Oxford University Press, 1946), pp. 3-42; E.C. Russell, *H.M.C.S. Haida: A Brief History* (Ottawa: Naval Historical Section, Naval Headquarters, 1959), pp. 3-7; and Martin Brice, *The Tribals* (London: Ian Allan, 1971), p. 130. For HMCS *Huron*, see Brice's *Tribals*, p. 140, and Mark Richard Venier, *Ready, the Brave!* (Woodstock: HMCS *Huron* Association, 1989), pp. 161-221, which also includes a transcript of Allied radio signals during the encounter with *Scharnhorst*. For *Athabaskan*'s story, see Len Burrow and Emile Beaudoin, *Unlucky Lady* (Toronto: McClelland and Stewart, 1987), pp. 52-69; and Brice, pp. 68-69. On *Iroquois*, see Brice, p. 150.

## Chapter 3: Plymouth Command: January–April 1944

Primary accounts of *Haida*'s redeployment to the English Channel and Plymouth Command are provided in the ship's ROPs for the period, along with the ROPs of HMCS *Athabaskan* for January to April 1944, *Iroquois* for January and February, and *Huron* for February to April. Further details are in RG24, Accession 1983-84/167 entitled "Movements – HMCS *Haida* – Tribal Class Destroyer (1943-1949)." Also useful is the Directorate of History & Heritage (DH&H) in Ottawa, which holds an extensive collection of archival material, including the fIles "Canadian Tribal Channel Actions" and an "Interview with Commander DeWolf, April 23, 1944, Plymouth." Published sources of primary information include the Admiralty Historical Section's "Cruiser and Destroyer Actions in the English Channel, 1943-44," *Battle Summary No. 31* (London: 1945); the memoirs of Commander Basil Jones, entitled *And So to Battle* (Battle: Jones, 1976); and Roger Hill, *Destroyer Captain* (London: William Kimber, 1975), a first-hand account of the disastrous "Tunnel" operation of October 22-23, 1943. For the recollections of *Haida*'s crew, see Alan Butcher, *I Remember Haida*, pp. 41-46.

Of the secondary sources available on the formation of the 10th DF and the activities of Canadian Tribals in the English Channel, the best account is provided by Michael Whitby's MA thesis, *The "Other" Navy at War*, esp. pp. 53-70. By the same author, "'Fooling' Around the French Coast," *Canadian Defence Quarterly* 19, No. 3 (Winter 1989), pp. 54-55, is also used in this chapter. Other accounts are Peter C. Smith, *Hold the Narrow Sea* (Annapolis: Naval Institute Press, 1984), pp. 206-207; Tony German, *The Sea Is At Our Gates* (Toronto: McClelland and Stewart, 1990), pp. 159-61; and Joseph Schull, *Far Distant Ships* (Toronto: Stoddart, 1950, 1987), p. 250, which describes the aim and conduct of "Hostile" and "Tunnel" operations. For the details of the Tunnel operation of October 22-23, 1943, see Smith, *Hold the Narrow Sea*, pp. 184-200. On the decision to adopt new patrolling tactics to counter the threat of German torpedoes, see Basil Jones, "Matter of Length and Breadth," *The Naval Review* 38, No. 2 (May 1950), pp. 136-42.

On *Haida*'s activities during this period, details are provided in Sclater, *Haida*, pp. 43-60; Russell, *H.M.C.S. Haida*, pp. 7-9; and Brice, *The Tribals*, p. 130. For HMCS *Athabaskan*, see Burrow and Beaudoin, *Unlucky Lady*, pp. 71-76, and Brice, *The Tribals*, p. 69. On HMS *Ashanti*, see Brice, pp. 59-61.

## Chapter 4: With Battle Ensign Flying: 26 April 1944

Primary sources for the Channel action of 26 April include the ROPs for *Haida* and *Huron*. NAC RG24, Vol. 11730 holds *Haida* and *Huron*'s Reports of Action (ROAs) for April 26, 1944. HMCS *Athabaskan*'s ROA appears as an appendix to Burrow and Beaudoin, *Unlucky Lady*, pp. 174-76. From DH&H, see "Canadian Tribal Channel Actions" and "German Channel Action Evaluation," the latter of which provides the details of the encounter from the German viewpoint and a translation of the 4th Torpedo Boat Flotilla's War Diary. Another German perspective is Wilhelm Zerter, "My Experiences During the Last Days of April 1944," *Haida Newsletter* (January 1983), pp. 5-6. The memoirs of Basil Jones, *And So to Battle*, pp. 74-79, give a first- hand account of the battle; and Alan Butcher, *I Remember Haida*, pp. 47-55, has statements by *Haida* crew members who witnessed the battle. The Admiralty Historical Section's *Battle Summary No. 31* is also useful.

Of secondary sources, Whitby, *The "Other" Navy at War*, pp. 76-101, gives the most detailed account. See also, Burrow and Beaudoin, *Unlucky Lady*, pp. 79-84; German, *The Sea Is At Our Gates*, p. 161; Fraser McKee and Robert Darlington, *The Canadian Naval Chronicle, 1939-1945*, pp. 139-41; Reinhart Ostertag, "Torpedo Boats in Battle with Destroyers," *Truppenpraxis*, p. 12 (1980), pp. 3-6; J. Rohwer and G. Hummelchen, *Chronology of the War at Sea, 1939-1945*, pp. 270; Russell, *H.M.C.S. Haida: A Brief History*, pp. 9-11; Joseph Schull, *Far Distant Ships*, pp. 251-53; Sclater, *Haida*, pp. 65-81; Smith, *Hold the Narrow Sea*, pp. 210-11; Venier, *Ready, the Brave!*, pp. 258-72; Michael Whitby, "'Fooling' Around the French Coast," *Canadian Defence Quarterly* 19, No. 3 (Winter 1989), pp. 54-59; and M.J. Whitley, *Destroyer!*, pp. 205-206. Brice, *The Tribals*, provides a brief summary for each of the Allied destroyers which took part in the battle: for *Haida*, pp. 130-131; *Athabaskan, pp.* 69-70; *Ashanti*, pp. 61-62; and *Huron*, p. 141.

For detailed accounts of the disastrous invasion exercise Operation Tiger, see Edwin P. Hoyt, *The Invasion Before Normandy: The Secret Battle of Slapton Sands* (Leicester: Ulverscroft, 1987); Nigel Lewis, *Channel Firing: The Tragedy of Operation Tiger* (London: Viking, 1989); German, *The Sea Is At Our* Gates, p. 162; Rohwer and Hummelchen, *Chronology of the War at Sea, 1939-1945*, pp. 270; and Russell, *H.M.C.S. Haida*, p. 11.

## Chapter 5: Tragic Loss of a Friend, HMCS *Athabaskan*: 29 April 1944

NAC documents pertaining to the loss of HMCS *Athabaskan* include RG24, Vol. 6890 "Sinkings – Warships – HMCS *Athabaskan* (1944-1945);" Vol. 11939 "Sinkings – HMCS *Athabaskan* (1944);" Vol. 11730 "Tribal Class destroyers – HMCS *Athabaskan*, loss of, personnel (1944);" and Vol. 6790 "Damage by enemy or other action – HMCS *Athabaskan* (1943-1944)." For *Haida*'s ROA on the night of 29 April, see RG24, Vol. 11730 "Tribal Class Destroyers – HMCS *Haida*, reports of action (1944)." The files "Canadian Tribal Channel Actions" and "German Channel Action Evaluation" at DH&H provide useful information, as does Zerter, "My Experiences During the Last Days of April 1944," *Haida Newsletter* (January 1983), pp. 5-6; H.G. DeWolf's recollections "An Afternoon with Vice-Admiral H.G. DeWolf," *Maritime Warfare Bulletin* (Department of National Defence, 1985), pp. 17-19; and Jones, *And So to Battle*, pp. 79-80. A contemporary newspaper article reporting the loss of *Athabaskan* is found in the *Vancouver Daily Province*, 1 May 1944, p. 1. The Admiralty's evaluation of the battle is in PRO, Adm 199/263; see also VAdmiral R. Leatham, "Report of Action on the Night of April 28th/29th;"and Captain St. J. Cronyn, "Minutes on Action of 29 April, 1944;" and "Cruiser and Destroyer Actions in the English Channel, 1943-44,"Admiralty Historical Section, *Battle Summary No. 31*.

Of the secondary sources available on the action of April 29, 1944, and the loss of HMCS *Athabaskan*, the best are Burrow and Beaudoin, *Unlucky Lady*, pp. 113-37; and Dixon, "I Will Never Forget the Sound of Those Engines Going Away: A Re-examination into the Sinking of HMCS *Athabaskan*, 29 April, 1944," *Canadian Military History* 5, No. 1 (Spring 1996), pp. 16- 25. See also, Brice, *The Tribals*, pp. 69-70, 131; German, *The Sea Is At Our Gates*, pp. 163-63; McKee and Darlington, *The Canadian Naval Chronicle, 1939-1945*, pp. 142-146; Reinhard Ostertag, "Torpedo Boats in Battle with Destroyers," *Truppenpraxis* 12 (1980), pp. 3-6; Russell, *H.M.C.S. Haida*, pp. 13-16; Schull, *Far Distant Ships*, pp. 253-58; Sclater, *Haida*, pp. 86-120; Smith, *Hold the Narrow Sea*, pp. 211-16; Michael J. Whitby, "'Fooling' Around the French Coast. RCN Tribal-Class Destroyers in Action—April 1944," *Canadian Defence Quarterly* 19, No. 3 (Winter 1989), pp. 59-61; and M.J. Whitley, *Destroyer!* pp. 205-206. For the details of the anti-salvage operation carried out against the wreck of *T-29*, see Peter Scott, *The Battle of the Narrow Seas*, pp. 182-83.

## Chapter 6: Normandy and After: "One Enemy Destroyer Beached off Île de Batz": 9 June 1944

*Haida*'s activities for May and early June are in the ship's ROPs. They also contain a brief note on the June 6 invasion as seen by *Haida*'s crew while patrolling the Hurd Deep. Another file, "The RCN's Part in the Invasion of France," is held by DH&H. The Admiralty Historical Section's "Operation Neptune: The Landings in Normandy," *Battle Summary No. 31* is also useful. See also the ship's log; a copy is in the *Haida* Archives. For the details of the encounter with the German 8th Destroyer Flotilla, see *Haida* and *Huron*'s ROAs for June 9 in NAC RG24, Vol. 11730. For Jones, see his *And So to Battle*, pp. 81-89.

Secondary sources of significance to *Haida*'s activities from early May to June 9 include Barnett, *Engage the Enemy More Closely*, pp. 810-31; Kenneth Edwards, *Operation Neptune* (London: Collins, 1946), esp. p. 108; Rohwer and G. Hummelchen, *Chronology of the War at Sea, 1939- 1945*, pp. 280-82; Russell, pp. 16-21; B.B. Schofield, *Operation Neptune*; Smith, *Hold the Narrow Sea*, pp. 216-25; and V.E. Tarrant, *The Last Year of the Kriegsmarine* (London: Arms and Armour Press, 1994), pp. 56-60. For Admiralty intelligence on German naval strength prior to D-Day, see Beesley, pp. 230-33, and for the invasion from the perspective of the German Navy, see Karl Dönitz, *Memoirs*, pp. 391-97, and *Fuehrer Conferences on Naval Affairs, 1939- 1945* (Annapolis: Naval Institute Press, 1990), pp. 395-404.

Various secondary sources were used to reconstruct the battle of June 9, but two stand out as being particularly useful. Michael J. Whitby, "Masters of the Channel Night: the 10th Destroyer Flotilla's Victory Off Île de Batz, 9 June 1944," *Canadian Military History* 2, No. 1 (Spring, 1993), pp. 5-21, gives an excellent account of the battle; and John Watkins, "Destroyer Action, Île de Batz, 9 June 1944," *The Mariner's Mirror* 78, No. 3 (August 1992), pp. 307-325, provides an in-depth look at the engagement from HMS *Ashanti*'s point of view. See also Brice, *The Tribals*, pp. 62-63, 122, 131 and 141; German, *The Sea Is At Our Gates*, p. 163; McKee and Darlington, *The Canadian Naval Chronicle, 1939-1945*, pp. 151-53; Rohwer and Hummelchen, *Chronology of the War at Sea, 1939-1945*, p. 282; Schull, *Far Distant Ships*, pp. 286-95; Sclater, *Haida, pp.* 141-60; Smith, *Hold the Narrow Sea*, pp. 237-41; Tarrant, *The Last Year of the Kriegsmarine*, pp. 60-5; Venier, *Ready, the Brave!*, pp. 303-313; and Whitley, *Destroyer!*, pp. 205-211. For Polish destroyers which took part in the battle, see Edmund Kosiarz, *Poles on the Seas, 1939-45* (Warsaw: Interpress Publishers, 1969).

## Chapter 7: The Killing of *U971*: 24 June 1944

Primary documents available from the NAC include HMCS *Haida*'s ROA for the attack on *U971*. HMS *Eskimo*'s Action Report is in the HMCS *Haida* Naval Museum. For the reminiscences of *Haida*'s crew, see Alan Butcher, *I Remember Haida*, pp. 71-73; and for DeWolf's recollections see "An Afternoon with Vice-Admiral H.G. DeWolf," *Maritime Warfare Bulletin* (Department of National Defence, 1985), pp. 20-21. Jones, *And So to Battle*, p. 88, also mentions the attack. A summary of *U971*'s last engagement, produced by her Second Officer Helmut Buchholz, is in Rainer Busch and Hans-Joachim Röll, *Der U-Boot Krieg, 1939-1945*, Bd. 4, *September 1939- Mai 1945* (Hamburg: E.S. Rittler & Sohn, 1999), p. 260.

Published accounts relating to the attack on *U971* include William McAndrew, Donald E. Graves and Michael Whitby, *Normandy 1944: The Canadian Summer*, Montreal: Art Global, 1944); Brice, *The Tribals*, pp. 122 and 131; Norman L.R. Franks, *Search, Find and Kill*, p. 116, which provides a list of the repeated air attacks on *U971* by Coastal Command; Paul Kemp, *U-Boats Destroyed* (London: Arms and Armour, 1999), p. 198; Ken Macpherson and John Burgess, *The Ships of Canada's Naval Service, 1910-1985*, pp. 42, 193; McKee and Darlington, *The Canadian Naval Chronicle, 1939-1945*, pp. 158-160; Marc Milner, *The U-Boat Hunters* (Toronto: University of Toronto Press, 1994), pp. 151-52; Axel Niestlé, *German U-Boat Losses During World War II*, p. 94, which confirms that *U971* was sunk by gunfire and not scuttled; Rohwer and Hummelchen, *Chronology of the War at Sea, 1939-1945*, p. 284; Russell, *H.M.C.S. Haida*, pp. 22-24; Schull, *Far Distant Ships*, pp. 302-303; Sclater, *Haida*, pp. 169-79; and Tarrant, *The Last Year of the Kriegsmarine*, pp. 84, 92. On sub-hunting, see Terence Robertson, *Walker, RN* (London: Evans Brothers, 1956). For the specifications of Type VIIC U-boats, see Robert C. Stern, *Type VII Boats* (London: Brockhampton Press, 1991).

On *Haida*'s "moonshine" operation of June 12-13, see Cave Brown, *Bodyguard of Lies*, Vol. 2 (New York: Harper and Row, Publishers, 1975), pp. 589-91; Charles Cruickshank, *Deception in World War II* (Toronto: Oxford University Press, 1979), pp. 199-201; Russell, *H.M.C.S. Haida*, p. 21; Sclater, *Haida*, pp. 161-68; and Venier, *Ready, the Brave!*, pp. 315-19.

## Chapter 8: In the Bay of Biscay: July–August 1944

Throughout this chapter, the ROPs for *Haida* and her sister ships *Huron* and *Iroquois*, were used extensively. See also *Haida*'s ROAs for the night of July 14-15 and August 5-6, and the Action Report of HMCS *Iroquois* for August 5-6. They are found in NAC RG24, Vol. 11731 "Tribal Class destroyers – HMCS *Iroquois*, reports of action (1944-1945)." The memoirs of Jones were used extensively throughout this chapter. In particular, *And So to Battle*, p. 91, mentions the engagement of *Huron* and *Eskimo* against enemy forces on 27-28 June and pp. 95-98 deal with July 14-15. Basil Jones, *The Tenth Destroyer Flotilla in the English Channel, 1944*, pp. 19-21, also deals with 14-15 July and provides an account of DeWolf's promotion (pp.17-18). Events of 5-6 August are retold on pp. 22-25. For recollections of this period by *Haida*'s crew, see Butcher, *I Remember Haida*, pp. 74-78.

For secondary sources on the importance of the Bay of Biscay to the German war effort in the summer of 1944 consult Barnett, *Engage the Enemy More Closely*, pp. 193-95; Schull, *Far Distant Ships*, pp. 347-48; and Tarrant, *The Last Year of the Kriegsmarine*, pp. 106-111. On DeWolf's promotion over Jones, see German, *The Sea Is At Our Gates*, p. 164; and Venier, *Ready, The Brave!*, p. 322. For more on *Huron* and *Eskimo*'s fight on the night of 27-28 July, see Brice, *The Tribals*, pp. 122-23 and 141; McKee and Darlington, *The Canadian Naval Chronicle, 1939-1945*, pp. 161-62; Schull, *Far Distant Ships*, pp. 339-40; Smith, *Hold the Narrow Sea*, p. 244; and Venier, *Ready, The Brave!*, pp. 241-42, 320-21. On *Haida*'s action of 14-15 July, see Brice, *The Tribals*, pp. 131, 240; German, *The Sea Is At Our Gates*, p. 164; Schull, *Far Distant Ships*, pp. 340-41; William Sclater, *Haida*, pp. 184-88; and Russell, *H.M.C.S. Haida*, p. 24. On the action of August 5-6, see German, *The Sea Is At Our Gates*, p. 164; McKee and Darlington, *The Canadian Naval Chronicle, 1939-1945*, pp. 154-55; Rohwer and Hummelchen, *Chronology of the War at Sea, 1939-1945*, p. 295; Russell, *H.M.C.S. Haida*, pp. 24-25; Schull *Far Distant Ships*, pp. 349-51; Sclater, *Haida*, pp. 192-199; and Venier, *Ready, The Brave!*, pp. 350-51.

## Chapter 9: "The Ship Whose Blazing Guns Have Written a New and Imperishable Chapter in Our Nation's History": August–29 September, 1944

For the details of *Haida*'s day-to-day activities during this period, the ship's ROPs were used, supplemented by those of her sister ships, all at the NAC. For official sources on actions fought by HMCS *Iroquois* whIle *Haida* was undergoing repairs, see NAC RG24, Vol. 11731 "Tribal Class destroyers – HMCS *Iroquois*, reports, general (1944-1945)" and "Tribal Class destroyers – HMCS *Iroquois*, reports of action (1944-1945)". Admiral Leatham's farewell speech to HMCS *Haida* is printed in Russell, *H.M.C.S. Haida*, pp. 26-28; and in Sclater, *Haida*, pp. 212-15. The CBC broadcast announcing *Haida*'s return to Halifax is in Sclater, pp. 218-21.

Secondary sources for the events of this period include McKee and Darlington, *The Canadian Naval Chronicle, 1939-1945*, p. 156; Rohwer and Hummelchen, *Chronology of the War at Sea, 1939-1945*, pp. 295-296; and Schull, *Far*

*Distant Ships*, pp. 351-53, which deal with the actions of HMCS *Iroquois*. On HMCS *Haida* and the return of *Jean Bart* and the French Provisional Government to France, see Brice, *The Tribals*, p. 132; and Russell, *H.M.C.S. Haida*, pp. 25-26. Details of *Haida*'s shore party that landed at Les Sables d'Olonne are reconstructed from Sclater, *Haida*, pp. 200-211, and supplemented by Alan Butcher, *I Remember Haida*, pp. 79-81, and Russell, *H.M.C.S. Haida*, p. 26.

## Chapter 10: A New Tour of Duty: Return to Russia, Liberating Norway: 1945

Primary sources for this chapter include the unpublished memoirs of the ship's former captain, Robert Welland, and the recollections of the ship's medical officer, David Ernst, who served in *Haida* during her second tour. Other crew recollections are contained in Butcher, *I Remember Haida*, pp. 83-88. These memoirs were supplemented by information from ROPs, and the original report of HMCS *Haida*'s attack on HMS *Trusty*, provided by the HMCS *Haida* Naval Museum. See also NAC RG24, Accession 1983-84/167 "Movements – HMCS *Haida* – Tribal Class Destroyer (1943-1949)" and Vol. 11730 "Tribal Class Destroyers – HMCS *Haida*, nominal lists (1944-1945)" for more on *Haida*'s movements and a complete list of her crew in 1945. ROPs for HMCS *Huron* and *Iroquois* provided supplementary details for this chapter.

For secondary sources on the Christmas Eve loss of HMCS *Clayoquot*, see German, *The Sea Is At Our Gates*, pp. 178-79; McKee and Darlington, *The Canadian Naval Chronicle, 1939-1945*, pp. 196-99; Milner, *The U-Boat Hunters*, p. 224; and Schull, *Far Distant Ships*, p. 384. For more on the accidental attack on HMS *Trusty*, see Paul Kemp, *Friend or Foe* (London: Leo Cooper, 1995), pp. 87-90; and Russell, *H.M.C.S. Haida*, pp. 28-29. On the sometimes-elusive Russian sub-chasers, see Martin Brice, *The Tribals*, p. 133; and Russell *H.M.C.S. Haida: A Brief History*, p. 29. Information on convoy JW-66 is found in Barnett, *Engage the Enemy More Closely*, p. 748; Brice, *The Tribals*, pp. 133, 153; Sir Ian Campbell and Donald MacIntyre, *The Kola Run*, pp. 188-89; Kenneth Poolman, *Escort Carrier: HMS Vindex at War* (London: Leo Cooper in association with Martin Secker & Warburg, 1983), pp. 18-87; Rohwer and Hummelchen. *Chronology of the War at Sea, 1939-1945*, p. 348; and Schofield, *The Russian Convoys*, p. 214. On *Haida* and the liberation of Norway, see Martin Brice, *The Tribals*, pp. 133, 142; Russell, *H.M.C.S. Haida*, pp. 30-31; and Patrick Salmon, ed., *Britain and Norway in the Second World War* (London: Her Majesty's Stationery Office, 1995).

## Chapter 11: Cold War Warrior: 1945–1951

Primary information on *Haida*'s movements, activities and operations during this period are in NAC RG24, Accession 1983-84/167 "General Information – HMCS *Haida* DDE-215 (1944- 1964)", "Collisions, Groundings, Mishaps – Warships – HMCS *Haida* – DDE-215 (1945-1963)", "Movements – HMCS *Haida* – Tribal Class Destroyer (1943-1949)" and "Movements – HMCS *Haida* – Tribal Class Destroyer (1949-1954)." From NAC RG24, Vol. 11525, see "[Flag Officer Atlantic Coast] – Reports of proceedings – HMCS *Haida* (1947-1950)" and "[Flag Officer Atlantic Coast] – Reports of proceedings – HMCS *Haida* (1952-1959)." On the B-29 incident, see Butcher, *I Remember Haida*, pp. 95-99; issues of the *New York Times*, pp. 17-23 November 1949; and Vernon Spurr, *HMCS Haida and Her Honorary Texans*, available from the HMCS *Haida* Naval Museum.

Secondary sources of relevance to this chapter include Brice, *The Tribals* (on *Haida*, pp. 133-35, on *Nootka*, p. 192); Butcher, *I Remember Haida*, pp. 89-94; W.A.B. Douglas, ed., *The RCN in Transition, 1910-1985* (Vancouver: University of British Columbia Press, 1988), pp. 186-204, 209-214; German, *The Sea Is At Our Gates*, ch.11, esp. pp. 204-207; John D. Harbron, "The R.C.N. at Peace, 1945-55: The Uncertain Heritage," *Queen's Quarterly* (Fall 1966), pp. 311-34; "In Hudson's Wake," *The Crowsnest* 1, No. 1 (November 1948) for more on *Haida*'s Arctic cruise; and Russell, *H.M.C.S. Haida*, pp. 31-33. For information on the new weapons and communications systems installed on *Haida* during this period, see Peter A. Dixon, *HMCS Haida Docent Manual* (Toronto: HMCS *Haida* Museum, 1994). On the rescue of the B-29 aircrew, see "Howdy Tex!" *The Crowsnest* 4, No. 12, (December 1949), pp. 33-34. On *Haida*'s 1952 recommission, see "HMCS *Haida* Commissions: Well-Known Destroyer Resumes Career," *The Crowsnest* 4, No. 7 (May 1952), p. 6.

## Chapter 12: Korean War, Train Busting, and Other Pursuits: 1952-1962

The most comprehensive primary source available on HMCS *Haida*'s activities during the Korean War is Norman Jackson, *Engineer Officers' Note Book and Ship's Diary, 1952-53*, from the HMCS *Haida* Naval Museum in Toronto. This record contains a day-by-day account of the ship's activities throughout her first tour in Korea. See also the monthly ROPs for 1952-1959 and NAC Accession 1983-84/167 "Movements – HMCS *Haida* – Tribal Class Destroyer (1949-1954)." For crew recollections of *Haida*'s first tour in Korea, see Butcher, *I Remember Haida*, pp. 101-135, and 136-49 for the second tour of duty.

Secondary sources relevant to *Haida*'s activities in the Korean War include John Bovey, "The Destroyers' War in Korea, 1952-53," in James Boutilier, ed., *R.C.N. in Retrospect* (Vancouver: University of British Columbia Press, 1982), pp. 250-70; Brice, *The Tribals* (on *Haida* pp. 135- 136, on *Athabaskan* pp. 72-82, on *Nootka* pp. 192-198); Edmond Cloutier, *Canada and the Korean Crisis* (Ottawa: King's Printer, 1950), pp. 7-13; Edward C. Meyers, *Thunder in the Morning Calm* (St. Catharines: Vanwell Publishing Limited, 1992), pp. 187-94, 212-14; Russell, *H.M.C.S. Haida*, pp. 33-36 for *Haida*'s first tour, p. 33 for her second; Thor Thorgrimsson and E.C. Russell, *Canadian Naval Operations in Korean Waters 1950-1955* (Ottawa: Queen's Printer, 1965), pp. 1-7 on *Cayuga*, *Sioux*, and *Athabaskan*'s departure for Korea and pp. 113-26 on train busting; and, for an overview of Canada's war in Korea, Herbert F. Wood, *Strange Battleground: The Operations in Korea* (Ottawa: Queen's Printer, 1966).

## Chapter 13: The Final Voyage: The Last Tribal: 1963 and After

Primary sources for this chapter include numerous interviews with volunteers, employees and associates of the HMCS *Haida* Naval Museum. Interviews were conducted with Peter Ward, Frank Stockwell, Alan Grant, Robert Willson, Carla Morse, Gord Shires, Neil Bruce, and Peter Dixon. Their comments and recollections formed the basis of this chapter. Also of use  was Peter Dixon's *HMCS* Haida *Docent Manual.*

Secondary sources include Neil Bruce, *"Haida." Sentinel* 8, No. 6 (June 1972), pp. 21-25; Butcher, *I Remember Haida*, pp. 156-63; various issues of the "Friends of HMCS *Haida*" newsletter; Carla Morse, "H.M.C.S. *Haida* Photo Essay" *Canadian Military History* 5, No. 1 (Spring 1996), pp. 85-89; William Schleihauf, "The Last of her Tribe: HMCS *Haida*" *Warship International* 4 (1996), pp. 344-77; Peter Ward *"Haida,* Inc." *The Crowsnest* 16, No. 9 (September 1964), pp. 5-8; and Peter Ward, "So...No-One Told You Who Brought *Haida* Up? Well...We Did!" *The Yorker* (October 1964).

# INDEX

# THE FRIENDS OF HMCS *HAIDA*

SINCE 1970 HMCS *Haida* has been preserved as a naval museum and maritime memorial at Ontario Place in Toronto. The ship is designated by the Historic Sites and Monuments Board of Canada, and is owned and operated by the government of the Province of Ontario.

Open from Victoria Day to Labour Day, the ship offers an insight into the life of Canada's seagoing sailors during the period from 1943 to 1963, and honours those who fought and died at sea to ensure the freedom of our nation. The museum houses artifacts of the period, and displays which interpret the role of the Royal Canadian Navy during the Second World War, the Korean War, and the early days of the Cold War. An extensive library and archives are located in the ship.

To support the museum and provide resources not available from government, Friends of HMCS *Haida* was formed as a non-profit organization and registered as a charity in 1988. Volunteer members act as docents and as skilled maintainers. All funds raised are dedicated to the preservation and restoration of Canada's most famous warship.

For information on how to become a member or to make a donation please contact The Friends of HMCS *Haida* at PO Box 405, 2-100 Bloor St. W. Toronto, Ontario, M4W 3E2, email hnmchin@planeteer.com or visit our website at www3.sympatico.ca/hrc/haida.

**DATE DUE**

| Nov 19/12 | |
| --- | --- |
| | |
| | |
| | |
| | |
| | |
| | |
| | |
| | |
| | |
| | |